THE TERROR AND THE TIME

THE TERROR AND THE TIME

Banal Violence and Trauma in Caribbean Discourse

PAULA MORGAN

THE UNIVERSITY OF THE WEST INDIES PRESS
Jamaica • Barbados • Trinidad and Tobago

The University of the West Indies Press
7A Gibraltar Hall Road, Mona
Kingston 7, Jamaica
www.uwipress.com

© 2014 by Paula Morgan
All rights reserved. Published 2014

A catalogue record of this book is available from the National Library of Jamaica.

ISBN: 978-976-640-496-3 (print)
978-976-640-537-3 (Kindle)
978-976-640-541-0 (ePub)

Cover and book design by Robert Harris
Set in Scala 10.25/15 x 27
Printed in the United States of America

TO MARGOT AND JILL IN RECOGNITION OF DECADES OF
INSPIRATION AND FIERCE CONVERSATIONS

CONTENTS

Acknowledgements / **ix**

Introduction: "Some Deep, Amnesiac Blow" / **1**

PART 1   ONTOLOGIES

1   "Re-membering Our Scattered Skeletons":
    Literary Representations of the *Zong* Massacre / **27**

2   "The Womb of My Otherness": Creolization in
    "The View from the Terrace" and "Barbados" / **49**

3   Lament of the Unhomely: Nationhood and Nonbelonging
    in the Work of V.S. Naipaul / **67**

4   "Something Inside Is Laid Wide Like a Wound":
    Walcott's City of Pain and Promise / **83**

PART 2   SOCIAL ISSUES

5   One Day for the Hunter, One Day for the Prey:
    State Criminality in Danticat's Fiction / **105**

6   "When Memory Is a Bruise Still Tender": Ageing and
    Alzheimer's in *Cascade* and *Soucouyant* / **129**

7   "Naked with Unknowing": Childhood Trauma and the
    Unmaking of Self / **146**

8   "Rum Till I Die": Discourses of Alcoholism and Death / **162**

9 "No Money, No Love": Representations of the
   Social Impact of Poverty / **189**

   Afterword / **203**
   Appendix / **207**
   Notes / **213**
   References / **223**
   Index / **233**

ACKNOWLEDGEMENTS

I would like to thank my colleague, collaborator and friend Valerie Youssef, my co-author for *Writing Rage: Unmasking Violence in Caribbean Discourse* (University of the West Indies Press); co-editor of the online collection *The Culture of Violence in Trinidad and Tobago* (Caribbean Review of Gender Studies) and joint lecturer for the course "Gender Violence and Trauma". We have put our heads together on these issues over the long haul and her thinking and linguistic training have enriched me greatly, and for this I am grateful. I need also to acknowledge the shaping influence of the students of my gender, cultural and literary studies courses who see the world through their own lens, challenge my positions and broaden my vistas. I do appreciate the University of the West Indies Research and Publications grant which has supported this work. To Bridget Brereton, Barbara Lalla, Patricia Saunders, Jennifer Rahim and Jean Antoine, all of whom took time out of their busy schedules to read chapters of this manuscript, I give thanks. I would like to pay tribute to Gordon Rohlehr, mentor and friend, who took the time to carefully read the entire manuscript and to make detailed comments. Finally I extend my deepest gratitude to my omniscient Creator and also to my husband, Michael, who has through our thirty-five years of partnership been consistently steadfast, supportive and wise.

INTRODUCTION
"Some Deep, Amnesiac Blow"

> Something inside is laid wide like a wound,
> some open passage that has cleft the brain,
> some deep, amnesiac blow. We left
> somewhere a life we never found,
>
> customs and gods that are not born again,
> some crib, some grille of light
> clanged shut on us in bondage, and withheld
>
> us from that world below us and beyond,
> and in its swaddling cerements we're still bound.
>
> – Derek Walcott, "Laventille"

THE NEW WORLD ISLAND societies of the modern Caribbean have been crafted by a traumatic encounter between worlds. In an early experiment of technologically driven global modernity fuelled by the largest mass labour migration in human history, Europe undertook to transform two-thirds of the then known world into its playground and factory. The imperial impulse which propelled the enterprise of the Indies drew together a multiplicity of non-homogeneous people-groups – indigenous Indians, Europeans, Africans, Asians – in minute island spaces to jostle for a place in an embryonic social order. This took place against a framework of genocide of indigenous tribes, oppressive systems of slavery and indentureship, racism and denigration, poverty, hunger and structural inequities – all buttressed by incredible excesses of terrorism and social violence. Contemporary legacies of these ignominious beginnings include widening gaps between haves and have-nots; paradisiacal upper-strata domestic retreats and touristic playgrounds alongside barrack yards and dungles; growing armies of illiterates alongside highly trained cadres of professionals; and regular mass eruptions of pure collective rage alongside gifts of resilience and celebration.

The island archipelago, which enjoys a favourable geopolitical location at the crossroads of the Americas, also faces the persistent threat of natural disasters – hurricanes, floods, volcanic eruptions, environmental degradation. Its social foundations face erosion via waves of voluntary migration and brain drain. The resilient island societies confront global economic strictures, currency devaluations and World Bank conditionalities, including structural adjustment. They are also undermined by their location, becoming drug transhipment points for narcotics en route to North America, with deleterious impacts on gun and gang violence, as well as on villages and towns clustered along vulnerable coastlines. Caribbean societies straddle paradox, balancing great potential with great depth of human suffering.

This enquiry reads literary, popular and media representations of a range of social scenarios and issues. It emerged out of a growing impatience with more esoteric academic endeavour within a season of spiralling crises. The text contests an assumption that scholarship in the humanities has little to bring to the table in terms of understanding and resolving our scenarios of individual and social suffering. It deals in part 1, "Ontologies", with representations of social and individual crises of being and becoming; part 2 adds a focus on real-life issues and scenarios, and more so on how these experiences are lived and perceived by the common person. The two closing chapters deal with banal violence and traumas induced by the outworking of structural inequities. The study is also concerned with the extent to which today's problematic social scenarios are bound up with unresolved traumas bequeathed by the violent origins of the New World societies of the Caribbean.

Caribbean Narratives of Trauma

For the peoples of the Caribbean and the creative writers and cultural practitioners who have charted their journeys, foremost on the agenda have been identity crises, with successive people-groups creatively exploring issues of "Who are we?" What is our relationship to ancestral and vestigial cultures?

How do we negotiate metropolitan cultures? How do we name ourselves and our landscapes? Caribbean artists and cultural practitioners have a long history of grappling with making meaning out of myriad crises and soul-sicknesses. Cultural critic Gordon Rohlehr indicates:

> The major work of Caribbean writers of the Twentieth Century was devoted to measuring the meaning of this complex and traumatic encounter of the peoples in the New World, and a great deal of the critical discourse that has grown out of and around Caribbean literature has been preoccupied with such crucial questions as the erasure, partial survival or hybridization of ancestral identities, traditions, languages and lifestyles; the latent potentiality of submerged memories and atrophied roots, the challenges of constructing and locating new identities out of the absence or ignorance of older selves or landscapes, and in the context of a process of continuous transformation; the problem of choice and political action which have beset nations that are small, globally insignificant, impoverished, subject to extreme pressures of imperialist domination as well as to recurrent natural disasters and drowning in the sadness of steadily sinking currencies . . . (Rohlehr 2007, 457)

A brief overview of seminal literary texts is exemplary. The protagonist of Jean Rhys's most acclaimed offering, *Wide Sargasso Sea*, grapples with identity and displacement traumas which resonate throughout the entire corpus of Caribbean literature. Antoinette asks: "who am I and where is my country and where do I belong and why was I ever born" (Rhys 1966, 61). This text explores the psychosocial fallout of the dismantling of the British Empire and particularly its impact on Caribbean-born white creole women. The planter class, rendered an economically disenfranchised minority, must confront the deep-rooted hostility of the newly freed slaves and face the brunt of the horrific dynamics of the plantation society which it created. The result is a people burdened with what Kenneth Ramchand terms a "terrified consciousness" characterized by personal and social disintegration, fragmentation and loss, with no way back "home" (Morgan 2003; Ramchand [1970] 2004). The incarcerated protagonist, labelled by the husband unchaste and intemperate, ends her untenable imprisonment in a cold British mansion by laying claim to resistance modalities of the enslaved: setting fire to the manor house and leaping to a violent death. Victoria Burrows, in *Whiteness and Trauma*, critiques Rhys for improper appropriations, arguing:

> mobilisation of a trauma narrative to explain the construction of Bertha's madness conceals the far greater traumatic historical conditions of enslaved African-Caribbeans.... In *Wide Sargasso Sea* marronage becomes a metaphor ideologically appropriated to represent both the intersubjective politics of a fraught mother–daughter relationship and the abandonment of white creole colonials by the "mother-country". (Burrows 2004, 9)

Rhys's work finds resonance in those of Michelle Cliff (*No Telephone to Heaven*, 1987) and Barbara Lalla (*Arch of Fire*, 1989), who express sympathetic identification with the pain and loss of the impoverished black majority, muted acknowledgement of complicity with the imperial order, and clear assertions of Caribbean belonging.

George Lamming's early engagement with the Prospero–Caliban encounter sounded a seminal note for postcolonial critique. His concern with the conquistador figure, the psychosexual dynamic of the encounter between worlds and its implications for decolonization and emergent Caribbean identities is reflected in *Natives of My Person* (1972) and *Water with Berries* (1971). These narratives probe the ideologies and cultural practices which undergirded the colonial encounter and its legacies. *Natives of My Person* questions what manner of man would leave his homeland and his family to make a life-pursuit out of murderous conquest and pillage. In an ameliorative gesture, the crew of the slave ship *Reconnaissance*, acknowledging the immorality of the Empire, seeks to break away from the colonizing Kingdom of Limestone to establish a more just and equitable settlement. The narrative indicates that uncanny repetition and loss are assured, because the men are unable to come to terms with their pasts and with the injustices and inequities embedded in their relationships with their women.

Water with Berries (1971) is a reworking of Shakespeare's *The Tempest*, which tests the potential for a reconstructed mode of being for the pre-independence Caribbean man and society. Working with a symbolic recreation of the Haitian Ceremony of Souls ritual, in which the living and the dead meet for fierce conversation as a basis for proceeding into the future, Lamming places the progeny of the colonizer and the colonized on a darkened heath to create opportunity for inter-subjective dialogue. At this stage of the encounter – the disintegration of empire and the birthing of the new nations – the sins of the imperial fathers who taught their animals to rape enslaved women have been visited on their own lily-white daughters. The darkness of the meeting ground is necessary so that persistent and pernicious notions of racialized embodiment do not disrupt or foreclose on dialogue. It is ground and groundation for approaching even the possibility of mutually transformative relations. Ultimately this text too deals with the failure to construct a just and equitable society, given the legacy of the past and existing deficiencies in male–female relations.

In these narratives Lamming exemplifies intersection between sexuality and power and the interplay between patriarchal, colonial masculine subjectivities and alternative subcultural masculinities within plural Caribbean societies. He contends that the enterprise of the Indies has thrust its fertile and bitter rhizomes into our myriad futures, and argues in favour of a necessary backward glance at the originary trauma for understanding contemporary social violence and emerging national and transnational paradigms of Carib-being and belonging. Should this notion appear to be losing its edge and relevance, it is persuasively fleshed out as the bedrock of a contemporary anthropological project. In *Exceptional Violence: Embodied Citizenship in Transnational Jamaica*, Deborah Thomas argues persuasively that "predatory violence and illegal forms of rule" were endemic to the colonial state and the plantation economy, and by extrapolation were foundational to postcolonial state formation. She traces correlations between these ignominious beginnings and contemporary manifestations of violence as manifested in cultural experiences and political modalities of working-class Jamaica (Thomas 2011, 14).

Narratives which return to the triangular slave trade which is at the root of modern Caribbean societies represent an unsilencing of the unspeakable, which is of immense therapeutic worth. The trauma of the Middle Passage was hitherto relegated to the subterranean realms of the supernatural, myth and metonym. Arguably, similar shadows attend the ongoing Afro-Caribbean struggle with the legacy of race colourism, one manifestation being a vague sense of shame at being unable to rise above the traumatic legacy of a history of enslavement.[1] Lamming's work bears comparison with that of John Hearne in *The Sure Salvation* (1981), Brathwaite in "Discoverer", Fred D'Aguiar in *Feeding the Ghosts* (1997), and the more recent female-authored offerings of Elizabeth Harrel Nunez (*Prospero's Daughter*, 2006) and NourbeSe Philip

(*Zong!* 2008). All engage the journey as an interstitial space within which the mechanisms and mindsets of conquest and dominance and subjugation were violently entrenched. Lamming's early representations lead in the hauntological project (as later delineated by Patricia Saunders in conversation with NourbeSe Philip) with their focus on initiating and articulating dialogue with spectres of blackness which have been denied subjectivity and voice. In these narratives, grappling with the unknowing and the unknowable is pivotal to the work of mourning in the aftermath of slavery.

Derek Walcott inscribes the wound generated by enforced separation from ancestral culture as a "deep amnesiac blow" which renders the New World inhabitant bereft of ancestry, moorings, ruins – but conversely in possession of a space of infinite possibility as Adamic Man, empowered to chart new beginnings. Fashioning himself as ruptured and genealogically poisoned by his European and African bloodlines, the poet/persona is simultaneously – as is the case for all proverbial well-trained Afro-Greeks – enamoured of European cultural forms and expressions. In relation to Laventille, a sprawling hillside catchment for the urban poor in Trinidad which sprang up when the slaves fled the estates and settled overlooking the city of Port of Spain, the poet/persona indicates: "The middle passage never guessed its end / This is the height of poverty / For the desperate and black." In his 1970 essay "What the Twilight Says", Walcott, though assured of the incurability of the wounding amnesiac blow, nevertheless greets the grim urban poverty, frenetic energy and eruptive violence of Port of Spain of the mid-1900s with the dissociation of the sublime, praising the sheer, almost mystical beauty of its ramshackle hoardings of wood and rusting iron as "gilded hallucinations of poverty with a corrupt resignation" (Walcott [1970b] 1998, 3). For here, Walcott states, "Desperation is made lyrical, and twilight, with the patience of alchemy, almost transmutes despair into virtue. In the tropics nothing is lovelier than the allotments of the poor, no theatre is as vivid, voluble and cheap" (4).

Amnesia, Walcott argues, is the "true history of the New World", which nevertheless entraps the colonizer and the colonized in cycles of condemnation and justification as they grapple to bring to the surface the enormity of loss:

> But who in the New World does not have a horror of the past, whether his ancestor was torturer or victim? Who, in the depth of conscience, is not silently

screaming for pardon or revenge? The pulse of New World history is the racing pulse beat of fear, the tiring cycles of stupidity and greed. The tongues above our prayers utter the pain of entire races to the darkness of a Manichean God. (Walcott [1974] 1998, 39)

Walcott argues that the enslaved surrendered to amnesia. Predictably spectral hauntings of a monstrous past, uneasily and tenuously confined beneath the surface of consciousness, have created an intrusive and persistent impulse to try to understand and justify a history of forgetting which coexists with the "awe of the numinous, this elemental privilege of naming the New World which annihilates history" (Walcott [1974] 1998, 40). In "What the Twilight Says" and *Pantomime*, Walcott expresses scepticism in relation to nostalgic impulses that seek to re-member and dignify an ancestral past, preferring a stance which embraces the perils and potentialities of a shattered archipelago and an uncertain future, with wonder and gratitude.

The adverse social condition and the quest for significance of the Afro-Caribbean urban poor are also a major focus for Earl Lovelace, who similarly traces the journey of the progeny of the enslaved from emancipation to the present. Conferring dignity and significance on the personal and socio-cultural pursuits of displaced and disoriented young male warriors, Lovelace explores the paralysis, even stasis, which grips a people dealing with ancestral loss of homeland, language, purpose, destiny and future. He eschews any discourse that blames young black males for the abject conditions of their daily lives without consideration of their historical legacies and contemporary adversities. He affirms the right of the people to rituals and acts of resistance and rebellion, and endorses the instrumentality of these forces in crafting a social order of benefit to all.

Erna Brodber is similarly concerned with disempowered Afro-Caribbean nationals, and with other descendants of the enslaved in the diaspora. She penned her first novel (*Jane and Louisa*, 1980) as a case study in abnormal psychology while seeking a medium to adequately reflect the myriad soul-sicknesses of Caribbean peoples, which could not be adequately encapsulated within Western knowledge frames. A sociologist turned creative writer, Brodber identifies herself as an intellectual worker and her work as fiction with activist intent, crafted to intervene therapeutically in legacies of trauma:

"It is about studying the behaviour of and transmitting these findings to the children of the people who were put on ships on the African beaches and woke up from this nightmare to find themselves on the shores of the New World" (1990, 164). The allegory *The Rainmaker's Mistake* (2007) debunks the imperial patriarchal mythologies which reduce the enslaved to brown yams born of the issue of the colonizer and entrapped in naivety, arrested development, juvenile sexuality and lack of responsibility. To shake off these shackles, the newly emancipated ferret out the wounding which denied them life, the primal scream which signals their traumatic initiation into its perils and potentialities, and face the imperative to assume responsibility for its outcome. Brodber's work with a focus on the African diaspora privileges ethnic inclusivity over Afrocentricity and eschews Western healing modalities in favour of interventions based on therapeutic folkways which address the spirit, soul and body. The work of Opal Palmer Adisa also follows in this vein.

Wordsmiths who have charted the journey of the progeny of indentees have also been eloquent in their evocations of social violence and trauma. For some, like V.S. Naipaul, the response to the tumultuous social order is ambivalent rejection and flight. His fiction and travelogues offer recurrent representations of flight from – alongside compulsive shame-ridden engagement with – his natal land and contempt for its myriad people-groups, bastardizations and miscegenations, but also an acknowledgement that its ethnic, religious, cultural and linguistic diversity has been a rich creative source. He affirms: "the island had given me the world as a writer" (Naipaul 1987, 153). The prevailing ancestral culture and the narrow provincialism of the "colonial backwater" of his birthplace holds a key both to the nature of Naipaul's "unhomeliness" – in the sense defined by Homi Bhabha – and to his lifelong creative project. As I argue in chapter 2, these traumatizing catalysts are primary shapers of Naipaulian characters and worldviews and a key formative element which has released their creator to become a world-renowned architect of the postcolonial house of fiction, which is pierced through with the lament of the unhomely.

Indo-Caribbean writers have been brutally frank in their evocations of identity, displacement and incest traumas. They carefully locate painful domestic dramas within the temporal, spatial and geopolitical contexts of the global movement of bonded labour to fuel the capitalist machinery of the Western world. Harold Sonny Ladoo's narratives *No Pain Like This Body* (1972) and *Yesterdays* (1974) constitute damning representations of horrific, mind-boggling family violence within a labour-based proletariat which has migrated from an ancient society, with its clear and strict norms and prescriptions, into the dislocation and anomie of post-indentureship Trinidad. Family becomes a microcosm of a social group in crisis. The central issue is an existential one. In this liminal space in the interstices of cultures, the migrants face the requirement of constructing viable modes of being, patterns of familial interaction, and dynamics of community which can empower and impart life and hope. A similar dynamic is set up in Shani Mootoo's *Cereus Blooms at Night* (1996), with its focus on racism, betrayal, incest, rape and patricide. The intense and sustained epistemic violence inflicted by the civilizing Presbyterian order plays a key role in the making of the abusive father, who in this narrative extends his violence to the level of incest. Mootoo, herself a victim of incest who turned to the visual arts to work through her pain, explores correlations among violence, trauma and loss of the symbolic referentiality of language. The novel, set in the indentureship period but written against the framework of contemporary gender politics, delves deeply into the complex interplay of identity and dislocation traumas and how these relate to the father–daughter incest and fluid gender constructions which are the core concerns of the narrative. Mootoo's sensitively portrayed and nuanced father nevertheless shadows Ladoo's horrific Pa. Together they inhabit the space beyond community, beyond hope, beyond redemption.

These Caribbean authors and countless others too numerous to mention work their way towards acknowledgement, expression and articulation of new modes of being human in the wake of horrific despoliation wrought by a history which refuses to be relegated to the past. As those seeds of early technology-driven globalization produce their prolific and strange fruit in contemporary Caribbean societies, they pose an ethical imperative of engagement and a compulsive impulse towards narrative, as successive generations of creative writers and thinkers seek to order its chaos and to bear witness to its atrocities. This, I argue, constitutes a collective, multigenerational, multiethnic endeavour to exorcise what Gordon Rohlehr has termed the malign unpropitiated duppy of history, and perchance to redirect its vengeful energies.

Frameworks

The imperative to engage issues of trauma, ethics and testimony in the wake of historical atrocities and their lingering, intrusive contemporary legacies is a major concern of this time. Globally, historical traumas overlay myriad contemporary manifestations of everyday violence and violation emanating from the environment; climate, economic, social, civil and geopolitical upheaval; terrorism; and health emergencies, which play themselves out on national and transnational stages daily. An unprecedented proliferation of crisis scenarios, which are a reflection of both the real and of media-transmitted "scripted" violence, is being mainlined into homes and sensibilities, creating lowering clouds of anxiety and dread. The media, working in tandem with world leaders in every sphere, have been accorded in our time a creative power to speak the word, which often delineates or defines but occasionally also creates crises globally. Either way, the perception is that we are currently engaged by unprecedented global crises which promise to escalate and which place a burden on our social and intellectual traditions.

The power of crisis to push knowledge beyond governing epistemes is widely acknowledged. In *Criticism, Crisis and Contemporary Narrative*, Paul Crosthwaite traces the etymology of the terms *crisis* and *criticism* back to their common root in the Greek word *krinein*, which means "to separate, judge, decide" (Crosthwaite 2011, 1). This interface between crisis and critique points to the potential of crises to rupture the way we have come to know ourselves and thereby demystify inherited intellectual traditions and generate new ones, which in turn produce their own mystifications. It works the other way too. Criticism, by pushing against the boundaries of received knowledge, puts the foundations of knowledge in crisis. In support of this position, Crosthwaite cites connections between psychoanalysis and the dissolution of the Austro-Hungarian Empire and the Great War; the Frankfurt School of critical theory and the global economic and social upheavals of the 1930s and '40s; existentialism and the post–Second World War physical and spiritual devastation in Europe; post-structuralism and unresolved issues of the Holocaust, the Vietnam War and looming threats of apocalypse; feminisms and radical disruptions of family, sex and gender of the 1970s and '80s; cultural studies and the collapse of Britain's social democratic postwar consensus; and postcolonial criticism and the tumultuous nationalist, ethnic and religious conflicts within both the New and Old Worlds. He argues: "The history of modern critical thought might, then, be best narrated as a history of attempts to register and amplify conditions of crisis in pursuit of a radical renewal of the intellectual and social order" (Crosthwaite 2011, 2).

Globally, the imperative to represent a painful past so as to alleviate forgetting, adjust misrepresentation, and admit subaltern perspectives has assumed great significance in this time. Fictional and other discourses of trauma point to the interface between social suffering and private disease and disquiet in multiple social and cultural contexts. Trauma theory, with its ethical focus, has gathered a substantial band of followers, reflective of a migration towards issues-based scholarship which is responsive to stakeholder needs. This school of thought was originally conceptualized in the response to the Jewish Holocaust. In the wake of activism by victims of the Vietnam War, feminists and trauma theorists have applied the diagnosis of post-traumatic stress disorder (PTSD) – the disturbing clusters of symptoms experienced by persons in the wake of trauma-inducing catalysts – to victims of sexual violence and survivors of extreme natural disasters and criminal acts. The commonly accepted symptoms of trauma are now well recognized: an event which overrides the body's coping mechanisms, triggering a response of fight or flight; intrusive memories caused by attempts of the conscious mind to bring the event out of the domain of submerged memory; belated hauntings caused by the inability of the victim to take in the horror of the traumatizing catalyst in one dose; cycles of uncanny repetition, hyperarousal, dissociated consciousness; and a fear reflex which is unrelated or disproportionate to any external causal factor (Caruth 1996; Hermon 1992).

In *Trauma and Survival in Contemporary Fiction* (2002), Laurie Vickroy argues that trauma narratives engage important social and psychological issues. These narratives demonstrate, first, the significance of trauma as a "multicontextual social issue as it is a consequence of political ideologies, colonization, war, domestic violence, poverty, and so forth". Second, trauma narratives challenge the Western notion of the "highly individuated subject by pointing to the limitation of subject so constituted to deal with "loss and fragmentation". Third, the narratives constrain the reader to confront fears "of death, of dissolution of loss of loss of control". Last, the narratives elucidate the "public's relationship to the traumatized, made public", taking into account public resistance to narratives of pain and the "psychic defences". Vickroy indicates that trauma narratives "internalize the rhythms, processes and certainties of traumatic experience with their underlying sensibilities and structures. They reveal many obstacles to communicating such experience: silence, simultaneous knowledge and denial, dissociation, resistance and repression."

The process by which collectivities construct themselves in relation to a violent history is debated in Ron Eyerman's notion of cultural trauma, which he defines as rooted in an event or series of events which may or may not have been directly experienced. He defines the characteristics of cultural trauma as mass mediation, allowing for spatial and temporal distancing; selective construction and representation through the intervention of media and knowledge workers as mediators and translators; and contestation over meaning, responsibility and nature of potential impact. Eyerman (after Alexander) points to a traumatic process by which "the collective experience of massive disruption and social crises become a crisis of meaning and identity . . . A traumatic tear evokes the need to 'narrate new foundations' which include reinterpreting the past as a means towards reconciling present/future needs" (2001, 3). Eyerman is careful to identify the collective traumatic memory as spatialized and vested in material culture and iconography, as well as in discursive formations. These are useful insights for part 1 of this text, which deals with fictional evocations of the complex cross-cultural interface of Caribbean ontologies from the perspectives of Euro Creoles and Afro- and Indo-Caribbean peoples.

The correlation between loss, subjectivity and history is the concern of Jonathan Boulter's *Melancholy and the Archive: Trauma History and Memory in the Contemporary Novel*. He takes as his point of departure Freud's incapacity to explain how mourning and melancholia work through the notion of "economics of pain" to allow the subject to "break free of his or her attachment to the lost object" (Boulter 2011, 2). Boulter also invokes Derrida's notion of the archive as a place of "commandment and commencement", "a place from which the order of things – let us call it for now the order of history – is governed"; the archive may be "a space, a site, a phenomenal presence just as it becomes a temporal and spectral entity" (3–4). Freud identifies mourning as the healthy way to grapple with trauma and loss. Through the work of mourning, the subject comes to accept that the loved object is no longer present. In the case of melancholia, on the other hand, the subject retains a continuous narcissistic identification with the lost object. The traumatic loss continually crops up because the subject cannot move past it. Boulter, in response to the contentions of Freud and Derrida, argues that, through melancholy, the individual subject becomes an archive, that is, "an effective response to the past; a place where history itself is housed, where the past is accommodated" (3). This, he posits, is a useful model for "thinking about the subject as he begins to negotiate a relationship to a disastrous history, to a past marked by loss and trauma" (9). Boulter's concepts may be usefully applied to the postcolonial subject and to the issue of how a radically decentred subject can respond to history. And conversely, what happens to history – remembered, reconstructed events of a disastrous past – when it has produced only decentred subjects?

Recently, theorists have engaged the discrepancy between trauma studies' stated commitment to cross-cultural ethical engagement and its ongoing focalization around the Nazi Holocaust. Alexandre Dauge-Roth, writing on the genocide of Tutsis in Rwanda, draws a possible correlation between excessive attention to the Nazi Holocaust and evasion of the challenges of the present: "the duty of remembering its uniqueness has now become our moral and political excuse for remaining blind to the ongoing genocide in Darfur and deaf to the long lasting needs of survivors of more recent genocides perpetrated in Cambodia, the former Yugoslavia, and Rwanda" (Dauge-Roth 2010, 4). Contributors to the 2008 issue of *Studies in the Novel* on postcolonial trauma novels were particularly vociferous in their call. Stef Craps and Gert Buelen, in their introduction to the volume, state: "If, as Caruth argues, 'history is precisely the way we are implicated in each other's traumas' (Caruth 1991, *Unclaimed* 24) then Western traumatic histories must be seen to be tied up with histories of colonial trauma for trauma studies to be able to redeem its promise of ethic effectiveness" (Craps and Buelen 2008, 2). Recent interventions have therefore applied trauma theory to the debacle of colonialism and its aftermath, in search of an understanding of its interplay between historical, public, communal and personal violations. This has led in turn to a shift away from limiting trauma theory's applicability to heinous events in favour of a focus on the traumatic impact of everyday violence (Morgan and Youssef 2006).

Theorizations of extended definitions of *trauma* in an attempt to shift away from an event-based model to a broader, more culturally applicable paradigm are itemized by Craps as type II trauma, complex PTSD or disorders of extreme stress not otherwise specified, safe-world violations, insidious traumas, oppression-based traumas, postcolonial syndrome, postcolonial stress disorder and post-traumatic slavery syndrome (Craps 2013, 44). And since trauma theory has far-reaching ontological and practical consequences, theorists are calling for adjustments in thinking and practice to enhance its usefulness. Michael Rothberg insists: "as long as trauma studies foregoes comparative study and remains tied to a narrow Eurocentric framework, it distorts the histories it addresses (such as the Holocaust) and threatens to reproduce the very Eurocentricism which lies behind these histories" (Rothberg 2008, 227). Craps is also critical of the capacity of the notion of trauma as an essentialized universal psychobiological response to lead to practical Western interventions which are disrespectful at best, if not downright harmful to deeply entrenched indigenous practices of remembrance, mourning, healing and reconstruction.

Postcolonial deployment and critique of trauma demonstrate both its usefulness and its limited applicability to social scenarios of the New World nations. The focus on the highly individualized subject of the Oedipal/familial narrative often does not take into account mass social suffering and the attendant collective nature of trauma. Politically motivated acts of violence assault entire racial minorities, classes and even nations when rogue states turn upon and eat their own children. The focus on trauma as inducing psychic incapacitation and loss of the facility for symbolic representation tends to minimize material dimensions of loss. Additionally, focus on the temporal dislocation inflicted by trauma can obscure the spatial outworkings of the traumatizing catalysts.

Irene Visser (2011, 273–79), addressing the issue of usefully conjoining trauma theory with postcolonial literary theory, focuses on definitions of trauma, streams of thought at the heart of the theory, and its Eurocentric orientation. A major disjuncture rests with the inherent historicity of the colonial experience vis-à-vis the supposed unknowability of the traumatizing catalyst. Visser points to the lack of historical particularity in Freud's theorization of the internal abstract, "unsayable" causation of trauma rather than a historically concrete, knowable external causation, which is a pivotal concern to postcolonial critique (Visser 2011, 273). Second, she posits that a viable postcolonial trauma theory would be predicated on a more comprehensive definition of trauma in order to "account more astutely for the aftermath of colonialism's systematic oppression, with its characteristics of prolonged, repeated and cumulative stressor events". Third, the concept of collective trauma needs a "more thorough and culturally astute formulation" (276).

Visser's fourth point is that postcolonial trauma theory would need to reject any orientation towards themes of "victimization and melancholia", which might serve to "obscure themes of recuperation and psychic resilience", thus foreclosing on the notion of a "melancholic, chronically weakened, socially divided postcolonial collective" (277). She identifies Caruth's aporia as too limiting a perspective, since many of the texts posit the need for political activism, social change and individual healing. "This is the movement away from melancholy and 'unspeakability' to resistance and recovery that accords with currents in trauma theory represented by Herman and La Capra." Visser also takes issue with the "fuzziness" attending notions of transmissibility, with its potential to blur distinctions between victims of historical traumas and their secondary witnesses, arguing that the collapsing of these distinctions has the potential to trivialize the experience. She advocates a definition of trauma as "the memory of an overwhelming, unassimilable and violent wounding directly incurred as a first-hand experience in order to differentiate it from secondary or vicarious traumatisation" (275). Fifth, Visser indicts the Eurocentrism of trauma theory's dismissal of the significance of religious belief systems as yet another matter that would need serious consideration in a further "rapprochement" between trauma theory and postcolonial studies (276). The Western trauma model does not acknowledge spirituality and the potential for regeneration through ritual and belief systems. She concludes: "Possible directions in which to reconstruct this framework to respond to postcolonial ways of understanding history, memory and trauma will involve reorientation towards narratives that are forward looking, striving for subversion of the traumatic experience rather than its containment in melancholia" (279).

Transferability and contagion are the focus of Balaev's engagement with prevailing notions of the workings of historical trauma. Balaev takes issue with theories of intergenerational trauma which "conflate loss and absence and collapse boundaries between the individual and the group", thereby suggesting that a person's "contemporary identity can be 'vicariously traumatized' by reading about a historical narrative or due to a shared genealogy that affords the ability to righteously claim the social label of 'victim' as part of personal or public identity" (Balaev 2008, 152).

> To claim that the traumatized protagonist expresses a specific, idiosyncratic response to trauma, while also functioning as a representative figure of a social group in order to relate the actions in the novel to a historical event, does not suggest that the protagonist asserts an essentialist, intergenerational identity based on a decades-old event. The novel demonstrates the ways that an experience disrupts the individual conceptualizations of self and connections to family and community, but the values attributed to the traumatic experience are largely shaped by cultural forces created within the world of the novel. (Balaev 2008, 156)

In other words, Balaev argues, the imputed silencing of trauma can readily be attributed to cultural values and communication rituals which allow or disallow the airing of certain topics and emotion, more so than amnesia in relation to submerged social suffering too grim to be articulated. "Yet, to what degree traumatic experience disrupts memory, self, and relation to others is mediated by cultural values and narrative forms rooted in a place that allow or disallow certain emotions to be expressed" (Balaev 2008, 156). This study pays regard to Balaev's contention in relation to the essentialized notion of intergenerationally culturally transmitted traumas: "trauma is not the definitive component of ethnic group definition; neither is its power of contagion so great that all descendants of an ethnic group are necessarily infected by its historical traumas". It acknowledges the potential for essentialized notions of group identity to transfix individuals perpetually in the roles of victims and perpetrators and to vitalize perceptions and discourses of violence, hopelessness and despair.

Building on a long tradition of literary and cultural practitioners and critical thinkers and activists acting as pointers to show us where we have come from and pathways we should be pursuing, this enquiry contributes to ongoing literary and cultural discourses which survey our current climate of crisis in the region and further afield. It contributes a focus on the construction and performance of personal and social crises as discursive phenomenon – the invocation and languaging of disaster scenarios, the power of the word to generate or subdue dissent, to purvey or alleviate fear. It is concerned with language, metaphor, metonymy, figuration, rhetoric, narratorization of trauma and the ideological functions served by discourses of crisis reality.

Media – print, radio and television – which provide fora and mirrors in which construction of the nation and transnation are being negotiated daily, are also influential purveyors of crisis talk. Internet chat rooms serve the same function. There is a high level of local and diasporic citizen participation in discourses of who we are, what we have lost and what we are becoming. Distinctive strands of crisis talk emerge, the dominant theme being "Look what we come to . . . we gon through or we gon clear." These Internet and media-based interfaces, like the traditional barroom conversations known as "rum talk" and the shifting mobile "taxi talk", are generally perceived as highly influential and effective barometers of "what tong [town] say". It assumes a substantial weight of authority and contagion, because "tong always know". Whereas taxi talk and the ubiquitous "shout-out" talk shows are features of everyday life, crisis talk typically spirals at points of wounding which pierce the body politic and generate doubts and fears about identity, safety, survival and a viable future.

The focus on trauma narratives and critique in this time points to a breakdown in generic delimitations and raises questions as to the correlations between polished fictional evocations, media representations, public conversational crisis discourse, testimony before a truth-and-reconciliation council, personal narratives of domestic abuse, and more. In essence, this focus points to correlations between narratives, constructed as factual or fictional, intended to represent and preserve, witness and memorialize trauma.

Pivotal to the argument is the assumption that modern societies of the Caribbean are built on a founding historical trauma, that all of its people have been indelibly imprinted by the cataclysmic encounter between worlds, and substantial cross-sections of its populations are still reeling from the force of that blow. In other words, legacies of that historical trauma erupt in successive generations and retain significance for the descendants of all ethnicities – victims and perpetrators alike. This study is by definition postcolonial but will engage only peripherally with the burden of paradox and ambivalence with which the term is invested and the contestation concerning its materiality, contemporary significance and relevance within a Caribbean framework, as opposed to within metropolitan academic institutions.

This study is historically grounded and socially situated. It recognizes that the colonial experience within the region and even within the anglophone Caribbean has been diverse – in terms of the values, ideologies and objectives of the enslaved peoples and of the dominant nations, the duration of conquest, the erasure of the indigenous inhabitants, the cultures of dominance and subjugation, the topographies of colonized island landscapes. The enterprise of the Indies has therefore yielded a substantial range of cultural legacies which colonizer, colonized and their progeny of successive generations are constrained to submerge or confront, evade or work through. The study deals with the interface between the psychological condition of having been colonized and surviving cultural and material practices. It draws its raw materials from texts, discourses and representations while retaining a sensitivity to concrete historical practices.

The discursive focus does not seek to evade existing political and economic inequities. Following the lead of the textual material briefly surveyed above, it reads beyond easy binaries of colonizer/colonized, colonial/postcolonial, them/us, self/other, settler/nomad, in the interest of exposing how these essentialized categories are deployed to support hegemonies. Formulations of creative writers have long since pointed to the postcolonial condition as predicated on mutually conflicted locations of both colonizer and colonized (for example, Jean Rhys's mirror imagery in *Wide Sargasso Sea* and Lamming's embrace of the colonizer in *Natives of My Person*), with complex evocations of split inner subjectivity, hybridization and mimicry. The colonized subject can no more effect a disjuncture from the worldview, language, cultural practices and political institutions of the colonized than the colonial master can erase that of the colonizer (as exemplified in Walcott's *Pantomime*). In its analysis of social issues, this study steers a careful path between commitment to nationalism – which retains serious symbolic currency within Caribbean nation-states and within its iconic institutions, such as the University of the West Indies – and recognition of the post-nation. The readings favour an interstitial subjectivity that is being constantly and ambivalently negotiated between complex cultural imperatives.

Following the lead of the primary material, much of which sets out to counter the epistemic violence of the hegemonic narratives and deliberate erasures of the imperial order, this study is sensitive to the ideological stakes and legitimizing forces implicit in acts of counter-remembrance. In other words, it locates all acts of memory, and even those more subtle acts of retrieval which are mediated through fiction, as socially negotiated and culturally determined. It is sensitive to the manner in which histories and narratives of becoming which legitimize particular representations of the past must also buttress a specified social order within the present. Hence, any act of inscribing a circumscribed visibility of the past within the present in turn institutionalizes its own gestures of forgetting.

The study therefore addresses the following: To what extent are existing conceptions of trauma useful for analysing the ruptures peculiar to Antillean history, with its attendant anxieties, identity crises and representational dilemmas? How can trauma be understood and worked through if it is inherent to group identity formation and schemes of representation? In other words, has trauma been normalized in Caribbean societies? The study is also concerned with the interface of trauma with the four existentials of lived experience – spatiality, corporeality, temporality, and relationality – which Van Manen argues ground the human interface with the world. Identifying in its primary material diverse representations of "unhomeliness", the enquiry poses these issues: Are their shared conventions of inhabiting space and time and how these ruptured in those who have been traumatized? What constitutes the experience of lived space in Caribbean literary and popular culture? How does one define the lived space in which Caribbean peoples circulate and find themselves at home or displaced, here, elsewhere, inside, outside, accommodated, exiled? Given the contemporary obsession with racialized and gendered embodiments, what do literary and cultural evocations reflect about the process of corporeal embodiment? How does the racialized and gendered body function under the gaze of the Other? And how does that gaze shape relationality? What does the body of primary material reflect about the lived experience of temporality when trauma cannot be relegated to the past? When the belated intrusiveness of trauma pushes insistently into the present and haunts tomorrows, what is the impact on hope, aspirations and expectations?

The title of this text is drawn from Martin Carter's lyrical poem "The University of Hunger", which deals with the impact of poverty and hunger on daily lives and its interface with mass migrations.[2] This poem is critiqued in chapter 9, which explores the social impact of poverty. The first part of the text deals with the impact of mass migrations and imperial ideologies on those who emerged from the nightmare of history to grapple with the constraints of finding themselves in the New World. This has proven to be a multigenerational project.

Chapter 1 explores representations of the originary trauma which marks the inception of the modern Caribbean social order – the slave journey, and specifically fictional representations of the *Zong* massacre, in which a slaver threw overboard between 133 and 150 sick enslaved Africans to facilitate collection of insurance coverage for property lost at sea. Several writers have evoked this incident as indicative of the social dynamics of the liminal space and the terrorist system which transformed free men into enslaved and enslavers and demonstrated the impact of the greed and dehumanization of the capitalist system, with its inherent devaluation of the human person. The major imperative is to recover and clothe with flesh, blood and narrative the submerged histories of the slaughtered, the disembodied and the voiceless. The narratives evoke the sea as amniotic fluid which birthed nascent cultures and social orders, bore witness to and engulfed grim human tragedy. The sea as archive becomes a resting place and catalyst of remembrance. Drowned ancestors anxiously seek a generation which will embrace the sacred imperative of re-membering their scattered skeletons. The narratives also point to the socio-sexual drama of the imperial project and to the power of racist stereotyping to transcend disembodiment of the part-born and aborted foetuses, whose ruptured life histories and silenced voices articulate the horrific legacy of empire.

The persistent personal and institutional legacy of racism and the mechanisms by which it infiltrated and embedded itself in the emerging Caribbean nation is the focus of chapter 2, which reads Olive Senior's "The View from the Terrace" and Paule Marshall's "Barbados" as evocations of the shifting of the power base from the Euro-creole to the Afro-creole contingent of Jamaican and Barbadian societies. The authors posit that the emergence of Afro-creole political and cultural sensibilities requires ontological erosion of the Euro-creole gatekeepers of the colonial order, embodied in desiccated light-skinned men who must face the onslaught of young, vibrant and sensual black women who personify the challenge of the emerging cultural and political order. The resultant ontological trauma leads to their unceremonious demise.

The third chapter deals with V.S. Naipaul's evocation of the challenges faced by Indian immigrants and their descendants in negotiating the journey away from a decaying ancestral culture and towards the tumultuous creole space of pre-independence Trinidad. It focuses on Naipaul's complex and ambivalent engagement with his natal land, which elicits in him a compulsive impulse towards flight, as reflected in his fiction, travelogues and essays. Referencing Bhabha's (1994) notion of "unhomeliness" as paradigmatic to the postcolonial condition, I argue that the impulse to transform shame and trauma into narrative holds a key to both the nature of Naipaul's unhomeliness and his lifelong creative project.

The following chapter, " 'Something Inside Like a Wound Laid Wide': Walcott's City of Pain and Promise", draws its title from Derek Walcott's 1970 poem "Laventille", which is dedicated to V.S. Naipaul. This chapter deals with Walcott's evocation of the outcome of the Middle Passage, which he claims delivered "a deep, amnesiac blow". The unbreachable gaps and fissures have nevertheless provoked an artistic and scholarly imperative to probe the depths and limits of this amnesia, and, in a functional sense, have left the poor and dispossessed of this hillside settlement reeling under cycles of poverty, dispossession and apathy. The chapter reads Walcott's 1970 representations of Laventille against contemporary newspaper headlines to probe the problematic of its ambivalent symbolic location as the birthplace of its major cultural export – highly successful and transportable carnival arts, which have spawned Trinidad-style carnivals in major metropolitan and other nations worldwide – and simultaneously as the symbol of the nation's incapacity to deal with its increasingly violent urban poor.

The second part of this text, which is focussed on more tangible social issues, uses as its primary material fictional and personal narratives, media and popular culture discourse. Chapter 5 begins with an exploration of the impact of state violence perpetrated under the Haitian Duvalier regime on the lives of victims and torturers alike, through a reading of Edwidge Danticat's *The Dew Breaker*. A member of a Haitian death squad is the common link in a series of stories of those who were maimed physically and psychically by a Tonton Macoute who has since reformed into a mild-mannered, diligent, successful Haitian migrant to the United States. The infamous rural militia was established to buttress the multigenerational rule of the Duvaliers; its henchmen were exempted from prosecution for any acts of violence carried out during the performance of this duty. This exploration of the ubiquitous, entrenched, social violence of the Duvalier regime is an effective access point for consideration of the culpability of states which enact policies and practices which devour and decimate its citizens. *The Dew Breaker*, which is also a migration and exile narrative, explores the meandering rhizomic tentacles of state and personal violence as they spread across generations, oceans and social orders. Danticat argues that alleviation of criminal activity and its consequences requires collective social action. Moreover, transgenerational intervention is required to expiate historical transgression in order to interrupt its violent present-day outworkings.

Ageing and Alzheimer's is the focus of chapter 6. Barbara Lalla's *Cascade* deals with the aching vulnerabilities of ageing and the challenges and imperatives it poses to loved ones and caregivers. This evocation of the crisis of forgetting within the framework of a loving, nurturing family and a fulfilled and productive life bears comparison with David Chariandy's *Soucouyant*. In the latter, ruptured cognitive schema and the intrusive belatedness of trauma are implicated in early-onset Alzheimer's. The catalyst is rooted broadly in the historical and communal violations wrought when First World nations seize the lands, human capital and resources of strategically located so-called Third World nations to service their warmongering objectives. The poverty and social inequity which made women and children vulnerable to prostitution during the establishment of an American base in Trinidad in the 1940s drives a preteen daughter to set her mother aflame. Early-onset Alzheimer's in this case releases fragments of submerged memories as the protagonist forgets to forget the piercing wounds of her past and negotiates the imperative to pass on the unspeakable narrative.

The final three chapters interrogate contemporary examples of banal violence manifested within the contexts of child-shifting, alcoholism and poverty. "Naked with Unknowing" explores the impact of trauma on the Caribbean child. It deliberately turns away from extensive examples of heinous acts of abuse against children in favour of a focus on the violence of everyday existence and its deleterious impact on the (un)making of self. Through a reading of Olive Senior's "Bright Thursdays", this chapter locates the child as caught up in a vortex of historical, communal and personal violations. It poses questions about the epistemological significance of psychic trauma in children, its impact on their worldview and their internal sense of being in the world, and their meagre attempts to rescue a shattered self and a shattered worldview in the aftermath of trauma.

Chapter 8, "Rum Till I Die", probes the outcome of a long-term historical relationship with rum which was a major by-product of the plantation economy and an anodyne for its dislocations, anomie and backbreaking labour. A resultant culture of alcoholism, chronic wife-beating, murders and high suicide rates developed. This chapter reads calypso, chutney, personal narratives and literary representations to explore the associations among ethnicity, rum and death. The final segment analyses an interview of a member of Alcoholics Anonymous, using a phenomenological approach to examine the lived and embodied experience of alcoholism.

The persistent poverty of segments of the region, exacerbated by seasonal hurricanes, droughts and other natural disasters, is the concern of chapter 9, " 'No Money, No Love': Representations of the Social Impact of Poverty". The chapter zeroes in on the deleterious impact of poverty on daily lives and its differential outworking based on period and gender. The primary material indicates that there was a season in which physical poverty did not necessarily mean emotional and spiritual impoverishment, and education provided a transgenerational escape route out of abject poverty. Those values and escape routes are not functioning as effectively today. Traditional avenues of poverty alleviation and upward mobility – through education, leading to a professional career – which undergirded the birthing of the new nations of the archipelago, are today proving increasingly distant or even unattainable for a widening cross-section of youth. The explorations of literary, popular and media discourses yield insights into the far-reaching social consequences of poverty, its intergenerational impact and prospects for alleviation. The chapter examines poverty's differential impact as dependent on the age, gender and social location of its victim.

Although the text zeroes in on social and/or banal violence in the

Caribbean, it is not grim and hopeless in its orientation. Instead it seeks to unveil the everyday brutalities and suffering in the ordinary in order to raise issues of ethical position in the face of violence, the requirement to collectively assume responsibility for who we are and what we are becoming, and the role of narrative in recuperating selves and constructing viable ontologies.

PART 1

ONTOLOGIES

1

"RE-MEMBERING OUR SCATTERED SKELETONS"
Literary Representations of the *Zong* Massacre

>   Columbus from his after-
>   deck watched heights he hoped for,
>   rocks he dreamed, rise solid from my simple water.
>   Parrots screamed. Soon he would touch
>   our land, his charted mind's desire.
>   The blue sky blessed the morning with its fire.
>   . . . Now he was sure
>   he heard soft voices mocking in the leaves.
>   What did this journey mean, this
>   new world mean: dis-
>   covery? Or a return to terrors
>   he had sailed from, known before?
>   – Edward Brathwaite, "Discoverer"

>   . . . but we were peaceful then
>   child-like in the yellow dawn of our innocence . . .
>   – Olive Senior, "Meditation on Yellow"

THE SEA JOURNEY IS the common experience which links the founders of the New World societies of the Caribbean. Recharting waters traversed by the region's indigenous inhabitants, slave traders, seamen, adventurers, explorers, merchants, missionaries, the enslaved and the indentured braved swelling oceans as they sailed away from relatively settled homogenous societies into what Wilson Harris terms the "happy catastrophe" of cultural confrontation which gave birth to the modern Caribbean.[1] This melee of people-groups, cultures and value systems has been yoked into a viable social order against the background of oppressive and unjust social systems, and in response it has generated networks of secondary migrations and vibrant diasporic communities. The sea journey has had pivotal actual and metaphorical significance for these islands' inhabitants since Columbus, that intrepid explorer, undertook his topsy-turvy endeavour of sailing west to reach the east.

Narratives of journey are sites at which we lay bare the weeping wounds of history. The journey to the New World haunts Caribbean writers who confront pressing contemporary social issues with the ongoing imperative to craft originary narratives. As if locking the island inhabitants into an ambivalent and contentious brotherhood of the boat, the sea passage refuses to be relegated to a historical time past, taking on instead the character of a haunting collective trauma which must be repeatedly recounted as writers of all ethnicities grapple with the legacy of the peoples, cultures, ideologies, institutions and material objects that came.[2] Notwithstanding the inexorable and creative ethnic admixtures which have since resulted, the current material circumstances of a cross-section of the respective people-groups bear direct relation to their beginnings. The racist ideologies of white supremacy and the cultural and mental inferiority of the Other undergirded the largest enforced labour movement in recorded human history – the transatlantic slave trade and the only minimally less violating indentureship schemes. Many permutations later, these ideologies lurk within the collective consciousness to accord social privilege and, conversely, to retard the progress of countless. The suffering endured on the journey is a significant factor in contemporary contestation over rights and belonging, including access to symbolic capital and national emblems. For, the argument goes, shouldn't the state extend greater patronage to those who endured greater hardship in the Middle Passage? The journey haunts centuries later because, until recently, it proved too grim to recount.[3] In Lakshmi Persaud's *Butterfly in the Wind* (1990), the tongues of the aged one are loosened to tell the horror of the journey only when the protagonist prepares to board a ship bound for Ireland – her passport to social upliftment through tertiary education. The successful journey redeems the shaming one and lifts the shrouds of silence.

This chapter explores the historical specificity of the slave journey for clues as to its relational dynamic in order to demonstrate the politics of slavery and its traumatizing legacy. It illuminates the slave trade's pivotal location in the formation of Western modernity. On the most basic level, many prominent material markers of Western civilization – as diverse as the Industrial Revolution and the Mansfield Parks of Britain – were constructed on the backs of enslaved Africans and their descendants. The imperative to swiftly accumulate wealth to fund its global ascendency propelled Britain to practise chattel slavery through an extreme terrorist system which superseded its legacies of "convention, morality and political procedure" (Beckles 2013, 203). A pivotal point of issue was whether or not the enslaved were human and therefore deserving of civil rights and liberties. Or, put another way, what strategies needed to be deployed to shore up the fiction that the enslaved were other than humans and therefore worthy of abuse and degradation? Sadiya Hartman opens her compelling exploration *Scenes of Subjection: Terror, Slavery and Self-Making in Nineteenth-Century America* (1997) by demonstrating how routinely acts of extreme violence constituted primal scenes by which the enslaved came to know themselves as beings in subjugation to the brutal power and authority of the Other. Hartman, taking an alternative stance, argues that it is not the certain conviction of the inhumanity of the enslaved that elicits the greatest excesses of violence; it is the insidious perception or claim to humanity of the enslaved that unleashes the beast in the enslaver. As argued by Cornel West, the transatlantic trade in enslaved Africans is located at the paradoxical ideological crossroads of Western modernity:

> The Dantesque journeys are the ignoble origins of Western modernity and the criminal foundations of American Democracy. African slavery sits at the center of the grand epoch of equality, liberty and fraternity, a center often concealed by modern myths of progress and liberation. And black doings and sufferings remain burdened by the unspeakable memories of the Middle Passage – the chamber of horrors enacted on slave ships. (West 1977, 8)

If we read the ship as Gilroy envisions – a "border crossing, transnational, microsystem of linguistic and political hybridity" which is a pivotal symbol of Western modernity (Gilroy 1993, 12) – then the slave ship, on which the terms of African–European encounter were brutally enforced in the interest of transforming free men into enslavers and enslaved, becomes a key signifier of the complex interface of cultural and political ideologies. The contemporary significance of the journey is reflected in Hilary Beckles's (2013) call to the Caribbean nations to seek reparation before the international courts for this crime against humanity. A similar note is sounded in Anita Rupprecht's impassioned work on the evasive measures being deployed by insurance companies as they selectively mine their archives in response to legal requirements to produce documentary evidence of their involvement in the transatlantic slave trade, as groundwork for considerations of reparation. Rupprecht indicates that representations of the *Zong* might also open out into "an alternative and politicized way of remembering with profound implications for contemporary global systems of finance" (2007, 346).

This analysis zeroes in on fictional representations of the journey of the iconic British slave ship *Zong*, which was purchased with 244 enslaved Africans on board and handed over to a ship's surgeon, Luke Collingwood, to captain, with the commission to enslave an additional 200 Africans. The *Zong* was bound from the island of São Tomé, off the coast of West Africa, to Jamaica in September 1781, with 442 slaves and seventeen crew members, when poor navigation lengthened the journey. This, coupled with excessive overcrowding, contributed to an outbreak of disease, which claimed the lives of sixty of the enslaved and seven crew members. In November, Captain Collingwood, in an effort to hedge further losses, took advantage of an approaching storm to dump approximately 133 enslaved persons into the ocean; he wished to benefit from insurance which would recompense for slaves lost at sea but not for those who succumbed to disease. Jettisoning human cargo was not unheard of, but it was not a common event. The risk of contagion was high within the cramped, unsanitary quarters, and the imperative to maintain the health and economic viability of the cargo, combined with inadequate medical knowledge, made the occasional dumping of sick slaves a viable option. Mortality rates on slave ships were extremely high, such that these vessels became floating sarcophagi reeking of waste and death; sharks tracked them through the oceans, lured by the promise of a steady diet of human flesh.[4] Collingwood, whose impending retirement may have provided the impetus to maximize profit, died seven days after the *Zong* docked in Jamaica. The ship's log disappeared, and dearth of knowledge adds to the mystique and fascination which attends the case.

The *Zong* atrocity provided grist for the mills of abolitionists on both sides of the Atlantic. Ironically, greed was once again the driving impulse which propelled this case into the public domain. The judicial proceedings which ensued (*Gregson v. Gilbert*, March 1783) hinged on whether the Liverpool merchants who funded the enterprise were entitled to collect insurance at the rate of 30 pounds per head for their property, which could be disposed of at will, or whether they had mismanaged the cargo. The ship's owners argued that the *Zong* incident was simply a case of disposition of "chattels and goods". The lower court ruled in favour of the owners. Lord Mansfield, in his judgement, indicated:

> What is this claim that human people have been thrown overboard? This is a case of chattels or good. Blacks are goods and property; it is madness to accuse these well-serving honourable men of murder. They acted out of necessity and in the most appropriate manner for the cause. The late Captain Collingwood acted in the interest of his ship to protect the safety of his crew. To question the judgement of an experienced well-travelled captain held in the highest regard is one of folly, especially when talking of slaves. The case is the same as if wood had been thrown overboard. (Quoted in Colley 2011)

The underwriters appealed, arguing that although disposing of the slaves was akin to disposing of horses, it was unnecessary to throw the chattels overboard, since there were sufficient provisions for their care. The massacre and the case have become iconic in the cultural memorialization of the Black Atlantic, for the horrific legally sanctioned violence which attended human trafficking; the brazen, premeditated massacre in the name of profit; and the broad-based legal, political and financial systemic which was foundational to its operation.[5] A critique of fictional evocations of this infamous historical event yields insight into the relationship between narrative and history, re-memory, testimony and survival. It identifies the journey as a transitional, liminal passage with its common burden of violation, physical and psychic loss, and muted potentiality.

Trauma, with its heavily symptomatic aftermath, looks into the past for root causes of contemporary disease and social dislocation. Its theorists have been concerned with two issues in the correlation between history and narrative. Even for historians, the essential issue in writing the past is not the fact or the truth of the event. As Dominic LaCapra argues, "Truth claims are neither the only nor always the most important consideration in art and its analysis . . . the interaction or mutually interrogative relation between history and art (including fiction) is more complicated than is suggested by either an identity or a binary opposition between the two" (LaCapra 2001, 15). Of greater significance is the politics of the ideological stance adopted by the historians as they select the details with which to recount their picture of the past. LaCapra, after Ankersimt, terms these pictures of the past "narrative substances" which are essentially "fictive and politically or ideologically motivated". Alternatively, LaCapra, after White, terms the pictures of the past "prefigurative tropes and meaning endowing projective narrative structures" (LaCapra 2001, 10). Fiction, released from the imperative of pursuing dates and times of historical events, delves into these tropes to arrive at submerged realities that would otherwise be lost to human knowledge. Creative writers, mining history for these projective narrative structures, clothe the gaps and erasures of this experience with groping for the meanings of what Erna Brodber terms in *Myal* (1998, 34) "the half" which has "never yet been told". The half that is subject to incapacity to fully articulate is as heavily infused with meaning as the half which finds its way into some measure of uneasy articulation.

This was the point of departure for the poet, novelist and playwright Fred D'Aguiar, born in London in 1960 to Guyanese parents, who testifies of his chance encounter with the *Zong* exhibit in the Liverpool Maritime Museum:

> The story left me with a feeling of deep depression and a desire to know more than the few facts conveyed . . . In the ship's log, it said one person climbed back on board without saying who it was. So I thought I'd make it a woman and once I'd done that it was hard just to make it a short story. I had to deal with what kind of journey a woman would have, and what if she survived, what if she got her freedom and other questions that came up that made it into a novel. It was a piece of history that then grew out of an absence of facts about it. (Hyppolite 2004, 4)

Fred D'Aguiar's *Feeding the Ghosts* (1997), rooted in social realism, interrogates the bedrock ethical, judicial and economic systems which undergirded the enterprise of the Indies. D'Aguiar grounds the lived experience aboard the slave ship within a range of contradictory philosophical and moral discourses and worldviews which governed the trade in human flesh. The social hierarchy of the ship is a microcosm of the broader society with its intersecting complex of racial, ethical and class relations. For the Captain, the bottom line remains the disposal of property for the sake of monetary advantage. The first mate struggles between his conscience, his blind obedience to the Captain's authority, and the compelling call emanating from a cross-section of the crew to intervene on their behalf in order to constrain the Captain's murderous intent and actions. Still other crew members vacillate between raw greed to multiply their share of the profit of the enterprise by destroying chattel and a sneaking suspicion of the shared humanity with the debased African. Looming above all is the evil institutional system which buttresses the merchandising, insurance and judicial conventions, all of which carry their own power to craft human motivation and action. The fundamental issue hinges on the energy it takes to maintain the illusion that the slaves are after all not human but chattels to be disposed of at the owner's will. The conundrum is, if perchance they are human, then to treat them as chattels and throw sick persons overboard is also to jettison one's own humanity. The implied question is, does the supposed inhumanity of the slave justify the brutal control system? Hartman argues that the very acknowledgement of the humanity of the enslaved, "rather than bespeaking the mutuality of social relations or the expressive and affective capacities of the subject, sentiment, enjoyment, affinity, will and desire, facilitated subjugation domination and terror precisely by preying upon the flesh heart and the soul" (D'Aiguiar 1997, 5).

The slave ship is portrayed then as a floating micro-society, based on terrorist violence, in which persons reinvent themselves relationally. *Feeding the Ghosts* makes it clear that slavers are equally trapped in a sadistic, debasing and dehumanizing micro-society, reduced by their role as exploiters and caretakers to an even lower level of bestiality than that of the slaves. They too breathe daily the filthy, contaminated air generated by unwashed masses and become habituated to cries of suffering such that "they were no longer heard as signals of distress, but as part of the whole, all-encompassing fabric of routine" (D'Aiguiar 1997, 10). On the slave ship, as is the case with every terrorist regime, systematic violence must not only be executed but it must be extreme enough and public enough to keep the masses in a state of perpetual dread. It is not sufficient to throw sick enslaved Africans overboard; they must be drowned in full sight of the queue of captives at mealtime to invest the action with its full intimidatory power.

One reading would argue that these excesses of cruelty become viable because of distance from the constraints of decency and the established social order. Conversely, these Western "emissaries of enlightenment" and "bearers of the spark from the sacred fire" (Conrad 1973) are arguably living out the dictates of the said Janus-faced social order. Spectacle and theatre are pivotal to the process and culture of debasement. Observations on the inner calibration of the enslaved African psyche are based on externalities. The black skin, which does not readily show bruising, is interpreted as demonstrating the Africans' suitability to a life of toil and physical abuse. Their skilled dancing indicates their enduring capacity for pleasure, even when the dance is enforced through whippings. Sexual access to enslaved bodies was considered a right to be enforced at will for the enactment of the enslaver's bizarre fantasies and unspeakable practices. Thousands of women arrived in the New World impregnated through acts of violence and violation. As for the pleasure of the gaze, when mass voyeurism of attempted rape is flouted by the flow of menstrual blood, the anticipated pleasure and subsequent disappointment of the spectators is matched by that of the perpetrator. Sadiya Hartman argues: "enjoyment was predicated on the wanton use of slave property. It was attributed to the slave in order to deny, displace and minimize the violence of slavery" (1997, 25).

The binary reads white–black; Christian–heathen; English–"gibberish"; civilized–savage; Prospero–Caliban/cannibal; literate–illiterate. The construction of the enslaved as ignorant, acquiescent, subhuman labouring bodies was crucial for the enterprise. Any assertion of the humanity of the enslaved was injurious to the cause. In *Feeding the Ghosts*, these binaries, which are difficult enough to maintain when the requirement is to massacre helpless, innocent captives, collapse when challenged by Mintah, to whom the first mate owes a debt of gratitude. She represents the ground on which illusions of Western modernity are challenged. The slavers are overwhelmed by a literate Christian slave who assesses their actions from a higher moral location than they occupy. Since it is impossible to strip her of these attributes, the slavers must take recourse to increasingly extreme acts of violence to dehumanize and silence her and teach her "her place". Paradoxically, even in D'Aguiar's economy, her capacity to challenge Europe's civilizing order rests on the extent to which she has already been socialized into its mores and dictates. For an enslaved African to carry the symbolic weight within the narrative, she must needs be creolized. Her capacity to intervene and act as an intermediary between the cultures is predicated on and commensurate with erasure of her alterity.

She is also emblematic of the potential of the slave to imbibe civilization. In a reversal of the Prospero–Caliban dynamic, Mintah the Christianized slave earlier nursed the sick first mate, Kelsall, on African soil, and in response to the amnesia induced by his illness, she imparted to him the gift of his name. In the vulnerability of illness and loss, he exchanged names with Mintah in an assertion of equality and reciprocity, free from the taint of supremacy. Significantly, this exchange is grounded in the Danish experiment with the potential for inter-ethnic encounter that is free of exploitation and fair to both parties. Within this re-membered context, she interpellates him as a fellow human being through her voice, emanating from deep within the bowels of the slave ship. A human demands, from a human, humane treatment and accountability for other human lives: "she shouted his name at those hands for the offence of beating, for the offence of holding a living body and slinging it over the side into an uncaring sea" (D'Aiguiar 1997, 38). Kelsall, fully understanding the nature of the requirement, suspends reason when a black body calls his name, and resorts to revenge. This is in keeping with Hartman's contention, "It was often the case that benevolent correctives and declarations of slave humanity intensified the brutal exercise of power upon the captive body rather than ameliorating the chattel condition" (Hartman 1997, 5).

As the massacre proceeds, maliciously and systematically, the power of naming becomes the only weapon left. The slave about to be drowned calls out her name to invoke her individuality, her uniqueness, nature, purpose and lineage within family and community. This is the call that must be silenced at all cost if the enterprise predicated on the subhumanity of the slave is to proceed satisfactorily. Unwillingness to acquiesce transforms Mintah into a dangerous body which must be subjugated. She is the body who refuses to be drowned and which is thereby infused with a supernatural power of transcendence. Her very existence is sufficient to display the potential for rebellion. But this potential remains muted. Coerced to dance by the whip, she dances the fertility dance, to no avail. Her lack of acquiescence proves too provocative to the slavers, who damage her fertility and quell her through the most extreme torture, by stuffing her genitals and her eyes with pepper. This induces so strong an impulse to escape her body that she lapses into woodenness, dissociation and apathy.

D'Aguiar's enquiry was triggered by a visit to the Liverpool Maritime Museum. Similarly M. NourbeSe Philip, in her attempts to plumb the absence and fissure generated by the *Zong* massacre, called the archives into service. Together they question whether the nameless, voiceless ancestor can be recuperated from the vast, amnesiac sea. Can the skeletal remains, which have long since suffered a sea change, be reconstructed for acknowledgement, for affirmation, for mourning? To what extent does the archive figure as uneasy resting place for the unburied, unpropitiated dead and as a point of interface for the probing artistic sensibility? The power of naming is invoked by Philip, who after exhausting archival searches for the names of the drowned souls on the *Zong*, names them herself. She recounts her inner devastation when perusing the *Zong*'s register to find the drowned humans listed as "man ... woman ... girl meagre". Her haunting reading of the manuscript calls up and foregrounds their humanity. The extended poem sets out to clothe the drowned in flesh.

The final and most evocative section of the *Zong!* collection was derived by outlining key words in the court transcript of the 1783 *Gregson v. Gilbert* judicial proceeding, and then fracturing the words to allow them to speak the depth of the atrocity the words originally set out to justify. The fracturing becomes the fragmented voices of the enslaved, who seek to tell a tale which is fundamentally unspeakable and hence can be expressed only in the gaps, erasures and interstices of the writing. For a reading at the University of Miami "Archaeologies of Black Memory" seminar in July 2007, Philip carefully removed her shoes as if for grounding and grunted the fractured words in hollow, guttural tones. She read as one possessed, constrained to articulate a glossolalia whose non-meaning conveys the essence of an experience which cannot be made to mean. Significantly, in commentary after the reading, NourbeSe Philip regretfully indicated the impossibility of telling this tale without recourse to expressing what might be interpreted as the growing descent into madness of the sea captain, who upon realization of the atrocity he has perpetrated, throws himself into the ocean, thus joining the community of the drowned. It seems a fitting indicator that imperial impulse and its carriers in successive generations must "die" if the human is to live.

Reflecting confluences with NourbeSe Philip's inner processes and writerly agendas in undertaking resuscitation of the *Zong*, D'Aguiar explains: "Fiction is working in a psychotherapeutic way. The writing of it is in the drama of it you feel both the hurt of the era and the memory and the recuperation of that memory. You also get the sense of *now* being fully in charge of your present because the gap that was willed away has now been bridged. I think fiction is trying to do that" (Hyppolite 2004, 4). The Middle Passage becomes a trope for the cataclysmic encounter between worlds. Mintah muses that life exists on land: "The sea is the place between lives: I float on it in the hope that my life can begin at some point in time. . . . The sea keeps me between my life" (D'Aguiar 1997, 199). It is an interstitial space on several counts – between land masses, between societies and cultures, between lives and, as D'Aguiar argues, between memories:

> the water became a new geography that they write their memory into. The memory is on the land you've left and the place you're going to is the unwritten text, and everything you do in preparation for getting there is done on water. Water then becomes this shifting library of sorts. I like to think of it as a library with books that can be rewritten since it is moving, never stationary. It gives you a chance to revise yourself. (Hyppolite 2004, 5)

The sea as archive – the repository and fluid, shifting ground of meaning and memory – is the central focus of David Dabydeen's extended poem *Turner* (2002), which is linked intertextually with the famous J.M.W. Turner painting modelled on the *Zong* massacre, titled *Slave Ship, or Slavers Throwing Overboard the Dead and Dying, Typhoon Coming On* (1840). Dabydeen's preface quotes the famous British art critic John Ruskin's acclamation of the work as "the noblest sea that Turner ever painted . . . the noblest certainly ever painted by man" (Dabydeen 2002, 7).[6] Ruskin terms the ship "guilty" in an oblique reference to the murderous act of dumping sick human beings for the sake of collecting insurance. The blood guilt of the enslaver is responsible in no small measure for the "multitudinous seas incarnadine" and sky and the judgement of the looming typhoon. *Slave Ship* was exhibited at the Royal Academy to coincide with the world anti-slavery convention held in London in 1840. Gilroy reads the painting as a "powerful protest against the direction and moral tone of English politics", citing in support of this view an epigraph which Turner draws from his own poetry: "Hope, hope, fallacious hope, where is thy market now?" (Gilroy 1993, 14).[7] Critical dialogue has focused on the manner in which the painting reflects the nineteenth-century aesthetic of the sublime, which submerges the subject in the interest of spotlighting the piercing illumination that is the focal point of the painting. In Dabydeen's words, "Its subject, the shackling and drowning of Africans, was relegated to a brief footnote in Ruskin's essay. The footnote reads like an afterthought, something tossed overboard" (2002, 7).[8]

One man's moment of intense beauty and contemplation is another man's carnage. Of interest to this analysis is the attempt to recover the submerged reality of the sea journey from the vantage point of slaves drowned at sea, as blatant sacrifices to the god of materialism. Dabydeen, reacting to the interface between this painting and nineteenth-century evocation of the amoral aesthetics of the sublime, sets about clothing the victims in flesh, formulating in the process an entire community of ocean dwellers who pick up the lament and articulate their memories, hopes, aspirations and reactions to the horrific events which determine their location. The testimony grapples with how to counteract epistemic violence that has relegated a people to an afterthought. How to give voice to what Dabydeen terms the "submerged head of the African in the foreground of Turner's painting" which has been "drowned in Turner's . . . sea for centuries" (2002, 7)? What is the potential for invention in relation to its quest for belongingness? How to shake off entrapment in a grievous history in order to begin anew?

The narrator of Dabydeen's poem is a slave drowned by Turner who encounters in Turner's latest victim and part-born offspring a catalyst for re-memory and reinvention of the past. The part-born thrown overboard becomes the wound that cries out a pain that is not otherwise accessible. The poem, which ends some thirty pages later with the statement "There is no mother . . . . No mother" (Dabydeen 2002, 41–42), places the acute pain of mother loss at the centre of the narrative. In the beginning, the cries of the birthing woman, like an eviscerated wreckage, is the only sound which pierces the stillness, except for the murmuring of women:

> Stillborn from all signs. First a woman sobs
> Above the creak of timbers and the cleaving
> Of the sea, sobs from the depths of true
> Hurt and grief, as you will never hear
> But from woman giving birth, belly
> Blown and flapping loose and torn like sails,
> Rough sailors' hands jerking and tugging
> At ropes of veins, to no avail. Blood vessels
> Burst asunder, all below-deck are drowned.
> Afterwards, stillness, but for the murmuring
> Of women . . .
> (Dabydeen 2002, 9)

The part-born itself cannot speak until it has been mothered into expression by the drowned slave, who is surprised by the joy of being accorded surrogate motherhood. The drowned slave is then mandated to become the wound that speaks.

The text presents an interplay of traumatizing catalysts which multiply with the identities of the drowned persona, the ship's captain and the victims of his infamous acts. For Dabydeen, the encounter between worlds is essentially of a psychosexual nature. Perverse interpenetrations abound, lending the fictional universe a multiplicity of Turners. Turner is the artist and doorkeeper of a Western aesthetic sensibility which would sublimate his civilization's horrific action in contemplation of an amoral sublime beauty; Turner is the gentle seducer of children who lures them to his ship with sweets and shada juice, even as they innocently wonder "why are the elders in chains" (Dabydeen 2002, 14); Turner is a paedophile who fondles boys in quiet corners and "finds" them tousled on his bed at night; Turner is the ship's captain, who, like Shakespeare's Prospero, imparts language, worldview and ideology along with furtive slimy interpenetrations, which he ministers to boys and women alike; Turner is also the sallow offspring of the Captain's black concubine, the part-born tossed overboard; Turner is the fable, the "miracle of fate, / This longed-for gift of motherhood", born of the drowned persona's persistent courting of the moon (9).

A fundamental catalyst of trauma is separation and individuation, which surfaces initially in the realm of personal history. Let us agree to admit the autobiographical dimension. Dabydeen owns the metaphorical part-born in an interview with Kwame Dawes, in which he indicates that he negotiated pitfalls of racism and shame in relation to his Indo-Caribbean heritage, from the vantage point of a ward of the British state. Dabydeen claims: "I feel like the stillborn child in *Turner* definitely. Or even worse than that, I feel like an abortion; messy and bloody and unborn, and that partly because of racism" (Dawes 1997, 219). Race as an overdetermined signifier is figured here as pivotal in the incapacity to bring latent potentialities to birth. Dabydeen purports that *Turner* is really about the absent mother: "the absence is the mother, not the life in the child" (Dawes 1997, 220). The drowned slave narrator, addressing the same lack, invents a personal, domestic and communal history which lends comfort of belonging: "I dream to be small again even though ..." (Dabydeen 2002, 12). Not even the fantasy of childhood is sufficient to subvert the fate of near-drowning:

> ... When I strip
> Mount the tree and dive I hit my head
> On a stone waiting at the bottom of the pond.
> I come up dazed, I ...

The comfort is that here he is shielded by mother love. In the constructed past the mother watches over the small boy with sorrow, hence the import of the final chilling statement: "There is no mother" (41). Encoded in *Turner* are severe mother–child individuation and autonomy traumas which find no resolution.[9]

The persona's longing for the mother is connected to the longing for motherhood, and this too is flouted by pernicious and persistent racism. Race is a catalyst of trauma when the material condition and consequence of racialized embodiment does violence to the soul and spirit of individual, community and nation. So deeply embedded are racism's tentacles that the floating woundedness of the half-breed part-born, without having attained embodiment and having been loved into speech by the narrator, in its first words declares its ancestry in Turner's abusive curses:

> This creature kicks alive in my stomach
> Such dreams of family, this thing which I cannot
> Fathom, resembling a piece of ragged flesh,
> Though human from the shape of its head
> Its half formed eyes, seeming jaw and as yet
> Sealed lips. Later it confirmed its breed,
> Tugging my hair spitefully, startling me
> With obscene memory. "Nigger!" it cried, seeing
> Through the sea's disguise as only children can.
> (Dabydeen 2002, 21)

Turner suggests that the trauma of embodied racism is so persistent and insidious it can survive even in the disembodied. In a symbolic economy, in which "it is the colour of a person's skin which to a large extent positions everybody in a social system of constitutive meaning . . . the inhumanity of slavery grew out of the binarized logic of free white bodies held in radical contra-distinction to the enslaved African black body" (Burrows 2004, 5). Why should the ideology of race supremacy flourish in the part-born, part-black, part-white progeny of the enslaved? The accusation "nigger" speaks to the persistence of Turner's legacy; it also declares the internalized self-hatred which would mask itself and organize into different hierarchies, and in turn evolve with changing historical circumstances and find reflection in fluid, ideological and material power bases. It is also a pivotal catalyst of intergenerational transfer of trauma and ongoing social injustice and inequities.

Dabydeen sets out to explore in *Turner* the notion that "Empire" was a pornographic project: "ultimately, the plantation experience had severe and traumatic psychic impacts that had to do with the loss of, or the traumatic changes in epistemologies and philosophies, but overwhelmingly had to do with what is the very ground of our beings, which is our body" (Dawes 1997, 220). It is with his body that Turner writes on bodies. A major objective of Turner's inscription on the flesh of the enslaved is to meet his victims at the crossroads where love encounters violence, and there to stun them into silence. Simultaneously Turner's language (read perspective and worldview) flows like the issue of oral sex into the perverted progeny of Empire:

> Turner crammed our boys' mouths too with riches
> His tongue spurting strange potions upon ours

> Which left us dazed, which made us forget
> The very sound of our speech.
> (Dabydeen 2002, 40)

For the women, Turner reserves the sadistic ministrations of whips, salt and stung wounds which seals Ellar into silence until he has "taken rage from her mouth. / It opens and closes. No word comes" (Dabydeen 2002, 39). This silence lifts only when Caliban learns a different language:

> ... Each night
> Aboard ship he gave selflessly the nipple
> Of his tongue until we learnt to say profitably
> In his own language, *we desire you, we love
> You, we forgive you.*
> (40)

Turner's narrative inscription is complete when he pours into the boys (along with the issue of anal sex) value judgements, occlusions, erasures – the gaps which would allow them in turn, to echo Ruskin's dialogue on the nineteenth-century aesthetic sensibility, "blessed, angelic, sublime" (40).

The final concern is the connection between trauma, forgetting and languaging. Dabydeen terms *Turner* the only thing that he has written so far with which he is satisfied. It represents a resistance of the compulsion to speak from a fixed and, by extension, exclusionary ethnic location: "I spent twenty years just trying to find an Africanness or find an Indianness or find a Creoleness ... now you settle for a world of your own making, and you settle for metaphor – the sheer beauty and autonomy of the metaphor" (Dawes 1997, 208–9). Indeed, *Turner* would seek to make of this extreme loss, lack and emptiness a radical reinvention rooted in metaphors of community and love and belongingness:

> ... I wanted to teach it
> A redemptive song, fashion new descriptions
> Of things, new colours fountaining out of form.
> I wanted to begin anew in the sea
> But the child would not bear the future
> Not its inventions, and my face was rooted
> In the ground of memory ...
> (Dabydeen 2002, 41)

The ground of memory disallows newness. The irony is that this world of beauty and autonomy is itself, at every level, pierced with lack. Every attempt to begin anew on a new ground is riddled with the old inequities. Even the inhabitants of the deep cannot escape the markers of race and class.

The transcendence, then, is in the creative expression. A primary objective of the terrorist acts which undergirded enslavement was to persuade the enslaved to adopt the location of subordination and inferiority, to persuade the subjugated bodies to imbibe the dictates and terms of their subjugation. The issue is, can the coerced dance on the slave ship be an effectual fertility dance? The transcendence is in the shaking off of this location and the bold self-assertion of being and knowing that escapes the denigrating epistemologies of the colonizers.

Where is the transcendence in D'Aguiar's account, whose title suggests the possibility of nurturing and nourishing insubstantial, fragmentary presences through narrative? Yet there remains the need to attach symbolic referentiality to the material. The symbol of transcendence in D'Aguiar's *Feeding the Ghosts* is to be found in the wood. The slave lies in intense intimacy with the floor of the slave ship; hence the wood – soaking up the blood, the sweat, the tears – becomes the primary witness and repository of suffering. The qualities of the wood also permeate the sufferers. The persistent torture reduces the protagonist to dense, unfeeling woodenness, an ossified state which obviates feeling and thereby shields the self from pain.

The clearest statement in the work of these writers is the imperative to transmute sites, objects and fixtures of suffering into sites of redemption. The child of a woodcarver who has been lovingly taught the craft by her father, who refuses to give up the ancestral gods in favour of Christianity, Mintah creates in her home 133 wooden creatures, plus ten representing the victims and the ten protestors who willingly threw themselves overboard in dissent against the torture. The spirits of the drowned come to live in and energize the carved forms. They become her children, her companions. They disallow forgetting as these their representations travel down the corridors of time. Oppression empowers the survivor to redeem herself. The medium of this expression is the repository of suffering, which is transmuted through creativity into life-giving entities.

In *Turner* also, the potential for transcendence lies in creative invention.

Indeed, the poem is an experiment in how to credibly invent that which was not experienced, how to tell the unspeakable. Creativity and invention are undermined at the end by the persistent gap between the telling and the reality: "There is no mother, family / Savannah fattening with cows, community / Of faithful men; no elders to foretell" (Dabydeen 2002, 41). D'Aguiar hints at the same when Mintah dreams of being reunited with her lover and her book in triumphant culmination of a life of brutish struggle. This is merely a nod in the direction of the romance. It is an ironic declaration that this tale cannot end "happily ever after". The implied author details the romantic ending as a dream and then writes a second ending in which the senile old woman meets her death by fire – no book, no lover, no acclaiming crowd of young people, just an incidental funeral pyre set while lighting a lamp. Both narrative representations of the *Zong* massacre speak to the incapacity of traditional narrative forms and conventions to tell the submerged narratives.

And this is where NourbeSe Philip's *Zong!* – subtitled "As told to the author by Setaey Adamu Boateng" (2008) – assumes its most profound significance. Lawyer, author and iconoclast, she penned the book-length poem using as her inspiration the five-hundred-word judicial summary of *Gregson v. Gilbert* 1783. In the absence of the ship's logs, which unaccountably disappeared before the infamous case, this was at the time assumed to be the primary surviving public documentation of the massacre.[10] The judgement becomes for Philip an archive to be mined to speak a grim reality that cannot be told but which demands a witness. After a seven- to eight-year incubation period and heroic struggles with internalization and possession, incredulity, grief and anger, Philip arrives at innovative narrative strategies to cause her reader to grapple with the incomprehensibility of the case and to enter experientially into a story which she explains "cannot be told . . . but must be told". The judicial summary becomes a word bank – a "particular and peculiar discursive landscape" into which she "locks" (Philip 2008, 191). Although she does not depart from the word store for the body of the poem, she responds to the impulse to break and enter the text – the better to do it violence, to fracture the smooth surface of the words, to expose their inherent irrationality and incapacity to mean what they legally purport to mean. The poem constitutes an iconoclastic act of resistance which unmasks the unassailability of the law and its agents to reveal its inherent injustice and alignment with the compromised hegemonic order.

Having revealed the lack of veracity in the system, Philip proceeds to pillage its word bank, fracturing words to create floating fragments divorced from any shared code of meaning, much like the floating corpses tossed off the *Zong*, as a deep and profound disavowal of shared humanity, purpose and meaning. The fragmentation is unrelenting and severe at every level of linguistic convention – sentence, phrase, word, syllable. If meaning cannot be found in words then they must found in the gaps, fissures, spaces which convey ontological and epistemological rupture. The speaking of the text undermines the rational mind, which relies on shared and highly structured linguistic and reading conventions, and points instead to a babel of shared experiential realities as a basis of meaning construction. It is an archaeological work, unearthing submerged memories and presences. And since the five-hundred-word judicial statement demonstrates so clearly the manner in which silence can be discursively produced in public documentation, the rupture of the silence becomes a political and liberatory act of possession for Philip. In a 2008 interview, she explained: "I finally felt that for the first time I had my own language. True it's fragmented and broken, but it's my own tongue. This totally ruptured, fragmented, dissonant language that is my mother tongue" (quoted in Eichorn 2011, 37).

The reader thus confronted with the responsibility of meaning-creation experiences wonder, humiliation, bewilderment, frustration and then some. The option that is closed is to escape from the responsibility of grappling with the task of making meaning; according to Philip (in an interview with Maria Preziuso, http://zong.site.wesleyan.edu.interview), "The reader is asked to make certain choices, so that in the end s/he is contaminated by the text and they become the co-creator and participant in this event." The indeterminate nature of the text is profoundly disturbing. NourbeSe Philip breaks the units of meaning into smaller and smaller shards and then sets them afloat, like dismembered bodies, on white space. The nature of the fragmentation is such that space assumes the consistency of water – the constantly shifting ground of new meanings. And the meanings are as unstable, proliferating like the near-infinite combinations of letters and words and phrases and fragments. Insofar as the slave ship itself would have been what Philip terms "a multilingual multicultural universe marooned in time on the sea", the search for meaning-understanding across multiple African and European languages would have produced a babel. Philip argues: "It suggests a polyvocality that is at times cacophonous in the extreme. It is a text of silence (of the ocean and the Middle Passage) and silencing (as in the historical silencing of this and similar stories) that is interrupted, fractured and fragmented by the human voice."

Water releases the evocation of the sea as history and the sea as archive. It is the archival repository of bodies, bones, members of drowned Africans, transmuted in so many mythologies into something rich and strange – vital communities beneath the seas. Water recalls the lying excuse put before the court: that the enslaved were dumped overboard because there was no water to sustain them. Water is the persistent rain showers which effectively washed away this spurious excuse; it recalls the "multitudinous seas incarnadine" of Turner's painting, and Macbeth's guilt-ridden plea:

> Will all great Neptune's ocean wash this blood
> Clean from my hand? No, this my hand will rather
> The multitudinous seas incarnadine,
> Making the green one red.
> (*Macbeth*, Act 2, Scene 2)

Dabydeen's *Turner* and D'Aguiar's *Feeding the Ghosts*, like George Lamming's *Natives of My Person*, John Hearne's *The Sure Salvation*, Erna Brodber's *Jane and Louisa, Myal, Louisiana* and *The Rainmaker's Mistake*, and Elizabeth Nunez's *Prospero's Daughter*, demonstrate the imperative of Caribbean writers to revisit the encounter between Europe, Africa and Asia which gave birth to the New World.[11] The brutalities of the encounter so overwhelmed the psychic resources of the enslaved at the point of occurrence that we are only quite recently, over the temporal distance of decades and within the safe enclaves of academic halls and conventions of discourse, beginning to grapple with them. Applying trauma's quality of belatedness to the issue of the periodization of colonialism, Burrows argues that it is only those whose material conditions allow them to escape the scars of colonialism who can embrace the "pastness" implicit in the term *postcolonialism*. Colonialism is certainly not over and done with for the populations who continue to live the aftermath of the enterprise of the Indies: "There are ongoing traumas for many millions of people whose lives are disproportionately circumscribed by the often intense suffering created by the changing face of power structures that have transmogrified into neo-colonialism, cultural imperialism and now the injustices (racial, gendered and classed) inherent in the universalistic notions of global capitalism" (Burrows 2004, 21).[12]

Incapacity to grasp the enormity of the trauma at the point of its occurrence brings both numbing belatedness and intrusive memory as the subconscious mind catapults it into the conscious, repeatedly demanding that it be confronted and addressed. The anthropologist Veena Das claims that "some realities need to be fictionalised before they can be apprehended" (2007, 39). The creative artists whose work we have been examining have outstripped other critical commentators in their willingness to give expression to the submerged and unspeakable. These critical minds have lagged behind in terms of finding a language for articulating the discourse.

This chapter was initially conceived as one of myriad backward glances conceived to mark the bicentennial of legislative abolition of the transatlantic trade in enslaved Africans (1492–1870). The legislation, which entered the statute books on 25 March 1807, made it illegal to engage in the slave trade throughout the British colonies, although the trade nevertheless continued between the Caribbean islands until 1811. Much of the discourse emanating from the former imperial centres which marked the recent bicentennial commemorations was, for the most part, self-congratulatory about the triumph of Britain's enlightenment and justice.[13] Rupprecht, in her essay "A Limited Sort of Property", which foregrounds the *Zong* as a "murder site" and a "space of untold trauma and loss", critiques the 2007 commemorative exercise involving sailing a replica of the *Zong* up the Thames River:

> Was the contemporary event a vivid spectacle of erasure and re-inscription in which the naval frigate confirmed British moral redemption and superior firepower in relation to the diminutive replica schooner? If it was, then it looked very much like the combined might of the military, church and state had come together to commemorate their own historic roles in the abolition of the slave trade. It also seemed to be a straightforward exercise in reinforcing the image of the British Navy as the global humanitarian maritime police swathed in imperial nostalgia. What did it mean to resurrect the *Zong*, to make the myth tangible, but to replace a slave cargo with modern Christians – white and black – singing hymns of liberation? (Rupprecht 2008, 267)

This stance prompts a broader application of Cornel West's statement in relation to America: "No other democratic nation revels so blatantly in such self deceptive innocence, such self paralyzing reluctance to confront the nightmare of its own history. Suffice it to say that another story must needs be told" (West 1997, 14). The creative writers of the Caribbean and the African diaspora are taking up this challenge with the insight and authority rooted in corporate suffering. Theirs, and by extension ours, is a collective work of mourning which is being executed with therapeutic care and precision in the interest of plumbing submerged repositories of black memory, as a basis for more empowering cartographies of self and society. They are masterfully wielding the authority to forgive but not forget. These writers are envisioning liberatory patterns of interaction which call Turner and Kelsall to account in the interest of preserving the human. Congratulations in this time properly belong to these creative writers who are grappling with the half which has never yet been told.

Anthropologist Deborah Thomas terms the outcome a minority report which differs from official histories, and which challenges received representations and memorialization of the past in national narratives and archives. It is foundational to mobilization of support for the contentious cause of reparation for slavery as a heinous crime against humanity, which is currently gaining ground in the black Atlantic. University of the West Indies historian Hilary Beckles, decrying Britain's unwillingness to speak honestly of the imperial past, contends that this region, which was the lynchpin of Empire, should lead the charge to legally call Britain to account for its criminal enrichment through the mass terrorist system of slavery.

This study will subsequently probe correlations between the forms of the originary violations and violence of chattel slavery and indentureship and their far-reaching tentacles within the modern social and political order. It will point to continuities between the gestational social order crafted under the shadow of the whip, the excessive and highly performative bacchanal of the domestic "cut tail", and the theatrical public killings which increasingly characterize contemporary gang violence and violence by the state against its citizens. The following chapter explores the persistent legacy of epistemic violence and racism which remains more or less muted in the contemporary order but is nevertheless persistent and resistant to erasure.

2

"THE WOMB OF MY OTHERNESS"
Creolization in "The View from the Terrace" and "Barbados"

> From childhood, therefore, creoleness made me aware of the complex labyrinth of the family of humankind into which I was born in the twentieth century.... I found myself on the edges or margins of a world, the estate of the world, that were shifting into numinous disorder in order paradoxically to alert us to shared responsibilities within the unfinished genesis of arts of survival.
> – Wilson Harris, "Creoleness: The Crossroads of Civilization?"

> plantation is my old and paradoxical homeland.... as a child of plantation, I am a mere fragment or an idea that spins around my own absence...
> – Antonio Benítez-Rojo, "Three Words Towards Creolization"

THIS CHAPTER READS OLIVE SENIOR'S "The View from the Terrace" and Paule Marshall's "Barbados" to interrogate pre-independence confrontations between representatives of the Caribbean Euro-creole elite and the emerging Afro-creole lower-strata population. It pays particular attention to the strategies deployed by these authors to narrate the politics of location and its ontological impact at this stage of the nation-building project. The reading zeroes in on the complexity of the cultural interface at the heart of everyday interactions within Caribbean societies: the persistence of the plantation dynamic, whose ideological reach remains vigorous and whose grim outworkings have far outstripped its historical and political tenure. The colonial state proved highly effective in producing segregated populations by invoking and maintaining racialized differences through epistemic and physical violence. The process was spatialized into territorial rights of belonging and gendered in relation to male–male contestation over access to women's bodies.

In his essay "Three Words Towards Creolization", Antonio Benítez-Rojo identifies the complex dynamics unleashed by plantation society as "the womb of my otherness – and of my globality. . . . It is the bifurcate centre that exists inside and outside at the same time, near to and distant from all things that I can understand as my own: race, nationality, language and religion" (Benítez-Rojo 1998, 54). The root and evolving social construction of this otherness in Caribbean societies has been hotly contested for decades. In his seminal work *The Development of Creole Society of Jamaica, 1770–1820* (1971), Kamau Brathwaite identifies creolization as an adaptive response to the social conditions of plantation society. Despite attempts to establish stringent boundary markers on which to rest notions of white supremacy, the respective ethnic groups underwent a process of mutual acculturation. Brathwaite saw potential for the emerging coloured population – the fruit of miscegenation – to become a bridge across racial and ethnic lines, functioning to cement the society with the potential for promoting social integration rather than divisiveness. Although mimicry of European forms was the order of the day, Brathwaite argues that African influences remained pivotal, contributing to the form of European adaptations embraced by the entire society: "There was developing a European oriented creole form (Euro-creole) and an African influenced creole form (Afro-creole); and they existed together within, often the same framework" (Braithwaite 1971, 231–32.) Wilson Harris, in "Creoleness: The Crossroads of Civilization?", similarly indicates that with the chasms and gulfs which divide cultures there exists "a storage of creative possibility that, once tapped, may energise the unfinished genesis of the imagination" (Harris 1998, 25–26).

Still very much in contemporary use, the term *creole* has been identified above all as a slippery signifier whose ideological and situated meanings can be multifaceted, diverse and even discordant. The term as defined by Indo-Trinidadian writer Samuel Selvon in the 1990s was inextricably intertwined with cultural nationality and racial indeterminacy. Selvon, in the essay "Two into Three Won't Go" (1987), describes his lived experience of the creolization process of his youth that propelled him away from Indian cultural forms and practices, which were then perceived as tribal and retrogressive. The term *creole* came to be seen throughout the region as referencing the indigenous, rooted new creation. Carolyn Allen, in the insightful essay "Creole: The Problem of Definition", indicates that the term was variously endued with social tensions as a manifestation of "the hierarchical structure of colonial society, the racial and social divisions which made the forging of national identities truly challenging across the region" and simultaneously construed as a "watchword of the nationalist movement", with its associations with natal land and adaptation: "Not unlike the plants and animals which grew differently in the tropical zones, humans were perceptibly modified by climate and surroundings. Habits of behaviour, attitude, speech, cuisine and more came to be identified with Creole populations" (Allen 2002, 52). She concludes her enquiry by pointing to seven underlying genetic characteristics in a bid to facilitate ongoing dialogue.[1] A salient node of enquiry for this argument is "the multiplicity of Creole forms/types making context and point of view crucial to understanding" (57).

These issues have been and will continue to be argued extensively and paradoxically. In practice, creolization, read as acculturation, is held to be inevitable. In ideological terms, creolization is held to yield multifarious prolific and creative intersections, joinings, collusions, hybridities without end, languages and cultural forms aplenty. In the service of the necessary, and occasionally even pleasurable, business of miscegenation, the term *creole* has become a gathering point for a proliferation of ethnic signifiers – *mulatto, dougla, quadroon, mixed, high-colour, red, Afro-Caribbean, Trinidad white, French Creole, Spanish* . . . and counting – each with its unique genealogy, historicity and dynamic social location. The genesis of the Creole is held to be located in an incident of history produced by an early wave of globalization, which brought in its wake hybrid models of humanity, a radical inclusivity which prefigured the challenges inherent in constructing individual and communal identities in contemporary globalizing postmodern times. Creolizations reflect the interaction between the macro dimensions of social contexts and interactions engineered by global geopolitical scenarios and the manner in which they shape micro dimensions of lived realities.

This reading sets out to glean what the selected short narratives indicate about the constitution and lived experience and discontents of being Eurocreole to the bone, and to locate the same within fixed temporal but divergent sociohistorical frameworks. In relation to Olive Senior's "The View from the Terrace", the study asks, what does it feel like to invade the castle of the skin of a light-coloured, deracinated, male, West Indian professional who has been carefully schooled in Englishness and established by the departing colonizers as the legitimate inheritor of the postcolonial kingdom? In relation to Paule Marshall's "Barbados", the focus is on the inner space of an ageing black-skinned "white man" whose negative response to emergence of the Afro-Caribbean peasantry into cultural assertion and self-government is mediated by a five-decade stint of migration to the United States.

Both female-authored narratives are located temporally at the point at which the old order, rooted in white supremacist ideologies, is on the verge of being supplanted, and the Afro-Caribbean lower-strata population is emerging into literacy, self-determination and mobilization in preparation for cultural assertion and political ascendency. They are loosely set within the transitional century delimited by Brathwaite when he argues that the assertion of folk culture after 1865 was to have "a profound effect upon the very constitution of Jamaican society. This assertion has become increasingly articulate since the gaining of political independence in 1962" (Brathwaite 1971, 212). The reading raises questions of cross-gender representation; of the interface of the strictures of patriarchy and colonialism; and of the impact of this subject construction on desire, on parenting and on lineage and inheritance.

Olive Senior's "The View from the Terrace" traces the anguish of an ageing Euro-creole protagonist, a retired senior public servant and agent of the colonial state, who scrutinizes from his terrace the life of a young Afro-Jamaican woman who overnight mysteriously takes up residence in the centre of his view. In a swiftly but soundly constructed house which clings tenuously to a barren rural mountainside, she breeds and cares for a growing brood of children. The narrative traces Mr Barton's responses as he variously eagerly awaits her downfall; emphatically predicts the destruction of her home by fire or flood; admires her tenacity and endurance; marvels at her housewifery and inventiveness; and responds sexually to imaginations of her sensuality and strength. Her thriving and refusal to go away come to symbolize the displacement of Euro-creole hegemony, aesthetic and worldview by a vigorous Afro-creole presence which refuses to be erased and "kept in its place". The final acknowledgement of its vigour, its longevity and its encroachments, through the woman's connection with his faithful servant, leads to Mr Barton's unceremonious demise.

Paule Marshall's "Barbados", set in 1958 and published in 1961, presents a similar dynamic played out on the island of Barbados, roughly within the same historical moment. It introduces into the equation North American migration – the mass movement of islanders and their cultures to North America from about the mid 1950s – whose impact on the host nation is expressed evocatively in *Brown Girl, Brownstones*: "Like a dark sea nudging its way onto a white beach and staining the sand, they came" (Marshall [1959] 1981, 90). Mr Watford, an Afro-Barbadian migrant who fled to the United States at age twenty, returns home some fifty years later to retire into the wealthy splendour of a lonely and barren life. He is challenged by the unwelcome intrusion of a beautiful young servant girl, who, because of the depth of her own loneliness, makes a silent yet articulate call for permission to breach his walls of silence and contempt in order to connect with him and quench her loneliness. He rejects her, only to be beset by desperate need after she connects emotionally and sexually with a youth her own age. The young man is in turn aligned with the emerging lower-strata Afro-Barbadian political force, which is threatening to overturn the Euro-creole political order and aesthetics that have hitherto governed the island. Mr Watford learns, too late, that all his life he has flown from love because he has refused to assume responsibility for his actions.[2]

Both short narratives illustrate how overlapping spatiotemporal locations shape subject and meaning constructions. Within the broadest geopolitical framework or centre of meaning, the narratives spring out of the shadow of *plantation* and its creolizing aftermath. I use this term in Benítez-Rojo's sense of constantly circulating, forming and reforming cultural fragments generated by plantation, "whose slow explosion throughout modern history threw out billions and billions of cultural fragments in all directions – fragments of diverse kinds that in their endless voyage come together in an instant to form a dance step, a linguistic trope, the line of a poem and afterwards repel each other to reform and pull apart once more" (Benítez-Rojo 1998, 55). Yet this notion of a merry creole dance of life and creativity, for all its soundness and validity, obscures the grim ontological contestation which engaged the respective combatants within the plantation and its aftermath, who sought variously to wrest or maintain diverse (read oppositional) cultural identities as the basis for ideological and political hegemonies. The issues remain the nature and constitution of the civilized and the humane, as well as the right to rule and to establish national culture in the face of ruthless imposition of foreign, culturally irrelevant forms. The pivotal point at issue in these narratives is, what is going to be the hegemonic culture of the new nations which are slowly making their way through a constricted and perilous birth passage towards the dawning of the independence era?

What then do these fictional scenarios demonstrate about the Euro-creole location, and correlations between ideological and spatiotemporal locations and political and psychic agendas? The major players in both narratives are typological. "The View from the Terrace" is fundamentally about the Euro-creole's focalizer Mr Barton, whose failing eyes and distorted vision are ineffective in terms of physically and metaphorically seeing the Afro-creole woman – the focalized – although he spends the closing years of his life gazing minutely upon her. She gradually comes to challenge every certainty which he holds dear and to undermine all that his life represents. The woman, who for the majority of the narrative is poorly perceived at a distance, carries all the symbology of the Afro-Caribbean matriarch: the quintessential larger-than-life mothering women who by dint of sacrifice and extravagant love raises a brood of children single-handedly. This is the Afro-creole mother whose task, as then defined in the national allegory, was to produce children fit to govern the burgeoning nations, hence the strong focus on the care she gives to her children and the primacy of their education – their neatness and readiness for school at all times, their happiness at play and general well-being.[3] Metaphorically, she is a good, nurturing and sustaining mother who stands implicitly in contrast to Mother England, who deforms and then distances herself from the sons of Empire.

Shades of this woman also manifest in the unnamed servant girl in Marshall's "Barbados". The aged protagonist's first glimpse of the beautiful servant girl is conveyed in allegorical language – a veritable ode to female *jouissance*. Arguably there is very little flesh-and-blood woman to be found under the weight of the overlapping allusions:

her bare feet like strong dark roots amid the jagged stones, her face tilted toward the sun – and she might have been standing there always waiting for him. She seemed of the sun, of the earth. The folktale of creation might have been true with her: that along a river bank a god had scooped up the earth – rich and black and warmed by the sun – and molded her poised head with its tufted braids . . . had sculptured the passionless face and drawn a screen of gossamer across her eyes to hide the void behind. Beneath her bodice her small breasts were smooth at the crest. Below her waist, her hips branched wide, the place prepared for its load of life. But it was the bold and sensual strength of her legs which completely unstrung Mr Watford. (Marshall 1961, 59)

This quintessential woman is a synthesizer and reconciler of opposites. She carries the quality of fixity and everlastingness and stillness, devoid of purpose outside of challenging and completing him. Forever waiting for him is the earth mother, the nature goddess, drawing her strength and power both from rootedness in the earth that she accesses through her feet and communion with the sun, whose light-filled energies she soaks in and exudes through her face. Her roots grow deeply into the rock-filled earth to draw up its reproductive energies into hips which branch in a proud display of procreative potential. The more-mythic-than-real woman embodies nature and is poised to be possessed as a magnet of male desire, repository of his generative potential and a womb for his progeny. Her gestures and the set of her head also awaken in him aching, long-suppressed memories of his mother. The mythic allusion emphasizes an essential female otherness and inscrutability. From his first glimpse of her, Mr Watford is assaulted with desire which threatens his impervious masculinity.

Although the gaze of the focalizers, and by extension of the reader, is kept tightly fixed upon the women who are the catalysts in both narratives, the entire process of adjustment is invested in the ageing Euro-creole males, both of whom are formally named with distancing signifiers: Mr Barton and Mr Watford. The girl of "Barbados" remains unnamed and the woman of "The View from the Terrace" is named only in the last segment of the narrative, by her close countryman during the revelation which substantively kills Mr Barton. Certainly in his eyes at the beginning of the narrative, it is all about him:

The house suddenly appeared to him one morning after he had spent two days in bed. Marcus wheeled him out to his accustomed place at the table on the terrace and the sight struck him immediately. How could it not? It was an abomination, a desecration, a heresy, a sight unbelievable. There was a house on the hillside. His hill, the one which overlooked the village and which his terrace faced. (Senior 1989, 90)

The opening paragraph signals much about Henry Barton's perspectival, spatial and ideological location and the Euro-creole order which he represents. It is told by an external focalizer whose voice and stance are fused imperceptibly with the character-bound focalizer in free, indirect narration; the phrase "how could it not" marks the shift from an objective focus to his thought patterns. The external focalizer uses this stance of peering over the shoulder and into the mindset of the protagonist to yield in-depth insight into his mind and then, rather than elicit sympathetic identification, which is how this narrative strategy tends traditionally to be used, the identification is used to create acceptance of the inevitable demolition of its mental strongholds.

Mr Barton is infirm, wheelchair-bound and given to periods of illness which lead to confinement in bed. The opening paragraph foreshadows the unfolding key events of the narrative, which are few and are triggered by unexpected changes to the house and which also occur when he has been confined to bed. In the opening frame, he is at his strongest – absolutely assured of his ideological location, reflected in the divinely ordained supremacy of his value system and worldview, as guaranteed by his race and skin colour as well as his proximity to European "civilization", his distance from African "savagery", his lordship over all he surveys. His diction captures his sense of this absolute right of mastery, as well as of sacrilege at the desecration of his view and his perspective on the rightness of things. The problem is that Miss Vie and the entire social strata she represents have forgotten their divinely ordained place – as Erna Brodber describes it, "In our Caribbean – where race, colour, and material wealth intersect with cultural orientation to form grids into which people are placed and into which they place themselves – it is important for social and psychological peace that one know one's place" (1998, 72–73). The Euro-creole sensibility, as aptly demonstrated by Mr Barton, executes a gate-keeping function. In the absence of brute force, the structures required to maintain and extend class and colour hegemonies stand strong only insofar as their ideological ramparts and foundations remain secure; as it turns out, it is not sufficient to place the Other in an "appropriate" location – the Other must be persuaded to be contained therein.

This is not to imply that Englishness and its bastardized offspring Eurocreoleness can be read as bastions of strength. They are equally fragile and imperiously mistrustful of difference. Senior imbricates the mores of colonialism and patriarchy until they cannot be disentangled. An apparent benevolence masks the impulse towards absolute dominance. He who must be obeyed maintains the imperviousness of his universe by a most obsessive self-centredness, so much so that Mr Barton inculcates from his English bosses studied poses of inattention, such as appearing to listen when he is miles away or asleep with his eyes open. The deliberate erection of walls and appropriation of masks to deny community bear fruit in splendid isolation within his family, an incapacity to acknowledge the individuality and personhood of his wife and children, and an inability to enter into intimacy or even acknowledge need.

In "Barbados" Mr Watford emerges from the very peasantry which would have been set aside for servitude by that island's then deep-rooted and stringent race and colour demarcations. Indeed, his stint in America would have solidified his position on the disadvantageous side of the fixed colour line by the negation in the United States of class, skin colour, education and other factors which would have contributed to the construction of ethnicity in the islands. This notwithstanding, he returns to Barbados, and by virtue of wealth and spurred on by internalized self-loathing, he swathes himself in whiteness – manifested in an unfinished, sparsely furnished "pure, proud, pristine white house Colonial American in design", white uniforms which are relics of his long years of working in the hospital boiler room, white sheets and white walls. All are iconic of his compulsive desire for whiteness, as well as his inner sterility. He tends stunted coconut trees, chosen because they reflect his own aborted self-development and desire to always appear young. He drives his body at a punishing pace, denying the accumulated weariness of his years and his need for rest. Emotionally inviolate, spiritually bankrupt, fighting the ravages of age, he is unable to make contact with people. He even steps into the mindset of the oppressor and projects a mindless hatred onto the villagers, the outgrowth of self-hatred born of the humiliation that the dominant class habitually meted out to the poor and black.

Both protagonists possess much of what Robert Young in *Colonial Desire* identifies as that paradoxical quality of Englishness of the past which tended to be represented in the writings of the colonized in terms "of fixity, of certainty, centredness, homogeneity, as something unproblematically identical with itself". Making reference to Rhys's male characters, he argues: "in the literary sphere such forms of Englishness are always represented as other, something other people possess, often as an image of consummate masculinity" (Young 1995, 2). Senior and Marshall probe the space between this rigid fixity and a paradoxical and gripping desire which ultimately pours out of the inner beings of these men, in such a compelling fashion that it destroys their investment in fixity and literally or figuratively ends their lives. In other words, their rigidly constructed inner beings and their internally generated life sources are destroyed by the intrusion of desire for the Other. In this sense they come to mirror the face which Young argues characterizes the constructions of Englishness/Europeanness in English novels, indicating that an insider's perspective presents the constructions of English masculinity as uncertain, fluid, vulnerable and sick with compulsive desire to consume otherness based on ethnicity and/or class (Young 1995, 2). Witness, for example, the uncontrollably passionate, teeth-gnashing, racially tainted Heathcliff in Brontë's *Wuthering Heights*, or the insatiably lustful Kurtz in Conrad's *Heart of Darkness*, incapacitated but crawling on all fours towards the compelling drumbeat of the African heartland.

Henry Barton's position, which is a direct reflection of his intense socialization in Englishness, requires that his meaning frame and process of formation must remain central at all cost. All things in his social and even his natural environment must be yoked to feed his delusions of central positioning. His relational manoeuvres present visages of politeness and conviviality intended to mask his essential disconnectedness. This ideological framework sweeps all who draw near into its ambit as servitors – the more excellent the servitor, the more effective the fulfilment of purpose and the more secure his or her place in Mr Barton's skewed framework of meaning. Mr Barton's primary and chief servitor is the wife of his youth, who loves him deeply, but he is unable to reciprocate because, in his view, her life purpose is first and foremost to provide him with the genealogical service of lending her fair complexion to his intergenerational skin-lightening project. Thereafter her task is to bring up his offspring to manifest his enlightened prestige and civility. In so doing she reflects the race and class dynamic of the time, which sociologist Lloyd Braithwaite identified as a veritable marriage lottery in which persons traded a light skin colour, with its capacity to ensure intergenerational upward mobility, for the benefits of enhanced financial wealth and class location. The attendant patterns of marital and sexual contacts, along with structured gendered roles in the domestic and public spheres, combine to form a grid within which persons are located – and it is crucial that at all times, persons are socialized to know their place. Mr Barton's perfect, fair of skin, subservient wife was attuned to the reality that her husband's public role was such that domestic requirements could never take precedence over his public pursuits.

If the wife's place is to lend her body and genetic advantage to status-enhancement and skin-lightening agendas, the Euro-creole's body-policing manoeuvres become even more subtle and virulent in relation to non-conjugal servitors. Indeed, the earliest inscriptions of European conquistadors standing erect, leaning on their weapons over the supine bodies of the "natives", demonstrates the significance and longevity of appropriate languaging of embodied power relations.4 The servile body was marked even more so, hence Mr Watford's suppressed glee when the servant accords him gestures reserved for the white man. Mr Barton's servant appears to know his place and role to exactitude. Born in his house, the son of his wife's maid, Marcus has been bred into generations of servitude as surely as Henry Barton's social trajectory has marked him as born to rule. Marcus is the ideal servant precisely because he has been socialized from infancy into the complex manoeuvres – speech inflections, body language, dress, guise, postures – which render him the perfect servitor. It appears that his every focus of attention is to please his master, care for him, medicate him, bathe him, pamper his ageing body, facilitate his sparse and sterile social contacts. Because of his ideological blindness, Mr Barton constantly misreads even those who are have the most intimate connection with him. Marcus's investment in the female-gendered role of domestic homemaker and caregiver leads Mr Baron to assume that he is womanized and potentially inclined towards homoeroticism.

Reflecting the interface between colonial and patriarchal oppression, the ultimate challenge to the problematic ideological position of both Euro-creole males comes from a most predictable locus of otherness and desire – gender and sexuality. Mr Barton's imperviousness is shaken by his second wife, whom he marries because her sexual abandon belies her snow-white skin. In the transnational marriage economy, race and place once again assume significance. Josie is constructed as a female predator who exchanges her odoriferous bedsitter in gloomy London for the position of wife of a wealthy government official in a tropical paradise. Patriarchal rule, which she defies at every turn, dictates that she live to please him according to his rules and under his control. The marriage ends disastrously.

These female-authored narratives intricately interweave a range of symbolic associations into the houses built and inhabited by their protagonists, until they come to be metonymically associated with their respective owners' essential unhomeliness. The house is a pivotal and enduring symbol in Caribbean literature – predictably so, as reflective of a society formulated out of multiple enforced and voluntary labour migrations. Houses carry the symbolic weight of deep-rooted longings for home, rest, shelter, protection, and even heraldic associations of every man's castle, lineage and cultural imprint. Much of both characters' (re)cognition is focused around the symbol of the house. Mr Barton's inner alienation is so great that he buys his land and plans a home without informing his wife of many decades about this aspiration. This house is for him, not about homely domesticity; it is an extension of his solipsism. He who could find no relief for his unhomeliness in the famous landscapes of Europe, during the "home" leave which every colonial craves, initially finds a measure of rest in his soundly built rural retreat facing a barren, inhospitable hillside. The terrace on which he spends most of his time represents the boundary between his house – in which he fashions himself the indisputable king of his castle – and outside, in relation to which he fashions himself as master of all he surveys: a sparse, sterile mountain which promises him the possibility of order, as opposed to the rich, riotous fecundity characteristic of the forested tropical landscape. His view from the terrace is just that – his – reflecting the inherited impulse of the colonial gaze which struggled to impose mastery, dominance and taxonomies. The landscape becomes an externalization of his desire as well as a projection of his inner psychic landscape – bare, barren, sterile, incapable of sustaining rich growth.

The alienation and otherness which are masked at the earlier stages of Mr Barton's life journey are revealed in his old age, when he fixes his gaze – initially in anger and contempt – on the woman whose stability and endurance constrain him to face the gaps and spaces of his inner being, his transience as an icon of a passing way of life, his lack of community. The apparently unattached woman on the hill poses a constant challenge to his notion that women exist to please men. Her men are invisible enough to appear nonexistent. Indeed, the only signs of their presence are the constant stream of diapers on the clothesline and the increasing number of neatly dressed children tumbling down the mountainside on their way to school. Significantly, the woman takes up residence in the middle of his view and gradually imposes upon Mr Barton, a revelation of his own marginality. The drier and more desiccated and cut off from human contact he grows, the more rooted she becomes. The impingement of one in relation to the other externalizes the takeover of the Euro-creole impulse towards civilization and governance by a contesting Afro-creole impulse, rooted in the creative medium of the indigenous, home-grown, communal and spiritual, all of which are invested with enormous growth potential. Although she is fleshy and substantial, Miss Vie comes to haunt his sensibility, like the duppy of Afro-creole mythology, which, like her, is held to live near the silk cotton tree.

The woman on the hill becomes above all the womb of Mr Barton's otherness, and his untapped potential for rebirth is offered in the dominant image of the house. Her presence lures him to re-vision and reformulate the lives he has missed. Temporally he becomes immersed in a series of overlapping time cycles – life cycle, rainy/dry season cycles, domestic cycles, and agricultural cycles. His diurnal cycle is measured by her activities and those of her children as he tracks their heads bobbing down the hill in the morning and returning in the afternoon. He who never gave credence to the domesticities of his household and left all such trivialities to his wife becomes immersed in their domestic rhythms, and this leads him to relive in flashback the gaps and elisions of his own home life.

The dynamic womb of otherness comes into play with the contradictory mix of contempt and desire which both protagonists come to harbour for the younger women, and the psychosexual dynamics which this sets up in relation to Afro-Caribbean males. In Senior's narrative, Mr Barton becomes immersed in the most female-centred of cycles – child-bearing – which seems miraculous, given the invisibility of men. This spurs him to vague stirrings of desire. His killing defeat comes when the hut is finally washed away by rain; he turns to his servant in grief to ask after the woman's welfare, only to be regaled with a slice of vigorous Afro-creole life. She has been mistress to multiple men; his own servitor, whom he had assumed belonged to him completely – with no purpose outside of caring for, soothing, medicating and pampering his master's ageing and ailing frame – had been in intimate connection with Miss Vie and had fathered two of her children. He learns that these several men are confident enough not to insist on exclusive rights of possession, and that despite her appearance of being solitary she is very much part of the community with its hierarchies, intimacies and modes of operation. The community had readily come to her aid in trouble.

Watford, like Barton, encloses himself in a deep and profound silence and unwillingness and even incapacity to know the Other. The only physical contact he allows himself is with his pet Barbary doves – which are generally white or light-coloured, with pale bills – with which he shares tactile and auditory affinity. He is comforted by the feel of their sound, a soft *ku-k'rroo*, which remains all day in his hands. Additionally, the derisive laughter with which he fends off human contact finds an echo in the birds' high-pitched, excited *heh-heh-heh* sound, like jeering laughter. Major disruption of his extreme isolation comes when the unnamed servant girl, who is initially innocent and full of hope and trust, comes to stake out a place of belonging in a hidden corner of his unfinished house, and in the submerged recesses of his truncated inner being. He is unable to acknowledge that the beautiful young woman stirs desire in his desiccated loins.

> But once, after many silent evenings together, he detected a sound apart from the night murmurs of the sea and village and the metallic tuning of the steel band, a low, almost inhuman cry of loneliness which chilled him. Frightened, he turned to find her leaning hesitantly toward him, her eyes dark with urgency, and her face tight with bewilderment and a growing anger. He started, not understanding, and her arm lifted to stay him. Eagerly she bent closer. But as she uttered the low cry again, as her fingers described her wish to talk, he jerked around, afraid that she would be foolish enough to speak and that once she did they would be brought close. He would be forced then to acknowledge something about her which he refused to grant; above all, he would be called upon to share a little of himself. Quickly he returned to his

newspaper, rustling it to settle the air, and after a time he felt her slowly, bitterly, return to her silence. (Marshall 1961, 20)

It is significant then that her call which he so effectively rebukes invites him to emerge into life. It triggers a series of reminders of his past, reconnects him to his mother, reminds him of community, warmth and conviviality. He begins to vaguely entertain the possibility that these may be centres of power, healing and self-affirmation. The power of this life and the emblem of its loss to him are represented by dance. Put another way, movement is the voice through which the subaltern speaks. Mr Watford and Mr Barton demand silence from the Other as "tongueless, earless, eyeless conveniences" (Hurston [1937] 1990, 1), as affirmation of their acquiescence to hegemonic values and their subordinate place in the Euro-creole social order. Yet given the potential of embodiment to convey social locatedness, this silence needs to be buttressed by a series of gestures, guises, poses of servitude and disciplining of the body to affirm complicity. On one hand, the servant boy affirms his subordination: "He came and stood outside the back door, his hands and lowered head performing the small, subtle rites of deference" (Marshall 1961, 8). Counteracting this, and compounding the irritation generated by the mere sight of his youthful, strong and supple body, the boy – who is associated with the emerging Afrocentric political order the Barbados People's Party – wears a declarative button that constitutes a deep assault to Mr Barton and his ilk: "The Old Order Shall Pass". This constitutes an act of defiance and self-definition, appropriation of agency, and assumption of the capacity to chart a future and a destiny. The potential for liberation speaks a stinging rebuke to those who would prop up the old order forever.

Mr Watford's killing blow comes when the servant girl whom he has silenced with all his accoutrements of power – his association with America, with its putative neo-imperial status; the whiteness of his colonial American plantation house; his practice of reading foreign newspapers, which locates him as enlightened and in touch with a higher order – finds her voice. All the markers which relegate her to being poor, mean, impoverished, uneducated, dark, ignorant and lacking in worth are undermined when she awakens to the immensity of her power and passion. Her emotional and sexual awakening, when touched by the defiant young boy with political aspirations, is accomplished through dance – a potent symbol in all Marshall's narratives.5 The courtship dance, which occurs spontaneously between the trees to the strains of the steel band on a stunning moonlit night – a theatre of Afro-creole embodiment, ritual and performance – speaks rootedness by both association with the indigenous cultural emblems and connection with the earth: "Dancing, the stones moiling underfoot, they claimed the night. More than the night. The steel band played for them alone. The trees were their frivolous companions, swaying as they swayed. The moon rode the sky because of them" (Marshall 1961, 23). Although the pursuit takes the form of leaps and spins and twirls in the air, the catch brings them to the earth, to grounding in each other's bodies in the ancient courtship rites of possession. Its fluidity and gracefulness speak both to their youth and sensuality and to the release of their bodies from circumscribing gestures of servitude and subordination. It transports them from the margins of their world into the centre of an explosive, sensuous universe of colour, beauty, strength, sound, passion and fecundity: "They were joined in a tender battle: the boy in a sport shirt riotous with color was reaching for the girl as he leaped and spun, weightless, to the music, while she fended him off with a gesture which was lovely in its promise of surrender" (23).

This celebration of the emergence of the new order is an embodied enactment of the unstoppable product of the encounter between worlds: the merry creole dance of life as celebrated by Benítez-Rojo, the flipside of the illusory tyranny of Euro-creole cultural impositions and policing of bodies and minds. The vitality, energy and cultural assertiveness as reflective of the inevitability of the new order penetrate Mr Watford's garrisons and expose him utterly. His inordinate pride and security in his capacity to work fall away to reveal a nameless dread. It reveals the mask behind which he hides weariness, fear of the unknown, the mythical terror which looms by night.6

The strength of these stories lies in their perspectival manipulations. The implied authors of both female-authored third-person narratives play with the otherness of their protagonists, based on patriarchal gender identities which are closely intertwined with their locations on the Euro- to Afro-creole continuum. The implied authors use in-depth insight into the psychology, mindsets and worldviews of their protagonists in order to reveal severe limitations of their sensibilities and vantage points, and even more so their diseased, pathological nature. The ageing men are so firmly vested in or constructed within the Euro-creole worldview that when the lower-strata women undermine their maleness, centrality and custodial control over this social order, even from a distance, the protagonists die. Yet the use of perspective is wielded skilfully by the implied authors to ensure that the protagonists emerge as entrapped, pathetic and needy rather than hateful. Readers are exposed to the deep-rooted and enduring self-hatred which is a fundamental legacy of the colonial order. As was the case for plantation society, the outcome is a skewed internal configuration which produces a toxic – though, to its adherents, plausible – world and worldview. The writer's countervailing perspectives, like the woman's hut, sprout in the centre of the barren male's vision, on a sparse, infertile hill which externalizes his inner being. Landscape and location become psychic landscape and internal configuration.

And here the African and the female presences, which despite deep-rooted denials, denigrations and marginalizations cannot be erased, emerge to take a position of centrality. The emergence proves inimical to the Euro-creole impulse. Given the dominant nature and absolute rule of the hegemonic order, the two cannot coexist. Both narratives assert that, given the insidious colonization of the inner being of the Euro-creole, the decolonization process must find its outworking in the private domestic realm. They are not alone in this assumption. This is a central tenet of Lamming's *Natives of My Person* (1994) in relation to the colonizer's quest to found a more equitable social order. Gender inequity is so foundational and all-pervasive that men cannot undertake to build a new social order until they first come to terms with their women – women are a future the men must learn. Dabydeen (2002) terms empire a pornographic project; hence, to eradicate the tentacles of empire, one must reformulate gender interactions. Senior and Marshall add to these insights. Since colonial and neo-colonial hierarchies were based on gendered ethno-political locations, dismantling of the region for the typological Henry Barton or Mr Watford requires that the womb of his otherness – a representative woman who fits to perfection the symbolic profile of the Other – should take up residence in his inner space, mirror his lack and stimulate a desire for the Other: for community, for fecundity, for wholeness, for flourishing, for sensuality. These Caribbean female-authored narratives point to a paradoxical bifurcate centre: it is vulnerability, insubstantiality and a submerged and unarticulated desire for the Other that produce the mask of rigidity and fixity.

Miscegenation, leading to mixing of bloodlines, has been endemic within the colonial encounter. At its root is the privileged European-descended male's inscription of his supremacy on the flesh of the disempowered female, to shame and to send a message to the disempowered African-descended male as to which cock rules the roost. The texts speak of the power of the female racialized Other to act as a bridge to release energies and to actualize the continuities implicit in the processes and lived experience of creolization. We return to Harris's contention that within the gulfs and chasms which divide cultures there is a storehouse of "creative energies which once tapped may energise the unfinished genesis of the imagination". He posits: "In that energy, eclipsed bridges and potential bridges exist between divorced, separated or closed orders that are sometimes precarious, never absolute, but which I think engender a profound awareness of the numinous solidity of space, inner space/outer space and the womb of simultaneous densities and transparencies in the language of originality" (Harris 1998, 25–26). The deeply entrenched psychic and experiential Euro-creoleness proves a discombobulating dwelling place indeed. In the final analysis, this process of dismantling the typological Euro-creole remains internal and isolated. In Senior's narrative, the representative major players never come into contact. Arguably, in real life they must.

3

LAMENT OF THE UNHOMELY
Nationhood and Non-belonging in the Work of V.S. Naipaul

> The nation fills the void left in the uprooting of communities and kin and turns that loss into the language of metaphor. Metaphor transfers the meaning of home and belonging across the middle passage . . . across those distances and cultural differences that span the imagined community of the nation people.
>
> – Homi Bhabha, *The Location of Culture*

A COMMEMORATIVE REPRINT OF the *Trinidad Guardian* broadsheet of August 1962, marking the fiftieth anniversary of independence in August 2012, bears the triumphant headline "Trinidad Now Becomes a Nation", with the subhead "Jubilant Scenes as the National Flag Signals New Era". The lead paragraph reads: "A noble red, black and white flag slid gracefully up the lofty white pole in the flood lit forecourt of the Red House, Port of Spain. A thunder of feverish applause from thousands of citizens . . . and a nation was born." Flush with the magic and giddy joy of the moment, the reporter proceeds: "Trinidad and Tobago –1,983 square miles – gained complete sovereignty at midnight last night to become the 15th proud nation of the British Commonwealth – the third member in the Western Hemisphere" (*Trinidad Guardian* 1962, 1). The potentialities and paradoxes of the moment are all apparent: exultation at the peaceful transition from an oppressive imperial regime into new, globally recognized political independence; the allure of the pomp, pageantry and iconography of nationhood; the joy, commitment and ownership of the people; the minuteness and vulnerability of the island state; the aspiration, perhaps more than affirmation, of "complete sovereignty"; the ongoing filiative relationship with the imperial motherland; the feverish moment of victory and the certainty of countless mornings after.[1]

This chapter, originally conceived as a contribution to retrospective deliberations fifty years later, explores the mornings after the triumphs of 1962. Trinidad and Tobago and Jamaica stepped into bittersweet nation-statehood as simultaneously the newly minted nations mourned the collapse of the West Indian Federation – a dream deferred. Of the countless architects of the nation-state – politicians, artistes, activists, creative writers, all involved in the ongoing highly contested project of imagining the independent Caribbean nations – this exploration focuses on perspectives offered by V.S. Naipaul. It uses as its point of departure a salient statement which he made in relation to Belize, which he terms "spectacularly decrepit":

> The politicians and some of the academics over there seem to think that they could abolish the deformities of that society simply by the use of words. And they use a special word there, their own magic word – and if you know the dereliction of that land you would understand that it was no more than magic. The magic word is "Belizean", an inhabitant of Belize, and they thought by baptizing everybody as "Belizean" they had healed everybody. (Naipaul 1999, 53).

Naipaul discounts in this statement numerous allegiances commonly associated with birthplace: being grounded in locality, landscape, seascape, weather systems, culture, dietary practices, faith, aesthetics, language and particular networks of grounded social relations, including but not limited to kinship, class and race. Arguably, depending on one's interpretative framework, Naipaul the essayist can be read as cautioning against facile constructions of nation as discursive anodyne, a play of words deployed by academics and politicians – spokespersons for the hegemonic order – which act as palliative and panacea to deep-rooted and divisive social ills. On the other hand, he can be perceived as privileging above all a pathological view of the social order as diseased and deformed beyond all powers of recuperation, hence as possessing little or no viability in relation to nation-statehood.

This is not an isolated indictment. In his travelogue *The Middle Passage*, Naipaul the travel writer opines:

> Nationalism was impossible for Trinidad. In the colonialist society every man had to be for himself; every man had to grasp whatever dignity and power he

was allowed; he owed no loyalty to the island and scarcely had any to his group. To understand this is to understand the squalor of the politics which came to Trinidad in 1948 when after no popular agitation, universal adult suffrage was declared. The new politics were reserved for the enterprising who had seen the prodigious commercial possibilities. (Naipaul [1962] 1969, 78)[2]

This statement, positively interpreted, by implication defines nationalism as collectively desired and engineered by the people for the people – a prize held more dear if it comes by dint of struggle. On the other hand, the statement can be interpreted as dismissive of the nation as a consensual grouping of persons who yearn for self-determination and for belonging to a collectivity larger than themselves, and as expanded and dignified by such belonging. By extension it denies the potential of political governance, which requires foundational integrity and a mutually responsible interface between a people and its leaders, as opposed to governors, who are essentially corrupt mercenaries interfacing with a near-ungovernable mass with an inveterate admiration for rogues – in short, a picaroon order.

Such is Naipaul's assessment of the outcome of mass enforced and voluntary labour migrations from Europe, Africa, India and the Middle East, which generated within tiny island spaces a microcosm of worlds in motion, oppressed people-groups jostling within an unjust, racist, Eurocentric social order for resources, for voice, for the right to be looked upon. For the enterprise of the Indies to function effectively, it was insufficient to trade in the bodies of humans. The subjugation of free women and men and their reduction to labouring bodies required erasure of cultural moorings; wrenching from ancestral norms; dismantling of ancient faiths; loss of everyday habits of dress, diet, kinship patterns and mourning rituals. In the aftermath of colonialism, the challenge has been to build viable and vibrant island societies. The national allegory goes like this: in the broad-based liberation movement of the mid-twentieth century which swept the so-called Third World into independence, self-determination and nation-statehood, the will to power had to be based on a foundational requirement – cultural certitude, crafted by creative imaginations and finely honed by practitioners who used the master's tools to dismantle the master's house.

Naipaul does not envision such a possibility. Wearing the guise of the travel writer and the essayist, he has repeatedly, eloquently and democratically characterized the new nations of the Caribbean as mean small backwaters populated by mediocre mimics who are fundamentally incapable of independent affirmation, self-validation and nationalist sentiment, construction and performance. And this his confessional protagonist and failed nation-builder Ralph Kirpalsingh constructs as particularly evident in relation to the fictional worlds against which colonials have been carefully trained to measure themselves: "We, here on our island, handling books printed in this world, had been abandoned and forgotten. We pretended to be real, to be learning, to be preparing ourselves for life, we mimic men of the New World, one unknown corner of it, with all its reminders of the corruption that came so quickly to the new" (Naipaul [1967a] 1969, 146). We the imitative castaways live on our islands; the real people live in substantial and tangible fictional worlds to which we are denied access.

Naipaul's relentless stance constrains admission that for the diverse Caribbean peoples, home – actual and metaphorical – carries a multiplicity of addresses. In *A House for Mr Biswas* ([1961] 1969) he critiques any attempt to locate the primary indicator of belonging in fading memories of ancestry, born again in adopted lands through debased collective rituals and re-enactments. Those who seek home in this location occupy an uneasy crossroads between coded cultural practices, themselves shored up with essentialized notions of fixed cultural and religious traditions, and inevitable, at times even radical, change processes. Alternatively, a primary locus of home has been the nation. Nationalism – that is, that notion that people-groups are divided into nations, each with unique identities, landscapes and political selves – has been a necessary driver of the region's independence movement. Yet given the racialized underpinnings of the nation-state and ethnic contestation over emblems of rootedness and belonging, as well as successive waves of secondary migration, nationalism has failed to give a substantial cross-section of citizens a psychic resting place of warmth and comfort to come home to.

If we accept that the nation can be a flawed symbolic receptacle into which to pour an innate and inherent longing for home, what is the nature of the house which Naipaul builds, given his foundational rejection of any potentiality for Caribbean nationhood, juxtaposed with an ambivalent connection to an island home which he despises but ultimately cannot disavow? Where is respite to be found from aloneness, alienation, anguish, fracture, isolation and loss? Where is the place of welcome, acceptance, fellowship, nurturance, shared vision, community and harmony? Where is Mr Naipaul's home?

Postcolonial theorist Homi Bhabha invokes unhomeliness as paradigmatic to the colonial and postcolonial conditions. In his essay "The World and the Home" (1992) Bhabha maps a psychic location which reflects the "uncanny literary and social effects of enforced social accommodation or historical migration or cultural locations". In this location, he argues, the home does not remain "the domain of domestic life, nor does the world simply become its social or historical counterpart". The sense of the unhomeliness is generated by the "shock of recognition of the-world-in-the-home and the-home-in-the-world" (10). This psychic location is

> a boundary: a bridge, where "presencing" begins because it captures something of the estranging sense of the relocation of home and world – the unhomeliness – that is the condition of extraterritorial and cross cultural initiation. To be unhomed is not to be homeless, nor can the "unhomely" be easily accommodated in that familiar division of social life into private and public spheres. The recesses of the domestic space become sites for history's most intricate invasion. In that displacement, the borders between home and world become confused; and, uncannily, the private and public become part of each other, forcing upon us a vision that is as divided as it is disorienting. (Bhabha 1992, 10)

Based on Bhabha's contention that "the unhomely moment relates the traumatic ambivalences of a personal, psychic history to the wider disjunctions of political ambivalence" (11), I argue that unresolved and submerged angst in relation to this condition remains at the root of Naipaul's continuous process of inventing, disavowing and reinventing the potential for New World statehood and the parameters of his engagement and (non)belonging to Trinidad.

For Naipaul, Trinidad proved a traumatizing catalyst which instilled an impulse for flight as early as his teens. As a Form Four secondary-school student at Queen's Royal College, he inscribed a desire for escape in the margins of a textbook. The experience of unhomeliness, which elicits fear of enclosure and entrapment, proves to be too overwhelming to be consciously grasped. Flight is his response. Yet demonstrating trauma's quality of belatedness and intrusive memory, Naipaul's natal land haunts the subconscious, surfacing in recurrent nightmares: "for many years later falling asleep in bed sitters with the electric fire on, I had been awakened by the nightmare that I was back in tropical Trinidad" (Naipaul [1962] 1969, 43). According to Cathy Caruth, in *Unclaimed Experience: Trauma Narrative and History*, "The painful repetition of the flashback can only be understood as the absolute inability of the mind to avoid an unpleasurable event that has not been given psychic meaning in any way. In trauma, the outside has gone inside without any mediation" (1996, 59). Identifying incomprehensibility at the heart of the repetitive seeing, Caruth (after Freud) argues that the point is not the avoidance of the unpleasurable event but rather "the peculiar and perplexing experience of survival" (ibid.).

From his youth, Naipaul has been marooned between worlds. In a 1954 letter to Henry Swanzy, producer of the BBC programme *Caribbean Voices*, for which the aspiring writer wrote while he was at University College, Oxford, he indicates: "The future is as blank as ever. Nobody loves me, nobody wants me. In England, I am not English. In India, I am not Indian. I am chained to the 1000 sq miles that is Trinidad but I will evade that fate yet" (Naipaul 1954).[3] The elements are all present: a dislocating history which generates a cultural and relational void, bespeaking loss of ancestral motherland; loss of all illusions of a filiative relationship with a nurturing colonial mother; the sense of an aborted future because of an incapacity to identify with where he came from and therefore disconnectedness in relation to where he may be headed; and a terrible and enduring sense of entrapment in relation to his island birthplace – even enslavement, as suggested by the chains which bind him to Trinidad – crowned by a compulsion to break the tentacles of an ill-fated connection which remains intact despite physical distance. Clear, penetrating and heart-wrenching longing for home is reflected in the child-like lament "Nobody loves me, nobody wants me."

For Naipaul the essayist, the root of the trauma comes to articulation only after he visits Trinidad briefly and subsequently regains a safe distance from this site of oppression. Only then does he set himself the task – on which his bread and butter as a commissioned writer depends – of ordering nightmare into narrative in *The Middle Passage* ([1962] 1969). As the ship docks in Trinidad, the sense of entrapment encloses him: "I began to feel my old fear of Trinidad. I did not want to stay. I had left the security of the ship and had no assurance that I would ever leave the island again" (Naipaul [1962] 1969, 44–45). The ship becomes its own ambivalent trope, an interstitial womb of space which enables travellers to arrive, and more so to leave. It is the liminal state of inbetweenness, a transitory, mobile place in which people group and regroup based on shifting allegiances of class, colour, language and race, meeting the unhomely conditions outlined by Bhabha: "We find ourselves in the moment of transit where space and time cross to produce complex figures of difference and identity, past and present, inside and outside, inclusion and exclusion" (Bhabha 1994, 1).

An intensely productive lifetime later, in his 2002 Nobel Prize acceptance address, the dyspeptic prizewinner attributes his prodigious creative output to the two worlds in which he lived as a child. The locus of one world is the ancestral Lion House of the Capildeo clan in Chaguanas, Trinidad, and the other world is outside its gates. From infancy Naipaul has occupied a precarious position between these two worlds: "The world outside the tall corrugated-iron gate, and the world at home. It was a remnant of our caste sense, the thing that excluded and shut out" (Naipaul 2001, n.p.). The impulse that shut the world out, based on fear of defilement, is the very impulse which generates the area of darkness outside the corrugated gates. This other world beckons and repulses, fascinates and assaults.

Much of the critique of Naipaul's acerbic vision responds to his skill at "othering" the island societies of the Caribbean. This reading mines Naipaul's relentless ambivalence and disavowal to elicit insights into paradoxes of belonging which are valid lived experiences, though not commonly perceived as ideologically and politically correct. Personal histories of ethnically diverse New World subjects have now been articulated from a range of sociocultural locations and by myriad voices. Together they tell of the interface of self and Other in the wake of the imperial enterprise. The narratives, when inscribed as felt life, emerge from the inexpressible domain to haunt the collective literary landscape with their shadowy presences, and therefore demand to be owned, digested, accepted and critiqued by all; in other words, having been voiced, they demand that we collectively bear witness.

The first fictional extract, which I have selected for its capacity to lend a plausible feel to the lived experience of suppressed histories and to convey the atmospheric immediacy of the unhomely, is taken from Naipaul's classic portrayal of post-indentureship to pre-independent Trinidad, *A House for Mr Biswas*. The extract zeroes in on Mohun's visit to his uncle, the estranged Bhandat, who, prior to the opening of the "corrugated iron gates" to overtly release the sheltered rural population into the creolization process, scandalously leaves the comfort of the prescriptive enclosure and does violence to notions of caste by choosing to live with his Chinese lover in Port of Spain. Decades later, Mr Biswas visits Bhandat in a Port of Spain slum and experiences an unhomely confrontation with extraterritorial and cross-cultural initiation. Submerged historical traumas, though unnamed in the text, collude and erupt to generate intense individual psychic pain and social dislocation.

Myriad historical parameters – articulated and unarticulated – undergird the extract. "In fact he lived in a tenement that lay between an importer of eastern goods and an exporter of sugar and copra. It was an old, Spanish style building. The flat facade, diversified by irregular areas of missing plaster, small windows with broken shutters and two rusty iron balconies, rose directly from the pavement" (Naipual [1961] 1969, 448). Biswas finds Bhandat jammed into a narrow enclosure among the outgrowth of the serendipity which accounts for the origins of modern New World societies – a location wrought by historical mercantilism, occasioned by Western lust for the spices of the East, which leads to an intrepid sea captain's misadventure of sailing west to reach the East, in the process discovering verdant tropical landscapes, which are transformed into Europe's wealth-generating factories and its playground. The derelict Bhandat is literally positioned between merchants representing the import and export arms of a global capitalist machinery which places little or no value on the human person outside of prefigured locations as producer and consumer. In this economy, the old Spanish-style building – a nod to the first imperialist power to appropriate these lands – is itself derelict, as if conscription in the interest of commoditization has debased its trademark elegant architectural statement.

The entrapped slum dwellers are inescapably enveloped by the pungent odours, which are laconically and comprehensively listed using parallel sentence structure:

> From the exporter came the rancid smell of copra and the heavy smell of sacked sugar. . . . From the importer came the many-accented smell of pungent spices. From the road came the smell of dust, straw, the urine and drop-

pings of horses, donkeys and mules. At every impediment the gutters had developed a wrinkled film of scum, as white as the skin on boiled milk, with a piercing, acrid smell, which, blended and heated by the afternoon sun, rose suffocatingly from the road and pursued Mr Biswas. (Naipaul [1961] 1969, 448)

The atmospheric tincture is generated by an assault to the olfactory sense, generated by an admixture of the products and processes of Empire – lusted-after spices of the East Indies, sugars and oils of the West Indies, and the filth and off-scourings of the process, which accumulate in odoriferous gutters of the colonies, covered in scum suggestive of the white-skinned architects of Empire. Unarticulated but latent in this fictional account is the mass importation of enslaved bonded labour to fuel imperial mills, generating loss of ancestral culture and languages, herding workers, irrespective of caste, onto migrant ships and later into impoverished rural villages, which are distanced from the multiracial anomie of pre-independent urban Trinidad, generating a prevailing insularity and defensiveness and eventually giving way to loss of cultural moorings. What is articulated is the pain of dislocation, fear of otherness, shame for weakness and loss.

The farce culminates when Bhandat spills hot tea and roundly curses his lover in Hindi, knowing well that she does not understand the language. She retorts in an unknown tongue. "No words came out of the mouth: only a clacking of the tongue that erupted, at the end, into a shrill croak . . . And Mr Biswas thinking of deafness, dumbness, insanity, the horror of the sex act in that grimy room, felt the yellow cake turn to a sweet slippery paste in his mouth. He could neither chew nor swallow" (Naipaul [1961] 1969, 458). The unhomely moment crystallizes. It ignites shame and pain at racialized embodiment – the impingement of colonial ideologies which thrived on finely tuned denigration of the non-white population, fear of miscegenation and ambivalence in relation to the wider society, which undermines any concept of a viable social order for the emergent plural New World society. The impact is felt viscerally, in the nauseating tactile and gustatory inbetweenness of a mouth full of sweet, slippery cake, offered by the Chinese woman as a gesture of welcome and hospitality, which Biswas cannot swallow. The extract explores the impingement of these suppressed historical complexes on the psychic configuration of the New World citizen.

The first extract focuses on the intrusion of the unhomely moment within the broader pre-independent Trinidadian milieu. The second fictional evocation selected to viscerally express suppressed histories is the intensely interiorized narrative "Tell Me Who to Kill" (Naipaul 1967b), which focuses on the outworking of shame and its interface with paradoxical non-belonging within the village environment, as reconstructed from exile within the colonial (m)otherland. This narrative of migration is instructive of the underlying dynamics and the haunting consequences of incapacity to commit to the emerging nation-state. It speaks to the persistence of a major traumatizing catalyst of the enterprise of the Indies, whose success at producing docile labouring bodies to fuel its endeavour was predicated on imparting shame in relation to embodiment, mores, ancestral faiths, family and kinship patterns, poverty and deprived living conditions – in short, shame in relation to every marker of home and belonging. This shame is coupled with its twin, narcissism: the intense visibility of selves which are perceived as deficient and incapable of ever measuring up to standards of beauty, self-worth, value and social acceptability.

"Tell Me Who to Kill" unfolds over the course of a day's journey in which an unnamed Indo-Trinidadian migrant to England, accompanied by a caregiver, is travelling to an unnamed location to attend his brother Dayo's wedding. This story has been assessed by critics as among the most unsatisfying and inconclusive of Naipaul's narratives. Nothing happens; the story goes nowhere; the central causative event of the protagonist's implied mental breakdown – his response to the young English hooligans who set out to vandalize his fledgling business – is never revealed. And there is no resolution. The reader is drawn experientially into bewilderment about what happens and the reason for the gaping hole at the core of the narrative.

During the course of the journey, the protagonist contemplates his life circumstances which have brought him to this day. He was born in Trinidad into an impoverished Indian family in an isolated village, at a pivotal period of social transition. Opportunities were then opening up for education abroad, as a point of access away from the meanness and menial labour of the rural village environment and into the upwardly mobile city-based business and professional class. While his parents and elder siblings settle for the obscurity of village life, in which insularity, scripted lives and caste certainties inure them to the worse assault of the shaming gaze of the arbiters of colonial values, the protagonist develops a driving ambition to escape, and with it, intense shame: "But I feel I become like the head of the family. I get the ambition and shame for all of them. The ambition is like a shame and the shame is like a secret and it is always hurting" (Naipaul 1967b, 65). The force of this ambition is focused on his beautiful younger brother Dayo, the hope for social upliftment.

In addition to the articulated and unarticulated parameters discussed above, this short narrative is also undergirded by histories of the perceived lack of viability of life options for many in the emerging plural New World society; secondary mass migrations to the metropolis in the quest for upward mobility and a better life; the colonial mother's rejection of her migrant subjects; and institutionalized and non-institutionalized racism in global metropolitan centres, intended to disallow West Indians from gaining access to avenues of upward mobility. All of these come to bear on the psychic configuration of the unnamed mentally disturbed individual.

In "Tell Me Who to Kill" the imparting of a concept of self as beyond the reach of civilization is a direct result of the unnamed but omnipresent gaze of the colonial social order and its neo-colonial adherents. This is the regulating gaze which fundamentally disallows the humanity of the subjugated. The hope invested in a foreign education is instructive. Education in the mother country symbolizes indoctrination into the core value system of imperial order as a prerequisite for insertion as the colonizer's emissary within the emerging social order. A key aspect of the crafting of these "mimic men" is acute shame about all things non-British. The imperial perspective, and arguably Naipaul's viewpoint, constructs the protagonist and his world as objects of contempt – fragile, ignorant, weak, deficient and dirty.

In *The Mask of Shame* (1994), Leon Wurmser (after Hegel) identifies three forms of shame: shame because one is a limited mortal far from an ideal of perfection, shame because a total and absolute union with another person is never possible, and shame as an attitude precluding naive self-exposure and self-expression (64). Wurmser points to a range of shame reactions, from mild forms of shyness and embarrassment through disgrace, dishonour, degradation and debasement. In its most extreme form, shame can become traumatizing: "Narcissistic mortification, a sense of terror (a sudden loss of control over external or internal reality or both) occurs when shame anxiety reaches traumatic proportions" (Wurmser 1994, 51). Naipaul's unnamed protagonist's growing unhomeliness propels him through all these forms of shame into the throes of narcissistic mortification.

The persistent and pivotal shaming scenario is yet another evocation of the unhomely moment, carefully set to flood the psyche through every door of perception: a fragile, beautiful younger brother who represents his unspoilt self, brimming over with potential; an inimical, threatening environment – sparse, poverty-scarred shelter, sweltering heat, blackened sky, incessant rain drumming on the galvanized roof; vulnerable body, subject to itching skin; the nauseating smell of smoke and food; marauding mosquitoes; inadequate sense of security and belonging, as represented by the impotent father; an overwhelming sense of looming harm and threat to life from disease.

> It is a bare room and the bare cedar boards have nothing on them except nails and some clothes and a calendar.... And my pretty brother is trembling with the ague, lying on the floor on a floursack spread on a sugarsack, with another floursack for counterpane. You can see the sickness on his little face.... It is how I think of my brother, small and sick, suffering for me and so pretty. I feel I could kill anyone who make him suffer. I don't care about myself. I have no life. (Naipaul 1967b, 61)

The protagonist, afflicted severely with shame at his poverty, squalor and vulnerability, envisages himself as beyond recuperation; he invests hope and prospects for the future in his alter ego – a brother, young and beautiful, who becomes the focal point of his desire and self-actualization. His brother takes up in his mind the complex location of a scapegoat who is suffering on his behalf, and as his shame mask, in whose personal success he will dissolve his debasement. This location awakens aggression, which is rage against his vulnerabilities such that he "could kill anyone who make him suffer" (61), and intense fear that his essential debasement and unworthiness will be exposed. Moreover, he embraces this life's work not simply as a personal quest but in fulfilment of a broader imperative, of supplanting the darkness of the debased, ignorant and impotent father and the elder siblings to save the family from shame – a task rendered impossible by the family's self-mockery and inverse pride in their debasement, which draws strength from insularity.

In the present time of the narrative, the first-person narrator has been severely traumatized by the loss of his brother to failure and the loss of his business, which represents his own bid for personal success. His pervasive spatiotemporal dislocation is related to haunting recurrence of that culminating shaming moment of childhood, which undermines his every effort to locate a home in the world. Constrained as he is to live with the recurrent intrusive memory, his mind-protecting erasure intervenes to disconnect the ever-present shaming recollection from spatiotemporal locatedness; indeed, the disturbing memory of home itself becomes displaced. The protagonist envisions the house, knows that it belongs to him, knows that, God forbid, it is located in an island, a village, a street, but since it has become all-pervasive, he cannot psychically locate it in a fixed geo-cultural location in the world. Even an illusory though sustaining childhood home – its intimacies, comforts, language, rituals, meals, landscape – is swallowed by horror, shame and revulsion. What remains significant is the tincture of the memory from which all the present experiences take their colouration: "But what I see in my mind is in no place at all. Everything blot out except the rain and the night coming and the house and the mud and the field and the donkey and the smoke from the kitchen and my father in the gallery and my brother in the room on the floor" (Naipaul 1967b, 62).

More significant, though, is the nature of the impulse which grips the protagonist. At the root of shame is fear of contempt.

> Contempt is a more global type of aggression . . . it constitutes a very strong form of rejection . . . a type of aggression that wants to hurt, to mutilate, to kill, to smash into pieces. In shame, one is held frozen, immovable, paralyzed, even turned into stone . . . . The loss of love in shame can be described as a disregard for having a self in its own right and with its own prestige. His aggression is a violent denial of any personal value, the degradation of one's value as a person equating him particularly with a debased dirty thing – a derided and low animal of waste. The thrust of this aggression is to dehumanize, really to change a person into excrement. (Wurmser 1994, 81)

Home is both a physical place and the locus for developing identity. This narrative demonstrates a now familiar Naipaulian paradox: a simultaneous imperative to flee home and an incapacity to leave home behind. His unhomeliness flourishes within. The unnamed protagonist appraises the dismal, dirty, cold, inhospitable England of the present through the lens of the dismal, dirty, hot, inhospitable Trinidad of the past. Constantly in motion, he is incapable of coming to rest or of belonging in either the actual or imagined landscapes, both of which amplify each other. Displacement is consistent in both localities: the remembered lost place from which he fled in disgust and relief and the present-day place in which he faces recurrent failure and future nothingness.[4] This stance resonates with Naipaul's explanation of his own journeys:

> I was a colonial travelling in New World plantation colonies which were like the one I had grown up in. To look, as a visitor, at other semiderelict communities in despoiled land, in the great romantic setting of the New World, was to see, as from a distance, what one's own community might have looked like. It was to be taken out of oneself and one's immediate circumstances – the material of fiction – and to have a new vision of what one had been born into, and to have an intimation of a sequence of historical events going far back. (Naipaul [1988] 2000, 17)

And as if to take respite from the relentlessness of the real, Naipaul, by his own confession, and also the protagonist of the short narrative take recourse in filmic representation, which lends a mysterious though dark glamour to the central enigma – what happens to an individual and to a people when life becomes too brutish and anomie rules the day? The films the unnamed narrator alludes to are *Jesse James* (1939), *Rebecca* (1940), *Waterloo Bridge* (1940) and *Rope* (1948), all dark gothic films dealing with unresolved hidden murders. Meaning congeals around fantasy. It raises the broader question of what can be the meaning of independence and self-affirmation when an entire nation can lose itself in mass flirtation with what Merle Hodge terms someone else's storybook – unabashed and untrammelled appreciation and mimicry of the style of the Hollywood actor. The movie theatre is the place of recourse from the frenetic world at home and the chaotic world outside the corrugated iron gate. Recalling his youth, Naipaul claims: "nearly all my imaginative life was in the cinema. Everything there was far away, but everything in that curious, operatic world was accessible. . . . I don't think I overstate when I say that without the Hollywood of the 1930s and 1940s I would have been spiritually quite destitute" (1998, 31). Arguably yet another imagined place amplifies the suffocating smallness of the natal space and existential angst at a world teetering on the brink of despair.

The central issue, as reflected in the title "Tell Me Who to Kill", is that of blame. Who is the enemy? Who is to blame? The central question of the narrative remains unanswered for two reasons. The responsibility for tragic lives laid waste resides in a complex of historical forces which cannot be unravelled to determine who is to be punished for its outcome. Naipaul answers this question in "The Overcrowded Barracoon": "Who is the enemy? The enemy is the past" (1972, 271). And so we leave the unnamed protagonist with neither ancestral, natal nor metropolitan home, no past and no future. His birthplace is reduced to a nameless placelessness from which he cannot escape because he has lost his way, a severed connection to a community to which he will never return. The loss is exhaustive; the loss is complete. This condition is not relegated to a physical location in the islands or in the tropics. Rather, it is a fundamental discomfort with self and community and modes of being in the world – the unhomeliness of psychic location, which condemns one to continuously wander through areas of darkness.

Arguably the impulse to transform trauma into narrative holds a key to Naipaul's creative expression. It certainly speaks reams to his location as a writer. In the author's thinly veiled fictional portrait of becoming an artist as a young man, fidelity to the autobiographical imperative leaves Biswas, a fictionalized version of the elder Naipaul, Seepersad, stunned into wonderment at his jerry-built house, within such a grim context that "to have survived is to have triumphed". The fictional house of Mr Biswas also releases the writer son Anand/Vidiadhar to begin his endless meandering through inhospitable landscapes, bereft of even the hope of a resting place, bound to repetitious cycles of wandering and bold experiments in telling a grim reality which he can never bring to complete articulation.

Would that we could happily relegate all such diagnoses of acute social pathologies to past challenges now successfully overcome. It appears that we cannot so do any more than Naipaul, seeking an explanation for the intense lifelong creative pursuit which won him the Nobel Prize in 2002, could fail to acknowledge that the island had given him his world as a writer; that his acerbic vision is shot through with vestiges of caste sensibility; that the dynamic interplay between that bastion of decaying Asiatic culture and the worlds beyond the corrugated iron gate equipped him to be a master architect of a postcolonial house of fiction pierced through with the lament of the unhomely, haunted by apparitions of former selves and shadows of identities yet to emerge. Naipaul declares himself to be "the sum of his books". His enduring legacy is foregrounding numerous ways of imagining non-belonging. These myriad modalities shine a light on how carefully we need to proceed with the current phase of the nation-building project: with acute awareness of the perilous process of making meaning of terms such as *nationhood* and – Trinidad and Tobago's current buzzword – *multiculturalism*.

4

"SOMETHING INSIDE IS LAID WIDE LIKE A WOUND"
Walcott's City of Pain and Promise

> The middle passage never guessed its end.
> This is the height of poverty
> For the desperate and black;
> – Derek Walcott, "Laventille"

LAVENTILLE, A SPRAWLING, MOUNTAINOUS magnet for the urban poor in the northern range that overshadows the prosperous capital city of Port of Spain, Trinidad, was a catchment for a substantial cross-section of the newly freed slaves who embraced emancipation in 1834–38 by fleeing the estates in pursuit of a better life. They were joined by waves of immigrants from other Caribbean nations who flocked to oil-rich Trinidad in the early and mid-1900s. Laventille and its inhabitants hold an ambivalent sociocultural location within the regional psyche. This chapter explores Derek Walcott's evocation of Laventille, a settlement which stands as an enduring legacy of the Middle Passage, in terms of both resilience, fortitude and rich creativity and poverty, hopelessness and disenchantment. The focus here is primarily on Walcott's representation of Laventille as symptomatic of an unrecoverable traumatic loss generated by "some deep, amnesiac blow" (Walcott [1970a] 1986, 88), with passing reference to its evocation in *Steel* ([1988] 2010) as the birthplace of the nation's primary cultural export – its carnival arts – and as a vantage point for virulent critique of the diseased social mores of the nation and region, in "The Spoiler's Return" ([1981] 1992). The final segment of the chapter reads Walcott's representations against a contemporary though emblematic media representation of Laventille. It explores the interface between Walcott's literary evocations of Laventille and its enduring overdetermined location in media reports, the popular imaginary and collective narratives of how the nation of Trinidad and Tobago has come to know and name itself.

The reading explores the legacies of slavery in a specific community, not as a historical event but as a cultural process. Pointing to slavery as a root of cultural identity and a primal scene for descendants of the enslaved, who have had no direct experience of it, Ron Eyerman, in *Cultural Trauma: Slavery and the Formation of African American Identity*, states: "As a cultural process, trauma is mediated through various forms of representation and linked to the reformation of collective identity and the reworking of collective memory" (Eyerman 2001, 1). The process memorializes the catalyst as a negative, threatening, violating and indelible event which becomes a cultural trauma in retrospect, as it is selectively repackaged and relived through mass mediation. In today's globalized world, its reach extends to diasporic populations. In the process, a cultural trauma has the power to generate a sense of collectivity, which in turn can ossify its adherents into notions of victimhood and/or afford opportunity for mobilization and agency in terms of redress. Such a scenario by its very nature involves the participation of a diverse array of knowledge workers, selective representations and contestation over meanings and attribution of blame. Eyerman (after Singh) indicates that transmission of cultural trauma can be conceived as the outcome of a shared communal meta-narrative, a dialogic process of negotiation between the individual and the collectivity by which "combined discourses of self: sexual, racial, historical, regional, ethnic, cultural, national, familial" intersect (2001, 7). Apart from its formation in discourse, Eyerman indicates that collective memory resides in material objects, customs, habits and spaces.

Salient issues for this chapter include these questions: What do the memory and representation of the community of Laventille mean as ground and groundation for evolving collective cultural identity within the nation of Trinidad and Tobago? If notions of trauma are being negotiated according to evolving historical and contemporary ideological imperatives, what are the spatiotemporal parameters that feed into the processes of reinvention and reinterpretation? If collective memory of historical trauma comes to be spatialized in a given psychosocial location, how is this "evil forest" mediated on an ongoing basis through contemporary fictional and mass-mediated discourses? And what is the impact of such psychosocial positioning on reproducing impoverishment and criminality? Derek Walcott's evocations of Laventille constitute the point of departure for beginning to grapple with this complex of issues.

Nowhere do the paradoxical impulses towards romanticization, lyricization, enervation and despair come to roost as decisively as in Walcott's evocation of Laventille, which he characterizes as the culmination of the Middle Passage for the descendants of the enslaved – "the desperate and black" – who remain entrapped in the aftermath of empire (Walcott 1970, 86). This district holds a pivotal place in the literary and social imaginary as the gathering point of the urban poor of African-Caribbean descent. The hills on the outskirts of the city embraced the newly freed Africans, who drifted towards Port of Spain to become a lower-strata population of employed labourers and craftsmen, the underemployed and the unemployed. It sits high above the increasingly prosperous, cosmopolitan city, which also became home to others of forced and voluntary migrations: Europeans (French, British, Spanish, Portuguese and their descendants) and Asians (indentured Indians and Chinese and their descendants). Laventille has today become iconic of the grim living conditions generated by persistent poverty, the emergence of virulent gun and gang violence and the challenge of bringing dis-eased communities to wholeness.

Looming over the city of Port of Spain, itself a melee of diverse cultural and physical miscegenations that generate rich creative potential, Laventille – as both physical landscape and cultural site of memory – holds an iconic location in the burgeoning multiethnic, multicultural nation's symbology and narrative of how it came to construct and know itself. For it was out of this hillside ghetto of the urban poor that denigrated young men – restless, violent and with nothing to lose – produced their enduring and compelling acts of resistance and creativity. Trinidad and Tobago's primary cultural export, the carnival arts, was crafted by this population, which was seen as uneducated, disempowered and even a threat to the security of the nation. Trinidad-style carnivals have grown exponentially; they have been exported to metropolitan centres to become the world's largest street festival and gathering place for migrants of the Caribbean diaspora and beyond (Guilbault 2005; Ho and Nurse 2005). More significantly, Laventille and its people have led the way in generating what Rawle Gibbons terms a theatre of self-liberation (1999, 150).[1] Stephen Stuempfle, in *The Steelband Movement: The Forging of a National Art in Trinidad and Tobago*, argues:

> Now social and cultural researchers are realizing what Caribbean novelists, poets, playwrights and essayists have understood for years: that traditional forms of expressive culture provide a means for disclosing fundamental aspects of the Caribbean experience. Through study of such expressive forms, we can gain not only an appreciation of the aesthetic qualities but a much broader and nuanced sense of how Caribbean peoples have perceived their worlds in the course of their histories of slavery, emancipation, peasantry formation, urbanization and decolonization. (Stuempfle 1995, 12)

Walcott published the poem "Laventille" and the essay "What the Twilight Says" in 1970, the year of the tumultuous Black Power revolution in Trinidad and Tobago. In his essay Walcott muses on two decades of toil on his chosen segment of the nationalist project: how best through the poetic sensibility and the dramatic arts to guide the twin-island state on its journey out of colonialism into independence. The precise focus of his attention is the creation of an indigenous theatre, with the power to point the way for a burgeoning nation desperately in need of direction and traumatized, insecure people seeking viable cultural identities and ways to be human. Its raw material was the youthful society's bare and impoverished slate of life, its absence of ruins, the hopes and aspirations of its peoples; its power was the potentialities of new beginnings. The essay constitutes both a backward glance and a visionary projection. The poet reflects on beginnings two decades removed, during a season in which gaping, suppurating fissures of woundedness are erupting in the form of the Black Power uprising, shaking the very foundations of the social order through staging its very own theatre of the absurd. Walcott, then suspicious of the volatile nature of this attempt to find grounding in ancestral culture, terms the youthful revolutionaries "reactionaries in dashikis" and relegates their protest to screaming "for the pastoral vision, for a return to nature over the loudspeaker" (Walcott [1970b] 1998, 24). Walcott, though deeply appreciative of the power of Afro-Caribbean folkloric traditions as a modality for communal self-definition – expressed in *Ti-Jean and His Brothers* (1958) – saw the incendiary nature of the Black Power movement as having the potential to tip futile recrimination into bloodbath and even genocide.

Decades later, Walcott's Nobel lecture, "The Antilles: Fragments of Epic Memory", uses at its point of departure a positive take on what he perceives as a more innocuous and generative lien on ancestral culture: re-creation of the Hindu Ramleela ritual. Here he identifies the task of Antillean art as reassembling fragments: the "gathering of broken pieces is the care and pain of the Antilles" (Walcott [1993] 1998, 69). The essay goes on to describe the city of Port of Spain as its own unique and fiercely creative chaotic, tumultuous and agitated gathering of fragments: "A downtown babel . . . mongrelized, polyglot, a ferment without a history, like heaven" (71). And the settlement of Laventille crowns the city and the "heavenly" ferment as its blessing and its bane. The nation, which has proven to be highly effective in incorporating the community's energies and creative potential, has failed spectacularly in terms of alleviating its ills. As the political constituency of Dr Eric Williams, the charismatic master architect of Trinidad and Tobago's independence movement and its first prime minister, Southeast Port of Spain (which included Belmont, Williams's birthplace) became the target of numerous upliftment strategies. Gordon Rohlehr, in "Calypso, Education and Community in Trinidad and Tobago from the 1940s to 2011", focuses on the backchat of the people's philosophers through the lenses of some one hundred calypsos, which echo or critique "official rhetoric about education, social transformation, and community-building" (Rohlehr 2012, 184). Referencing the didactic impulse of the committed intelligentsia mobilized by the People's Education Movement (PEM) and the nascent People's National Movement (PNM), aimed at "uplifting and illuminating their less fortunate brethren in the rural and peri-urban borderlands, the calypsonians, fierce guardians of independent grassrooted opinion, assume the right to dialogue, to talking back" (184). Rohlehr points to the gap between Williams's earnest attempt to carve out a curriculum within his constituency of Southeast Port of Spain and the self-fashioned curriculum of the ever-proliferating ghetto – a curriculum generated in a crucible of "constant crises and survivalism – its alternative economy of cutting and contriving and its own hierarchy of muscle and blood" (184). Rohehr argues that Williams faced a constituency which was impervious to his curriculum, comprising "unmanageable rebels, outcasts, knife-and-razor technicians, gunslingers, and blood-and-sand gladiators

... who have created their own cinematic lifestyles, counter-cultural mores, values, and modes of earning, granting respect, and self-recognition" (184). Rohlehr's enquiry, which probes the rupture which destroyed the trust and the tenuous connection between the intelligentsia and the masses during the early Williams years, is instructive in terms of understanding what Laventille has come to mean to the progeny of these failed educators and gatekeepers of the evolving norms, values and directions for the burgeoning nation.

Walcott's poem "Laventille" was published almost two decades after these failed interventions. It records a journey of the poet persona and a companion up the hill to participate in a christening ceremony in the Catholic church, in which he is to stand as godfather for the child of a friend. The physical surroundings externalize the grim quality of the people's lives:

> we climbed where lank electric
> lines and tension cables linked its raw brick
> hovels like a complex feud,
>
> where the inheritors of the middle passage stewed,
> five to a room, still clamped below their hatch,
> breeding like felonies,
>
> whose lives revolve round prison, graveyard, church.
> Below bent breadfruit trees ...
> (Walcott [1970a] 1986, 86)

Walcott sketches in highly compressed word pictures an external environment which reflects grim socioeconomic and psychic realities. The electric wires convey both the dense interconnectedness of the people in the community and the inevitable tensions generated by overcrowding, poverty, frustration, flouted desire and hopelessness. The journey uphill causes the poet to envision another circular journey that sent a people into futile repetitive cycles of time, space, oppression and loss, which undermine attempts to plot a trajectory for escape. The journey finds a metaphorical parallel in the Middle Passage – the traumatic loss, engendered by transportation of the enslaved into an alien and alienating New World, that resists forward movement and throws its inhabitants into repetitious spatiotemporal cycles of displacement and oppression. Walcott tersely makes the point often echoed by theorists who argue about the *post* in *postcoloniality*. The Middle Passage is a present horror for this segment of the population, for whom to go downhill from Laventille is to ascend (Walcott [1970a] 1986, 85). The horrific journey cannot be relegated to the past if two centuries later its survivors still live the legacy of its horrors daily: heat, entrapment, oppression, disempowerment, despair. Here the descendants of slaves are still "clamped below their hatch, breeding like felonies" (86). A pervasive culture of criminality emanates from both the historical blow and the contemporary social environment.

The opening lines, which locate Laventille within the framework of another slum conglomeration – Rio's favelas – allude briefly to the emblem of hope, creativity and potentiality hammered out from this terrible crucible: "It huddled there / steel tinkling its blue painted metal air, / tempered in violence, like Rio's favelas" (Walcott [1970a] 1986, 85). The persona ascends the hill for the christening of a child destined for a journey between the "habitual womb" – the repository of seed sprouting from loveless, passionless, mechanical couplings – and the "patient tomb", which is content to wait quietly, certain of its harvest. The life of this child will follow a trajectory "fixed in the unalterable groove / of grinding poverty" (86). The persona attributes this condition to psychic disease, and to gaping lack suffered because of the ruptures of the Middle Passage (ibid.):

> Something inside is laid wide like a wound,
> some open passage that has cleft the brain,
> some deep, amnesiac blow. We left
> somewhere a life we never found,
>
> customs and gods that are not born again,
> some crib, some grille of light
> clanged shut on us in bondage, and withheld
>
> us from that world below us and beyond,
> and in its swaddling cerements we're still bound.

The originary trauma of the Middle Passage though oceans, ideologies and myriad savageries is represented here as inflicting a deep wound through a violent blow which has cleft the brain and thereby generated the amnesia, which Walcott identifies in "The Muse of History" as the "true history of the New World" ([1974] 1998, 39). This is responsible for rupture of personality and being and the resultant enduring identity crisis. Walcott represents a rupture so extreme as to erase customs, faith and enlightenment and to create liminality as its inherent condition. This state finds fuller representation in the bolum of *Ti-Jean and His Brothers*, a mythical douen-like creature which is poised between the world of the living and the unborn, unable to die and powerless to be born. The notion of history as a wound that creates an enervating loss of African heritage, and by extension Afro-Caribbean identity, and entraps its victims in a state of perpetual underdevelopment is also evoked in Brodber's *The Rainmaker's Mistake* (2007). In Brodber's representation, the amnesiac rupture, executed with deliberate and surgical precision and manifested by a scar on the head, creates perpetual juvenile underdevelopment, along with a deep dependency on and longing for the return of the imperial patriarchy of Mr Charlie.

Walcott's socially grounded representation moves beyond abstract transgenerational transfer of trauma mediated through discourse recollection, memorialization, scholarly enquiry and cultural representation. It is vested in place. Laventille becomes the site of raw pain in which poverty, denigration, hopelessness and despair are created anew with every passing day, given the cognitive dissolution of time and the belated intrusion of the past into the present. The amnesia and shame generated by the African presence in aspirants to the hegemonic Euro-creole sensibility must bear Laventille's intrusive enactments of cultural rituals of transcendence and resistance, the embodied assertion of the ancestral danced faiths of the Orishas and Spiritual Baptists, the rhythms and energies of drumbeats transmuted into "steel tinkling its blue painted metal air, / tempered in violence" (Walcott [1970a] 1986, 85). The poet persona, ever divided in the vein between his African and European heritage, rages against the Roman Catholic ministrations enacting by a fawning verger, earlier foreshadowed in the opening of the poem as the carrion scavenging on the remains of empire: Episcopalian buzzards circling over the doomed life cycles from womb to the tomb.

The symbols of entrapment abound in the poem. The protective crib of the newly christened child, intended to nurture and protect for a season, will in time become a confining structure from which there will be no escape. The "grille of light" is the illumination supposedly offered by Christianity, and the baptismal ritual, which symbolically delivers the infant out of the kingdom of darkness and into the illumination of faith in Christ, also encloses the spirit. The crib and the grille of light fuse to generate estrangement and essentially to lock away the inhabitants of the hill – themselves emblematic of the desperate, black, urban poor throughout the Caribbean – from a broader world of comfort, opportunity, potentiality, upward mobility and transgenerational progress, which has been accessed by more privileged descendants of slaves and indentees. While this social condition is not the full nature of the sprawling leviathan released by the Middle Passage, it is certainly its dark underbelly.

The high vistas of the Laventille hills give access to panoramic views of the sea, which function throughout the poem as a catalyst of vision and insight, initially as a "hot, corrugated-iron sea" of horrors for ships that became floating sarcophagi. The descendants of the enslaved know the grim reality through transgenerational transmission conveyed through vital life fluids: "The salt blood knew it well / you, me, Samuel's daughter, Samuel, / and those ancestors clamped below its grate" (Walcott [1970a] 1986, 86). Patricia Ismond points to the centrality of the sea:

> Behind this expressive sequence of images – open passage, wound, limbo condition – it is the sea itself which remains the primary, generative symbol in this definition of history as soul-bruising amnesia. The sea, a vast and multifaceted symbol in Walcott, represents here the space/time vacuum between the Caribbean and the ancestral world from which it was separated; it is ... the visible image of the hiatus between Africa and the Caribbean. ... Ultimately, healed of history, it becomes in the mature Walcott the custodian of both regional and world memory. (Ismond 2011, 72)

Who then are the rulers and poets of this domain? Walcott's "The Spoiler's Return" ([1981] 1992) assumes the voice and the mask of the people's poet, the calypsonian. The poet persona dons the guise of the calypsonian Mighty Spoiler (Theophilus Philip), known for his hit "Bed Bug", or "Reincarnation" (1953).[2] In this playful, rhythmic song he declares his intention to return from the grave, not as a creature that needs to work for its keep but as a parasitic bedbug dedicated to biting fat young ladies:

> Ah want to bite them young ladies, partner
> Like a hot dog or a hamburger
> And if you know you're thin, don't be in a fright
> Is only big fat woman that ah going to bite

Walcott spins this mild and playful post-death sexual fantasy into "The Spoiler's Return", not as an incongruous bedbug with grandiose sexual fantasies but as a fearless, doom-speaking moralizer with macabre humour, incisive wit and percipient turns of phrase. Spoiler has returned from Hell to the hills of Laventille for two weeks to sing what he has always sung – the truth – which in practice becomes delivery of scathing critique of the institutionalized hegemonic structures of the day. He sends a message to the steelbandsmen who are the kings of the hill: "Tell Desperadoes when you reach the hill, / I decompose, but I composing still" (Walcott [1981] 1992, 432). Whereas the poet persona of "Laventille" focuses on a philosophical and psychic statement on the root of the poverty and its connection to the violations of history, Spoiler picks up the traditional anti-establishment stance of critique in relation to the new rulers of the now independent republic, to voice the plight of the poor and oppressed as neglected and exploited by the establishment; to critique the oil-rich nation's imperious manner of dispensing handouts throughout the region; to rail against the insensitivities of the people's representatives in relation to the electorate; to condemn the compliance and silencing of the people in response to abuses of state authority:

> 'fraid to take side,
> they say that Rodney commit suicide,
> is the same voices that, in the slave ship,
> smile at their brothers, "Boy, is just the whip"
> (434)

The complicities of the journey, which may have been vital to survival, transmute within the new post-independence context and leach away incendiary responses which can potentially produce change.

The poet persona stands above these compromises. In short, nothing escapes his acerbic tongue, not even the self:

> So, crown and mitre me Bedbug the First –
> the gift of mockery with which I'm cursed
> is just an insect biting Fame behind,
> ... bound to bite
> its saving host, ungrateful parasite,
> whose sting, between the cleft arse and its seat,
> reminds Authority man is just meat,

> a moralist as mordant as the louse
> that the good husband brings from the whorehouse,
> the flea whose itch to make all Power wince,
> will crash a fête, even at his life's expense
>
> (434)

Spoiler mocks the emerging order and the new political directorate, whose promises have dematerialized and left in their space an all-too-familiar range of unjust practices. Indeed, the new domain has turned into an animal kingdom with a range of dishonourable behaviours:

> The shark, racing the shadow of the shark
>
> . . .
>
> Is crab climbing crab-back, in a crab quarrel,
> and going round and round in the same barrel,
> is sharks with shirt-jacs, sharks with well-pressed fins,
> ripping we small-fry off with razor grins;
> nothing ain't change but colour and attire
>
> (433)

These are predatory creatures known for their painful bite. The bloodsucking bedbug from Hell goes up against the savage authoritarian predators in a David and Goliath–style battle fought with words and wit of tremendous bite. Change for the new leaders is both skin-deep and transient. In the 1970s the shirt-jac, a nod to the tropical climate, replaced the suit as business and formal wear for a brief season; it became characteristic of a move towards indigenizing the wardrobe. The short-lived moment is emblematic of decolonization gone awry. Images of ascendency remain. In the upside-down ethical order, the poet-calypsonian's enlightened stance, high on the hill of deprivation and disempowerment, looks down upon the deficient political and moral order and from his elevated viewpoint laments: "I see these islands and I feel to bawl, / 'area of darkness' with V.S. Nightfall" (433).

The final segment of this chapter will focus on the prophetic nature of Walcott's poetic enquiries in relation to the iconic settlement of Laventille – which remains today a pivotal social barometer in the popular imaginary – in the context of a media report from 2009. The front page of the *Daily Express* of 29 December 2009 featured a prominent red headline: "Despers Flees the Hill", with the subhead "Crime Forces Laventille Panorama Champ to Seek Shelter in Belmont". This was supported by a large composite photograph of a decrepit bassist dressed in a bedraggled red outfit decorated with blue and yellow ribbons. This image is a vast departure from more characteristic portrayals of youthful pannists as vigorous bodies dancing in gay abandon. The photograph represents the band through a solitary individual, advanced in years, with sad eyes trained inwards in deep reverie suggestive of mourning. The background is also instructive. The venues in question are open-air spaces: the National Insurance Board car park in the Belmont Valley replaces the lofty panyard with its wide vistas. In a discussion of the move, an online commentator posted: "Going to Despers panyard was something unique though. It was a curious feeling . . . anxious in terms of the reputation of the hill . . . and then getting there, seeing & hearing the band in action in the most gorgeous setting was almost surreal" (Soca Warriors 2009).

In the large front-page photo, the red of the gloomy pan man's costume is repeated in the rows of seats in an auditorium, a reminder of what the steel pan has accomplished as the premier (some would argue the only) percussion instrument to be invented in the twentieth century, a marvel of the creativity that emerged out of the crucible of poverty and denigration to gain international acclaim in the most prestigious concert halls of the world. It also images the grand Trinidad and Tobago National Performing Arts Centre, an elaborate glass structure which artistes have complained has not taken into account local performance needs and style. The photo echoes a then ongoing debate, with its censure of a government that was more concerned with grand buildings and First World architectural structures and skylines than with the needs of its populace.

The enormity of the loss is reflected in the disjuncture between the newspaper feature and the lyrical opening of Stephen Stuempfle's ethnographic study of the steelband movement, which subtly and intimately links performance and process with place:

> Above the eastern edge of Port of Spain, Trinidad, rises Laventille Hill, with densely built houses clinging to its steep slopes. A narrow road winds up the hill, and from it radiates a maze of paths that lead to individual locations with names that only the inhabitants know. On top of the hill, and across from the Laventille Shrine, are a spacious lot and an open concrete block community center which together serve as the *panyard*, or practice site, for the Desperadoes Steel Orchestra. . . . Scattered about the yard are young men from the neigh-

borhood, some of whom observe the band intently while others banter among themselves. In the yards of nearby houses, people tend to laundry and other morning chores. Boys fly small homemade kites that rise so high as to almost disappear in the cloudless sky. (Stuempfle 1995, xi)

Stuempfle conveys the sense of an orderly community, with its place of worship, its daily rituals and its recreation, with its cultural products and practitioners enjoying centrality and pride of place.

The newspaper report quotes the band's spokesperson: " 'Because of the crime situation, you know, our supporters and panmen are reluctant to come out on the hill, so we decided to come down and meet them. By leaving there and coming down here the people feel more secure,' Holder said." The loss is reflected as a sense of displacement which constitutes also a loss of pride and identity and self-fashioning. Holder is reported as saying: "The people from the hill, the people who live on the hill itself, they don't like the idea of coming off the hill because Despers is a proud band, the people of Laventille are a proud people but we have no other choice . . . It is very painful, it is very hard to leave Laventille but we really have no other choice" (*Daily Express*, 29 December 2009).

This is a far cry from the time when the Despers were feared anti-establishment warriors – the bad-johns of the hills. Telling elements thread through the media report which lend a measure of sensationalism. The abstract cause – *crime* has forced Despers to flee the hills – evades the issue of who or what is responsible. The band, notorious as fierce performers, warriors and kings of the hill, has given way to constructions of defensiveness – they must *flee* from their homes to seek *refuge* in what in time past was the turf of rival bands. Vestiges of bad-john culture are expressed in the nickname of the assistant leader, "Warlord", but the fight which he now superintends is for survival and for the safety of players and supporters. The aggression of Warlord and the band's executive is now reduced to this "bold" move to address dwindling support and player safety.

The online commentaries on this article are also instructive. One poster laments the action but sees the beautiful music as a positive, transcendent dimension that lives on: "Ironic & sad dat de bad john band forced to leave dey home by badder johns but I for one am thankful that at least the band survives and it's [sic] music is still alive no matter the venue. Play on Despers . . . live long and prosper" (Soca Warriors 2009, reply #3). The power of the music and the communality of the people transcend place. Another commentator makes a distinction between the band's having to leave the hills for the safety of its players and patrons and the fact that players resident in Laventille return home every night after practice. The band may have migrated for practical purposes, but the people remain "at home".

Yet another commentator makes the all-too-common symbolic leap that constructs Laventille as a social barometer for the entire nation:

> Pan started in those hills. Men died to play. Their deaths marked the path that pan took to reach this place, in this time. Now, in its birthplace, people are simply being killed and a pivotal, iconic band has to tear up roots. It's just pan I know. There are more important things like food and shelter and clothes on your back. Those people who are doing the crimes don't really see what pan has to do with anything. An old piece of tin can't stop a fella from hacking off your wrist for that watch or slamming a bullet in your belly becuase [sic] you looked at him the wrong way.
>
> They big and strong and armed and dangerous and ruling the hills now. And where once the pan identified Trinidad and Tobago, they are now the symbol of what we have become. (Soca Warriors 2009, reply #1)

Here, as is invariably the case in the popular imaginary, the commentator synthesizes the competing legends and narratives of origin, and the diverse experimental processes which rolled out in numerous panyards in and around Port of Spain in the late 1930s and early 1940s, into a single understanding: "Pan started in those hills."[3]

The second synoptic statement, that "men died to play", constructs the establishment of steelpan as exacting the blood of martyrs. At the inception of the steelband movement, when it was perceived by representatives of the colonial hegemonic order as the noise of unruly hooligans, there was police harassment alongside confiscation of instruments, skirmishes and violence against the players. Even greater violence was generated by inter-band rivalries. Stuempfle notes that in the 1940s conflicts frequently broke out over female supporters of the bandsmen – many of whom were engaged in prostitution – when they were seen consorting with men of rival steelbands. Competition for the attention and earnings of these women was a major source of inter-band rivalry and violent skirmishes, on Carnival days and year-round. The conflation of anti-establishment resistance and association of the movement with violence and bloodshed is reflected in the assumption that men died to play. This oversimplification and romanticization feed into the logic of the following statement: "Now, in its birthplace, people are simply being killed and a pivotal, iconic band has to tear up roots." The word *simply* implies that people are being killed for no just cause. On the surface it appears that the killings are motivated by greed and by ego boundaries which are so fragile that people are taking lives because of a slight, or any real or imagined act of disrespect.

By constructing the panmen as victims of the hegemonic order and of a younger generation of bad-johns, the online commentator recognizes no continuity between the violence of the past era and the present. There is a lack of any sense of communal responsibility for historical or contemporary causal factors for outbreaks of crime. And where once the pan identified Trinidad and Tobago, it is now a symbol of what we have become. The iconic symbolic identification and high international profile given to the pan as a symbolic locus, the location of which is the hills of Laventille, has overreached itself in an equation which goes like this: if Laventille and its cultural inventions are symbols of accomplishment, resistance and assertiveness which have been embraced by the entire nation, then its lacerations, violence and eruptions in crime are symptomatic of the contemporary state of the nation: "they are now the symbol of what we have become".

The final sample of print media discourse is a commentary on the *Trinidad Express* front page coverage of the issue. The commentary makes links between the photo analysed above and two other sub-headlines that shared front-page billing on that day. The first sub-headline article is titled "Beyonce Tickets from $450 to $1600 . . . on Sale Today". The second sub-headline announced "Acting DPP Gets Second Three Month Extension". Journalist Lennox Grant, in a feature article (29 December 2009), develops some salient connections. The global entertainment industry points to huge gaps in the distribution of wealth; it accords high value to the representative foreign entertainer Beyonce; such is her intensity of appeal as a locus of desire that, as subsequent news reports indicate, the $1,600 tickets sell out in a flash. The Despers and Beyonce articles are placed opposite each other; the downcast panman stares at the subhead and draws the eye to invite an unwelcome connection. The conspicuous expenditure required to attend a Beyonce Knowles concert will inevitably trigger an entirely new wave of crime as the impoverished, their desires stirred to fever pitch by global advertising and entertainment strategies, seek to gain access to tickets and the appropriate dress for concerts which are beyond their means. Deep-rooted identity crises exist in profligate admixture with advertising "truth" – that access to name brands will clothe the dispossessed and disempowered with worth, such that youths thus persuaded are prepared to rob, maim and even murder for the privilege of pouring their ill-gotten gains into the gaping maw of consumerism and conspicuous consumption.

And this is where the final headline of the day – "Acting DPP Gets Second Three Month Extension" – becomes significant. In a context of politicization of crime and recrimination of governmental authorities – for their studied inattention to the correlation between crime reduction in traumatized communities and the roles of families, churches, schools, community organizations; the impartation of values, ethics and morals; the requirement for therapeutic interventions – the belaboured and largely inadequate criminal justice system is fingered as the fundamental root of the problem. Indeed, how effective can an acting Director of Public Prosecution be if he is functioning on a series of three-month extensions?

Today the nation of Trinidad and Tobago is located quite some distance from the problematic laid out in Walcott's "Laventille" and "What the Twilight Says". After more than five decades of intensive development fuelled by oil wealth and two oil booms, emblems of conspicuous consumption reign, from the highest levels of governance to the lowest levels of the social order. The common perception of politicians and the political will to engineer change that would benefit the people runs dangerously close to Walcott's statement in "The Spoiler's Return". Laventille, commensurate with its excessive visibility on the hills overlooking the capital city, is a tangible and overdetermined symbolic receptacle for the vibrant, persistent bedrock rhythms and energies of Africa; for indigenous transformation through suffering and other strange alchemies into the gifts of creativity and celebration in face of grim adversity; and for loss of yet another generation to structural poverty, enervation, despair and the wastage of gun and gang violence.

Award-winning iconic steelbands, which have brought great acclaim to the nation, are seeking refuge; profligate government spending continues apace on high-profile buildings designed to transform the Trinidad and Tobago skyline; essential services are strained to their limit. Development spells highly visible structures of glass and steel and fails to spell an effective focus on people. The psychic disease and the grim social condition which Walcott then envisioned as a legacy of empire have proven resistant to decades of independence and mammoth expenditure on education and social programmes. The nascent violence reflected in traumatized, displaced and dispossessed Afro-Caribbean warriors has ripened into full-scale urban gang warfare in which ascendancy is marked out in turf. Rival gangs slaughter each other, largely untroubled by police intervention; entire communities are being held to ransom; children and infants are being felled by stray bullets or in revenge killings; and vigilante justice is taking root.

And in this regard the downward spiral for a cross-section of displaced and disempowered warriors and their progeny, who as yet have not found a viable and generative place in the New World order, knows no bounds. Rohlehr, commenting on the flagrant disregard for life demonstrated by a cross-section of the lower-strata Afro-Trinidadian urban male population, has coined the term *culture of terminality*. This urban phenomenon, particularly among lower-strata Afro-Caribbean nationals, allows them to casually take life and equally casually to surrender their own, because to them life has no value. Pointing to decades of rural–urban migration into the region's strangled cities, underdevelopment, unemployment and underemployment, persistent denigration, hunger and food survivalism, Rohlehr identifies a dangerous countercultural ethos that is fuelling gang violence, feeding on the transnational drug trade and bent on terminality.

Deborah Thomas, surveying the same demographic in urban Jamaica, ties exceptional gang violence even more directly to the spectacular atrocities of slavery's terrorist systemic. Arguing that the historical legacy has created a "repertoire" of techniques of embodied violence as a "potential resource" for the display of power, she indicates that there is a historical precedent for contemporary practices of disfiguring and dismemberment, mutilation of corpses and burning black bodies alive. No act of spectacular violence in relation to Jamaican gang culture, no matter how heinous and shocking, draws an effective line of demarcation: "What we have instead is a series of events that provide ever increasing levels of shock and disbelief but that nevertheless are quickly enfolded into the realm of imaginable possibility" (Thomas 2011, 110). This, she argues, is how the enslaved must have come to terms with the ever-proliferating excesses of discipline and punishment which characterized their everyday lives.

It is a strange alchemy which transmutes rage, disorientation, denigration and disempowerment into powerful cultural resistance. It is an even stranger alchemy which transforms the instrument that they, the despised and wretched of the land, created into the iconic collective symbolic inheritance of all. The interface of this heavy metaphorical burden with collective amnesia, erasure and perhaps even shame in relation to the African presence in the Caribbean constrains the body politic to carry the burden of Laventille as its ubiquitous albatross.

The literary and popular representations point to the notion of place as archive. As surely as a recurrent dismal rural scene of displacement, woundedness and loss crops up in Naipaul's fiction, such that it loses spatiotemporal groundings to become omnipresent, Laventille has come to be a significant locus of meaning for the national community, rooted in latent personal and communal histories which reflect the traumatized consciousness of the nation's peoples. The deeply rooted psychic lacerations generated by the known as well as the silenced and submerged abuses of the colonial and neo-colonial social orders travel underground like rhizomes, linking people-groups into complex networks of relations and of unresolved hurt. These roots of rejection, bitterness, acrimony and loss crop up where we least expect them. It explains why every contestation over national emblems proceeds with fresh rancour as the unhealed wounds erupt and suppurate anew, generating original pain. It is trauma's re-experiencing, created by the inability to take in all at once the enormity of the pain and loss in its entirety. It is trauma's hyperarousal which generates an intensity of response which is disproportionate to its catalyst. It is trauma's uncanny repetition which causes this complex of issues to crop up repeatedly, intra- and inter-generationally. For a substantial cross-section of our society it is simpler to resort to avoidance of thought and feeling and distancing of shame through collective amnesia. It is more painful to deal with *hypernesia* – trauma's intrusive memory of haunting ancestral presences that intrude centuries later. It remains to be considered whether acknowledgement of the role of trauma in the symbolic construction and self-fashioning of Laventille and its inhabitants would alleviate the nature of its ills and lend success to the myriad interventions into this troubled community.

It is recognition of a similar dynamic operating in Kingston which led Brian Meeks, in *Envisioning Caribbean Futures* (2007), to call for a truth and reconciliation commission to address the "near civil war of the 1980s", including violent "excesses of politically aligned ethnic cleansing", which "haunts" Jamaican social and political life. The blood feuds generated in those violent days have fed into the marrow of urban communities and continue to exist in the saliency of areas and zones of exclusion long after the memory of the era has passed (Meeks 2007, 117). Expressing faith in the therapeutic potential of such intervention, Meeks suggests that haunting outlives the memories; the ghosts of the past must be put to bed (117). Would that such fora would provide incisive opportunity, as prescribed by Eyerman, to work towards a new foundational narrative, to reconstitute the torn social fabric, and to point to the possibility of a new future.

This segment began with a reading of narratives of journey which pose an imperative to collect scattered ancestral skeletons. It ends with analyses of contemporary Caribbean cities of pain, traumatized urban communities in which blood feuds have seeped into the marrow. Part 2 reads a range of social issues through the lens of trauma.

PART 2

SOCIAL ISSUES

5

ONE DAY FOR THE HUNTER, ONE DAY FOR THE PREY
State Criminality in Danticat's Fiction

HAITI OCCUPIES A UNIQUE location in Caribbean imaginaries. It is variously celebrated as the site of the only successful slave rebellion in history, the first black New World republic, a stronghold of African retention, and a land – and, for its diaspora, a cultural memory – which evokes intense patriotism and loyalties. Conversely, Haiti is emblematic of the devastating impact of decades of underdevelopment, the consequences of the unbridled excesses of despotic megalomania, and a grim contemporary sociopolitical scenario which poses an imperative of escape so urgent that Haitian boat immigrants risk fortune, the threat of deportation and their lives. Haiti under Duvalier also resides in Caribbean imaginaries as a site in which state criminality had free play, banal violence reached its zenith and political torture became normative.

State criminality can be defined as a nation-state's acting through its agents to violate civil, criminal and international laws. The focus of this chapter is not on the macro domain of illegal invasion and unjust wars but on the long-term intergenerational impact of state violence on both perpetrators and victims. In *State Criminality: The Crime of All Crimes*, Dawn Rothe quotes David Frederichs: "the worst crimes – in terms of physical harm to human beings, abuse of civil liberties and economic loss – have been committed by individuals and entities acting in the name of the government or the state". She continues: "During the twentieth century, it has been suggested that 170 million people have been killed in 'conflicts of a non-international character, internal conflicts and tyrannical regime victimization' (Bassiouni 1996). Since the beginning of the twenty-first century there have been hundreds of thousands more killed, maimed, tortured, displaced, and/or raped" (Rothe 2009, 76). Rothe classifies forms of harm wrought by state violence as physical, psychological, financial, environmental, cultural, social and political. She points to the incredible toll exacted by state violence in terms of maiming, mass fear, torture, post-traumatic stress disorder, depression, physical and mental illness, depression, sexual dysfunction and suicide.

This chapter focuses on Edwidge Danticat's engagement with the Tontons Macoutes, the death squads set in place by President François "Papa Doc" Duvalier, who ruled Haiti between 1957 and 1971. This dreaded militia was wielded by a corrupt totalitarian directorate to induce political compliance through mass terror. Established by the president in the wake of an attempted coup in 1958, the militia was founded in 1959 with a single objective: to squash any and all political opposition to the regime. For this service they were granted automatic immunity from prosecution for all violent crimes performed in the line of duty. The Macoutes continued their terrorist rule under Papa Doc's son and successor Jean-Claude ("Baby Doc") until a spontaneous people's uprising in 1986 toppled the Duvalier regime. The legacy of unrelenting underdevelopment and of gross human rights abuses persists in contemporary Haitian society, such that the United Nations established a mission to Haiti in 1994 intended to alleviate the human rights abuses which accompany civil unrest.[1]

Danticat's evocation in *The Dew Breaker* (2004) is the culmination of the author's long fictional engagement with the Haitian stage, which was initiated in her first novel. In *Breath, Eyes, Memory* (1994), a faceless Macoute features centrally as the shadowy catalyst for the events of the novel – a masked rapist assumed to be a Macoute attacks a young virgin in a cane field and thereby fathers the protagonist. The state criminal finds fullest development in *The Dew Breaker*, which is named after a lyrical Creole term inspired by the nocturnal activities of torturers: *choukèt laroze*, translated as "he who breaks or shakes the dew".[2] The text comprises a series of interrelated narratives of persons who have been touched by a particularly objectionable member of the nefarious death squad, who has refashioned himself as a taciturn, mild-mannered, law-abiding immigrant to the United States. The central issues are the following: What goes into the making of the terrorists? How do the Macoutes locate themselves within family and community? How do state-sanctioned criminals perform their duties? In view of their violent hostilities against the community, how can a Macoute find love and reconnection to family and society? What are the border-crossing transnational and transgenerational consequences of torturous regimes on individual lives? Danticat argues that alleviation of criminal activity and its consequences call for collective social action. Moreover, transgenerational intervention is required to expiate historical transgression in order to interrupt its violent present-day outworkings.

"Who invented the Macoutes? The devil didn't do it and God didn't do it" (Danticat 1994, 138). Danticat locates the Tontons Macoutes first and foremost as agents of an increasingly murderous state. Anthropologist Michel-Rolph Trouillot (1970) identifies the Duvalierist state as an outcome of the nation's historical evolution, attendant upon increasing disjuncture between political and civil society and an unjust economic system carried laboriously on the back of the rural peasantry. The latter were heavily taxed producers while the profits were gathered by an import-export bourgeoisie dominated by foreign nationals. In the political sphere, urban elites systematically pushed the rural majority to the periphery of social life. Trouillot argues that the disequilibrium between the state and civil authorities, which was nascent from the inception of the republic, was kept in uneasy balance until the US occupation of Haiti from 1915 to 1934 tilted the balance, by increasing forced contribution of the peasantry to the state coffers, centralizing the "state apparatuses, especially the army", and disarming the provinces "both militarily and economically":

> The US-trained army led the way to totalitarianism when the crisis re-emerged in the late 1950s. Between 1956 and 1960, the entire system began to go off its traditional guide rails. The manifest location of civil and political society spurred panic and confusion, especially among urbanites. Using that confusion and state-sponsored terror, President François Duvalier succeeded in providing what was, in Haitian terms, an unconventional response to the crisis: The transformation of the authoritarian political model of the past into a totalitarian apparatus. In so doing he pitted the state against the nation. (Trouillot 1970, 17)

The Duvalier regime, which spanned the period 1957–86, saw the nation's already besieged social, political and juridical structures dismantled and replaced by a predatory system, largely via a process of state-sponsored terrorism. Through the agency of the Macoutes, the Haitian state turned against the nation, appropriating for itself the legitimacy to create or fabricate crimes, select guilty parties, pass judgement, abuse and humiliate its targets, and execute enemies or, conversely, exact tribute from already impoverished citizens for sparing their lives. Having established a reign of terror, the Macoutes' reputation served to generate ever wider reaches of fear, complicity and subjugation.

The instrumentality practised in the implementation of state-sponsored terrorism strains the boundaries of credibility to such an extent that several have commented that the surreality of the horror of Haiti under Duvalier feeds readily into the blurred space at the interstices of fiction and reality.3 Graham Greene, in the foreword to Bernard Diedrich and Al Burt's text *Papa Doc and the Tontons Macoutes,* notes of Haiti during the Duvalier regime: "There is something peculiarly Roman in the air of Haiti: Roman in its cruelty, in its corruption and in its heroism . . . . Haiti is the scene of a classical tragedy. . . . We feel sometimes that we are witnessing a tragedy by Racine played by coloured actors – or at the worst moment *Titus Andronicus*" (Diedrich and Burt 2005, 7–8).

The sudden fall of the dictatorship which Papa Doc passed to his son Jean-Claude in 1986 was termed as containing the vital ingredients of an "insurrectionary melodrama" engineered by starving unnamed masses who had simply "lost their fear and demanded their right to 'justice and freedom'" (Ferguson 1987, viii). According to Diedrich and Burt, Papa Doc had repeatedly declared himself to be an immortal and immaterial being, so much so that he had difficulty relinquishing dictatorship even to protect his health, and his subjects had grave difficulty believing that he could actually die.

The location of Tontons Macoutes in the popular imaginary draws heavily from the interface between criminality and fiction. Macoutes drawn from every sphere of society were recruited to detect subversion and generate fear. Traders, criminals, former soldiers, goons, thugs and opportunists of every kind were recruited, handed uniforms, guns and assignments, and occasionally given payment. Originally conscripted as a coercive force to influence the course of the elections, the *cagoulars*, the semi-secret police who operated at night with the aid of *cagoules* (ski masks), traded in their masks for slick clothing and dark glasses. The regime also conscripted women who were reputed to be incredibly loyal and incredibly cruel. Particular value was derived from the conscription of voodoo priests, *hougans*, who added deep spiritual dread to their arsenal of weapons. Duvalier himself mined spiritual sites, rituals and symbols for supernatural embellishments and endorsement of his reign of terror:

> Relying upon *hougans* for detailed accounts of provincial developments, Duvalier willingly cultivated his own image of the omniscient voodoo priest. The inscrutable expression, the sombre clothing, the secretiveness surrounding his movements: all these deliberate affectations and strategies were calculated to inspire respect and fear among the Haitian masses, who Duvalier hoped would view their president as the incarnation of the voodoo loa Baron Samedi, the frock coated guardian of the graveyard. (Ferguson 1987, 52)

Their naming also drew from mythologies which support child-rearing practices based on fear and intimidation. Before the Macoutes stalked the land, they inhabited the psychic terrain, living in mythology as the Haitian counterpart of the universal bogeyman used by generations of parents to threaten badly behaved children with the fate of being carried off. Haitian lore holds that good children are visited and rewarded by Uncle Christmas, while bad children are snatched by the Tonton Macoute, which is a Creole transliteration of Uncle Gunny Sack. "In the fairy tales, the *Tonton Macoute* was a bogeyman, a scarecrow with human flesh. . . . In his knapsack, he always had scraps of naughty children, whom he dismembered to eat as snacks. *If you don't respect your elders, then the Tonton Macoute will take you away*" (Danticat 1994, 138). This relatively benign traditional mythological figure predated the walking nightmares who fed in turn into a contemporary mythology of state terrorism, creating a cycle in which myth, nightmare and reality achieved a seamless blending. Within this dark space in the imagination, the death squads settled comfortably to carry out their nefarious acts.

Much of the power of Danticat's evocation can be attributed to her seamless interweaving of factual, mythical and fictional strands in this grim narrative. The Tontons Macoutes have long haunted Danticat's artistic sensibility. Her formative years were spent in Haiti during the Duvalier regime. In an interview with Robert Birnbaum, she roots the fictional exploration of the Dew Breaker in an impulse towards understanding a malignancy which must have been both dreadful and mysterious to her youthful mind: "What interested me in the stories and in these people and in this era because it was the last era that I lived consistently in Haiti was to understand these people so at least try to get as close to understanding these people as possible. The country and other countries, too, where things are difficult, keeps repeating or keeps recreating this environment that creates these kind of people" (Birnbaum 2004).

Traditionally, state violence is exerted on those perceived to be enemies of the regime or opponents of its chief functionaries. This tacit rule absolved women and children and the aged from the worst excesses of torturous regimes. This was not the case with the Duvalierist regime. The enormity of the terror was magnified by the complete disappearance of the protection traditionally conferred by political innocence. Indeed, the sexual desirability and vulnerability of women made them the target of diverse, well-honed strategies of sexual violence which Danticat takes pains to carefully document and explore, with an insistence which borders on an obsessive act of re-memory lest these atrocities sink into oblivion.

One Day for the Hunter

Danticat paints the Macoutes as democratic, fulsome and generous in their malignancy. In *Breath, Eyes, Memory*, an innocent coal vendor – significantly named Dessalines, after a heroic father of Haitian independence – is murdered by a group of Macoutes in full public view, ostensibly for stepping on the foot of one of their members:

> "My foot, you see, you stepped on it!" The baby-faced *Macoute* was shouting at a coal vendor.
> He rammed the back of his machine gun into the coal vendor's ribs.
> "I already know the end," said my grandmother.
> . . .
> I turned back for one last look. The coal vendor was curled in a fetal position on the ground. He was spitting blood. The other *Macoutes* joined in, pounding their boots on the coal seller's head. Everyone watched in shocked silence, but no one said anything.

> My grandmother came back for me. She grabbed my hand so hard my fingers hurt.
> "You want to live your nightmares too?" she hollered. (Danticat 1994, 118)

The murderous violence – even that inflicted by youthful "baby-faced" recruits against their elders – is explosive, unpredictable and entirely unrelated to any "harm" done. The population of the busy market, and by extension the entire society, is disciplined by terror, because there is no rationale to the attacks. In this bizarre scenario, no one is safe; no one is absolved; there are no innocents; there is no correlation between violence and wrongdoing. The objective is not simply to murder all perceived dissidents but to practise scattershot gratuitous violence with such flair and flourish as to destabilize and terrorize the entire society.

It was not enough for the Macoutes to kill their victims. They adopted a range of theatrical devices to support macabre dramas of their own cultivation. They left their dead hanging in public places as evidence of their operations. They habitually wore masks, dressed like goons in dark clothing and glasses, and ploughed the psychic domain to cultivate the image of being voodoo demons. Their arsenal of terrorist strategies was designed to strike dread into the entire society and to dismantle the humanitarian basis of community. The grandmother's remark – "I already know the end" – speaks to oft-repeated acts of violence which lend to each outbreak a predictive quality, such that the observer is dulled by habituation and rendered impotent to intervene, because to do so would be to risk life and limb. The intrusive, nightmarish recurrence is inevitable. The impulse to avert the eye is powerful, for even to watch would send an invitation to realize a horror which is already vibrant and alive in the psychic domain – that is, to live one's nightmare. The practice of rape often results in the fathering of progeny who, but for the healing power of community, would be the walking powder kegs of a new generation.

Danticat probes delicately beneath the façade of this monster in her quest for intelligence on who made the Macoute. Persistent connections emerge in the narratives between the monstrous subject's formation and fathering. The narratives present the Macoute as a torturer first and foremost, but besides that, his most persistent identity markers are those of orphan, son, father and, more precisely, lost father. A major catalyst in the subject formation of the Dew Breaker is the loss of the father and the reformulation of paternity via an engrafting into a corrupt, illicit paterfamilial order. For many, the process begins in infancy. Danticat sensitively reveals perpetrators who themselves become victims of state violence as their childhood innocence and place in family and community, with its potential for service, balance and judgement, are replaced by an implacable blind and murderous heartlessness. The murderous paterfamilial regime picks the young out of destitution and arms them with guns, uniforms and state permission to rape, pillage and prey on the population. In "Monkey Tails", set during the collapse of the regime, the narrator observes that the flight of Baby Doc has orphaned Haiti's death-dealing squads of terrible infants (Danticat 2004, 140). The child narrator says:

> I couldn't help but be frightened. I was twelve years old, and, according to my mother, three months before my birth I had lost my father to something my mother would only vaguely describe as "political", making me part of a generation of mostly fatherless boys, though some of our fathers were still living, even if somewhere else – in the provinces, in another country, or across the alley not acknowledging us. A great many of our fathers had also died in the dictatorship's prisons, and others had abandoned us altogether to serve the regime. (141).

The "something political" which steals fathers away is manifest when the philosophical eighteen-year-old Romain searches in vain for his father, the Macoute Regulas, who is at risk of mob assassination after the flight of the dictator and the collapse of the regime orphans him and his fellow henchmen. The son disappears without ever finding his father, while the narrator protagonist identifies his own lost father, a prosperous merchant neighbour who has failed to acknowledge his existence. The anguish of father loss is also reflected in the first line of the narrative, when a young Haitian artist in the United States discovers both her sculptural representation of her father as presumed victim of torture and her actual missing father. The collection begins with a simple statement of loss: "My father is gone" (Danticat 2004, 3). The sentence points to a painful process, and one response to the key question posed in the narrative: Who made the Macoutes?

Systemic corruption is working feverishly to actively create violence and thereafter to sustain itself by feeding off the corruption and defilement which it produces. A key by-product is vulnerability to the seductive pull of the corrupt and corrupting father of the state and the paterfamilial network. In the case of the Dew Breaker, the loss of his father's land to the officials of the regime for their country homes and the subsequent despair and insanity of the father do not insulate him from corruption. Conversely, the vulnerability and hopelessness he experiences draw him magnetically into evil paterfamilial connection with the dictator, garbed to represent supernatural power. He is sucked into criminality because he is dazzled by the public face of power, which seamlessly fuses thuggery with grandeur. Layering symbols of power drawn from diverse realms, the president parades dressed in the trappings of supernatural power of the voodoo *loa* of death, Baron Samedi, complete with the *loa*'s characteristic white (heavily powdered) face and nasal voice, "like a guardian of the cemetery in a black suit and coattails, a black hat". His multiple guns are reflective of physical firepower: "a .38 visibly attached to his belt, and a rifle at his side" (Danticat 2004, 192). His verbal violence erupts in grandiose promises of bloodshed should one seek to topple his regime, which echo the carnivalesque grandiloquence and hyperbole of the midnight robber: "the land would burn from north to south, east to west. There would be no sunrise and no sunset, just one big flame licking the sky" (193). It is in the service of this grandmaster's death-dealing performance that the Macoutes stage their petty dramas.

Danticat's Dew Breaker effects a series of responses to powerlessness when he opts to become a hand extended in the service of this drama. Rendered hungry, frightened, orphaned and lacking in purpose, as a young recruit he seeks to instantiate and externalize his power, initially in a coarse physicality which he enhances by gorging himself on food exacted from restaurants under the guise of protectionism: "He ate eagerly several times a day because he enjoyed watching his body grow wider and meatier just as his sense of power did" (Danticat 2004, 196). It is this gross and exaggerated externalization of power which he extends spatially, financially, sexually and socially, across class barriers. This terse description is telling: "Bourgeois married women slept with him on the cash filled mattress on his bedroom floor. Virgins of all castes came and went as well. And the people who had looked down on him and his family in the past, well, now they came all the way from Leogane to ask him for favours" (196). His tiny office and torture chamber work on the same principle: his large desk and corpulent frame gobble up all the space and render the torture victim diminished in a low, vermin-infested sisal chair.

Danticat is careful not to portray the Dew Breaker as totally heartless. His location is initially a mask for and subsequently an antidote to vulnerability and powerlessness. While others use the position for personal vengeance, he prefers to mask any culpability behind anonymity. He exerts torture on persons whom he does not know, as an impersonal viciousness in the service of a higher order. He also learns to extend torture beyond the physical to become psychological manipulation. In order to steel himself to kill, the Dew Breaker must create a series of fabrications which render his victims enemies who are inimical not only to the state but also to the body politic. It is important to him to work around people he does not know so that his personal knowledge of them does not interfere with his fabrication of "evil tales" (Danticat 2004, 187).

The unmaking of the Dew Breaker is initiated by events which crack this façade when he is assigned to kill a minister who has been preaching against the president's injustices, demanding, "What shall we do with our beast?" From the vantage point of the political directorate, the basis for the assassination order is clear. But it is not a sufficient cause for the Dew Breaker to identify his opponent as inimical to the Duvalierist state; he must also invoke difference which is meaningful to him and then make that difference punishable by his torturous acts. His skewed rationale goes incrementally as follows: the man he is to kill is a Protestant and not a Catholic like himself; Protestants distort the Bible, practise brainwashing and use religion as the colonizers did, to keep people in subjugation and to turn them against ancestral religions; therefore, to kill the preacher is to undermine his destructive influence and do people a favour.

The Dew Breaker, having fashioned himself into an avenger of a higher order, responds to the command to kill the pastor but botches the assignment and imprisons him instead, so that he stands to resemble a martyr. Complexity increases when the sister of the pastor, who is running to the aid of her brother, collides with the bloodied Macoute, who is running away from reprisal for his botched assignment. She misreads him as the victim and gives him the first line of the fabricated script for the rest of his life. It is this incident which must be mined for Danticat's insight into the danse macabre that locks torturer and tortured together in grim manoeuvres. The turn is initiated as the Dew Breaker considers withdrawing from his line of work and encounters a young boy who reminds him of his own subverted potential for a different destiny. Wishing for a better possibility for the child, he paternally gives him money for running errands and questions him about his homework. He fails to kill the preacher in the street because of concern for the welfare of the boy, who is at risk of being hurt in the process. As an alternative, he takes the preacher into his office and torture chamber and is constrained to encounter a process which reverses the torturer/tortured power dynamic.

The objective in the art of torture is to magnify the torturer far beyond human measure, culpability and vulnerabilities and to objectify the victim into the lowest possible state of shame and abjection. The lower the abjection of the victim, the greater the powerlessness; the more diminished the body and stature of the victim, the greater the corpulence of the torturer, who seeks to fill all things with himself; the greater the "world dissolution" of the victim, the more expansive the world construction of the torturer. The torturer's role is to remake the victim into an inimical and alien enemy, to use pain to obliterate the victim's sense of significance, purpose and social locatedness, and to impose as an alternative his own skewed worldview and framework of meaning. It is pivotal that the tortured and torturer arrive at agreement that the power to impose pain be perceived as supremacy. The objective is to so magnify the enormity of the pain that all other complex facets of the victim's world are melted down into this single, all-encompassing, inescapable reality: a human, despite strategies of dissociation, ultimately cannot escape embodiment. The torturer would also seek to destroy the voice – the primary avenue of self-expression and social connection – by yoking, ventriloquizing and eventually silencing the speech of the tortured.

The preacher defeats the Dew Breaker by retaining his strength of purpose, which he derives from the spirit of martyrdom, despite the dissolution of the body. On his way to the church where he expects to encounter his assassin, the preacher is undergirded by community – a solid phalanx of greeters and well-wishers who energize him with their very ordinariness. After his imprisonment, the preacher moves through an environment of disembodied voices, all signalling or responding to actual or projected pain: the woman's voice which screams, "Jean! Jean! Is that you?" (Danticat 2004, 212), the assistant who drags him to and from the cell and whom he experiences only as "the Voice". Indeed, he draws small measures of comfort from other disembodied functions and voices. "Goodness" is manifested even in the cellmates who piss on him in the hope of sealing his wounds, in the prisoner who whispers *"bonne chance"* as he passes. As he is dragged from place to place, the preacher experiences a dissolution of self and world which is akin to defoliation: "He felt as though he was shedding skin, shedding voice, shedding everything he'd tried so hard to make himself into, a well-dressed man, a well-spoken man, a well-read man. He was leaving all that behind now with bits of flesh in the ground, morsel by morsel being scraped off by pebbles, rocks, tiny bottle shards and cracks in the concrete" (213). Through the infliction of pain, the victim constructed as inimical to the body politic is made to experience an inversion such that he comes to experience the dissolution of all other dimensions of self, and to experience his body as an alien and alienating object which is inimical to the self but from which he cannot escape.

The preacher assumes agency through refusal to give voice to his sense of dissolution and through taking away from the Dew Breaker the only force which could eventually break him. The pastor, who well understands the power of the voice to shape reality, refuses to scream and thereby strike fear into other victims of the enormity of the power of his torturer; he refuses to beg and thereby affirm the Dew Breaker's success at transmuting pain into power. Locked into what he envisions as a spiritual conflict between his god and the agent of the beast – who appropriates the disguise and authority of the voodoo *loa* of the cemetery, names himself the "Sovereign One" and reframes the Lord's Prayer as "Our father who art in the national palace" – the preacher is well prepared for the swift, grand gesture of martyrdom. He nevertheless stands to be broken by unrelenting extremes of torture until pain subsumes every other reality, his mind seesaws between false hope and plummeting despair, and his body becomes host to unabated stink, filth, and parasitic vermin. His determination to choose martyrdom gives him the courage and power to wrest control from the torturer and to lay down his life through an act of aggression which precipitates his murder.

It is this act which destroys the identity construction of the Dew Breaker and changes his psychic location in relation to the works of his hand. He murders the preacher not as an agent of a higher order but in a fit of rage and personal vengeance. He finds himself in the process transported into a subordinate position in the torturer/victim cycle of opposition identified by Scarry: "The pain is hugely present to the prisoner and absent to the torturer; the question is, within the political fiction, hugely significant to the torturer and insignificant to the prisoner; for the prisoner, the body and pain are overwhelmingly present and voice, world and self are absent; for the torturer, voice, world and self are overwhelmingly present and the body and pain are absent" (Scarry 1985, 46).

The wound which scars the Dew Breaker for life ambiguously locates him. It transfers him from the one who inflicts to the one who is vulnerable to and receives pain – first the pain inflicted by the preacher who rakes the wooden spar though his face, and later the pain inflicted by the doctor who pulls the silver thread through the wound: "It seemed like some kind of torture, the type you might inflict on someone you truly hated" (Danticat 2004, 238–39). Pain is pivotal to the healing process. The wound to which Anne reacts with sympathy becomes his new mask, allowing him to remake himself as the victim, the prey as opposed to the hunter. The wound is an inescapable, life-long signifier to him, every time he looks into the mirror, that he has fabricated himself into a lie. He is made keenly aware of the vulnerabilities of his embodiment, for as long as he is clothed in flesh he must continue to inhabit the mask. He develops a habit of shielding the scar with his hand, which is representative of his agency – the hand with which he took the oath to serve Duvalier, the bone-crushing hand with which he restrains his daughter. In this sense the preacher has succeeded in leaving his mark on the beast: "Every time he looked in the mirror, he would have to confront this mark and remember him. Whenever people asked what happened to his face, he would have to tell a lie, a lie that would further remind him of the truth" (228).

Body and pain are overwhelmingly present to the Dew Breaker. Voice, world and self are overwhelmingly absent. The requirement to constantly hide his identity leaves him bereft of a world, a family framework and background. His Haitian legacy is effectively lost to him and his progeny solidly enough to undermine his sense of being in the world. He who has imposed himself on his surroundings with gross corpulence and an eloquent voice, which he exerted to capsize the world and worldviews of others, has become slender, taciturn, uncommunicative, bent on erasing his material presence as far as humanly possible. He is constrained to live with haunting nightmares of the evil he has done, bound to constant vigilance and fabrication to prevent discovery.

Finally, the questions which are paramount to those who are constrained to interact with him are the very ones he would erase. His daughter whispers: "Manman. How can you love him?" (Danticat 2004, 24). His wife, faced with the prospect of confronting another torturer, asks herself: "Would she spit in his face or embrace him, acknowledging a kinship of shame and guilt that she'd inherited by marrying her husband? . . . What if he considered himself innocent? Innocent enough to go anywhere he pleased? What right did she have to judge him?" (81). His would-be avenger grapples with the question "of harming the wrong man, of making the wrong woman a widow and the wrong child an orphan" (107).

The question which the Dew Breaker is constrained to grapple with is this: How can I negotiate the afterlife carrying this enormous burden of guilt and shame? As may be fitting for a once loyal follower of the leader who modelled himself after Baron Samedi, *loa* of death and the cemetery, the Dew Breaker is obsessed with the immortality of the soul and the requirement to account in the afterlife for deeds done in the flesh. The conviction of this reality, which lent the preacher strength to choose the dynamic of his dying, haunts his murderer, as manifested by his obsession with the ancient Egyptian Book of the Dead – a book of mortuary spells which the wealthy in that society paid to have transcribed and entombed with their remains to arm them with the knowledge and rituals necessary to negotiate the afterlife.

One Day for the Prey

As persistently as Danticat has carried the figure of the torturer through her works of fiction, she has also engaged his prey – victims who decades later are still forced to bear in their bodies and their psyches the imprint of their physical and psychic pain. Through this process she is inscribing facets of the social history of the impact of the Duvalierist regime which would otherwise remain unwritten, silenced or told haltingly in whispers that can barely penetrate shrouds of shame. This work then becomes an act of re-memory which seeks to substantiate remembrance and appropriate responses to traumatic historical events and to agents of repressive regimes. Danticat is clear on the damage done to the social order by this state that rapes and eats its children. Indeed, the very naming of the Tontons Macoutes speaks to the fabled Uncle Gunny Sack who snacks on morsels of naughty children.

The body becomes the point of access for destruction of the moral and ethical order. Danticat consistently portrays damage to the social and moral fabric, as effected through the body, as the primary human interface with the material world, and through perversions of the basic needs and appetites of the body which are essential to healthy human life. This becomes particularly significant in the lives of women, for whom female embodiment generates gender-specific atrocities. Macoutes break into homes and demand food and sex with mother and daughter. The impact is not only to devastate and despoil women but also to break the social order, in which men's sense of self-respect hinges in part on their capacity to protect their families from harm. The point of access is the body, but it is the very soul of the social order which comes under attack when men are constrained to break deep-rooted taboos by having sex with their own daughters or mothers and thereafter face arrest for vice. These devastations persist long after the body has healed, generating a siege mentality and changing the world of the traumatized into a hostile and violent place.

The torturer's skill is reflected in his capacity to shift responsibility for his actions from himself to the victim. Elaine Scarry, in *The Body in Pain*, conceptualizes the moral inversion which becomes pivotal for the act of torture and which shapes its long-term deleterious impact on victims. Scarry identifies torture as constituting a primary physical act – "the infliction of pain" – and a primary verbal act – "the interrogation" (1985, 35). In Danticat's title story, a tiny octogenarian describes the Dew Breaker's interrogation strategies:

> "He'd lean close to my ears to tell me, 'Valia, I truly hate to unwoman you. Valia, don't let me unwoman you. Valia, tell me where your husband is and I won't cut out your . . . *I can't even say it the way he said it. I refuse to say it the way he did.* He'd wound you, then try to soothe you with words, then he'd wound you again. He thought he was God." (Danticat 2004, 199 [my emphasis])

As Scarry theorizes,

> The question is mistakenly understood to be "the motive"; the answer is mistakenly understood to be "the betrayal". The first mistake credits the torturer, providing him with a justification, his cruelty with an explanation. The second discredits the prisoner, making him rather than the torturer, his voice rather than his pain, the cause of his loss of self and the world ... the one is an absolution of responsibility; the other is a conferring of responsibility; the two together turn the moral reality of torture upside down. (Scarry 1985, 35)

Language is a major avenue for self-representation and connection to community, pivotal to an assertion of being in the world. Bearing wounds that speak and impaired capacity to verbally articulate her loss, the victim, who refuses to identify the precise nature of her violation, is robbed of far more than an unnamed physical appendage. Thirty years later, the magnitude of the horror is demonstrated in ongoing loss of verbalization: she "would stammer for an hour before finally managing to speak, pausing for a breath between each word" (Danticat 2004, 198). The torment becomes a trauma-inducing catalyst so great as to become submerged into the subconscious mind as an unspeakable act which evades apprehension and articulation. Enormity of pain causes the sufferer to revert to elementary pre-linguistic signifiers – whimpers, moans, groans, grunts, hisses, screams. "The tendency of pain not simply to resist expression but to destroy the capacity for speech is in torture re-enacted in an overt exaggerated form" (Scarry 1985, 54). As an act of resistance to the Dew Breaker's naming, Valia struggles towards articulation, but significantly, given the notion of trauma theorists who privilege a narrative cure, also refuses to speak and to name as act of agency; she rejects his languaging as reflective of her own agency to reject imposition of his worldview.

Danticat's collection also explores the working of cycles of uncanny repetition in response to trauma. The conviction of a haunting presence, which she is unable to escape thirty years after her encounter with the Dew Breaker, constantly discommodes the protagonist of "The Bridal Seamstress". Arrested and tortured because of her refusal to date him, Beatrice Saint Fort's incapacity to move beyond this incident is reflected in her constant drive to change residence in order to escape. His ubiquitous and overdetermined presence, and her loss as a result, is exteriorized in her conviction that he is inhabiting empty houses in every neighbourhood in which she takes up residence. Trauma's uncanny repetition ensures that every move enables her to encounter afresh his absent haunting presence. In this case, clear memory of the encounter and vehement articulation free of self-blame are insufficient to free her from the haunting. The traumatized woman has been robbed of the capacity to fashion a teleological developmental narrative; she is constrained ultimately to fashion her life in relation to empty houses which host spectres of the torturer. In short, her inner being is the haunted empty house, and she proves incapable of exorcising the spectre.

Dragging her internal woundedness, the scarification branded on her body, and his absent presence like a doppelganger through her life, Beatrice has become in essence an unaccommodated woman, exiled from lasting relationships, simple domestic pleasures, roots, community, marriage and children. The dynamic of living to accommodate an absent presence permeates every aspect of her life. She is a superb maker of bridal dresses that she will never wear but which she lovingly crafts for girls who call her the mother that she will never become in the flesh. She reasons that when wedding guests see the creativity and beauty of the dresses she makes, they are seeing the absent her. This makes for a dynamic interplay with the Dew Breaker, who sought to assuage his sense of powerlessness with gross corporeality and violent mind games aimed at disallowing space for others. A spectre that now subsists on nothingness remains mammoth in the seamstress's mind, while the actual man has become a mere shadow.

In this narrative, Danticat posits another avenue for persons coping with "tremendous agonies" which fill "every blank space in their lives". When the past is an unendurable pain which intrudes in an obtrusive and unseemly manner into the present, one strategy for coping is to live intensely in the present. Images of falling leaves permeate this narrative: "It was an odd yet beautiful sight, the leaves seemingly suspended in the air, then falling ever so slowly as if cushioned by air bubbles" (Danticat 2004, 133). This state of suspended animation and Beatrice's practice of doing everything slowly and painstakingly are strategies for inhabiting the interstices of time between a painful past, endlessly recycled, and a relentlessly encroaching future. It is here, moment by moment, that the trauma victim finds an (albeit fleeting) measure of peace.

The fullest evocation of post-traumatic stress disorder is inscribed in *Breath, Eyes, Memory* (Danticat 1994), which I have discussed at length elsewhere. Of significance for this chapter is the manner in which Danticat conveys continuities between the gender-based violence meted out to women under colonialism and that under post-independence terrorist regimes. After sixteen-year-old Martine Caco is raped by an unknown masked assailant in a cane field, she learns his face only when she sees it reproduced in her daughter. Decades later, when she conceives a child in a loving relationship, the haunting rapist appropriates the voice of her unborn child to torment her with cursing. The location of her rape "points to the abuses inherent in forced and voluntary labour within the death generating cane fields in a process which is akin to 'the farming of bones' (Danticat 1998, 55). Moreover, the location points backwards to the sexual abuses endured by generations of women in cane fields as part of slavery's mechanism of dominance. It intimates that, generations later, the daughters of the diaspora are not free from this grim legacy, wielded now by new recipients of "power".

Manifesting classical symptoms of post-traumatic stress disorder, Martine nightly relives the rape, the full horror of which is seeking to rise into her conscious mind. Trauma's quality of belatedness is rooted in the conscious memory's protective device of dissociation and distancing while the event is taking place. Yet the body remembers, even when the mind cannot immediately take in the full horror. The body remembers the plunder, the facelessness, and the eyes of the attacker as he plunges deep for rage and for pleasure. And the sensorimotor memory of the panic, the fear and the vulnerability triggers an almost nightly reliving of the nightmare of rape, which can be stilled only when she plunges a knife seventeen times into the fetus which has become the enemy, assuming the identity of the rapist, entrenching her shame, cursing her as a filthy whore. The unborn child articulates the rapist's disavowal of blame for the violent sexual encounter, and the victim's appropriation of self-blame for that which she could not avoid.

Potential for Recuperation

The nine interrelated stories which constitute *The Dew Breaker* point to intergenerational cycles of repetition which entrap both victims and perpetrators, at the same time retaining focus on the humanity, belonging and redemptive potential of the most violent of perpetrators of state injustice. The text touches on the multiplicity of roles which tie the mild-mannered scarred man to the Dew Breaker who relishes inflicting extreme torture. He appears variously as an attentive husband, an awkward but loving father, a successful entrepreneur, a corpulent mass murderer and torturer, an elusive, haunting personal spectre to his traumatized victims, and a human-rights puzzle to relief workers and the media. Each fictional construction is offered to the reader as an act of re-memory and representation based on recollection of predominantly personal grim events, anecdotes, memories, gestures, actions, myriad ways of knowing and experiencing, escaping, evading, reconfiguring traumatic realities which escape orderly spatiotemporal continuities. The knowing of this grim, silenced, submerged, shameful reality becomes of necessity dialogic and, even for those at the core of the experience, shifting, uncertain and unknowable.

The stories also pose a diverse range of moral, ethical and relational issues around the perpetrators of state-sponsored torture. It proffers muted representations of the potential for redemption through love, community and family. Although the disaffection of young males that makes them targets is constructed as relating to an absence of fathering, potential redemptive reintegration into community is related to the capacity to receive the healing grace extended by women. Immediately after he is wounded by the preacher and comes to the point of conversion away from his criminal lifestyle, the Dew Breaker dreams about idyllic reconnection to the land and to his mother, who has mysteriously disappeared. In a paradisiacal dreamscape of a cool morning bathed in golden mists in a rich, verdant garden, his mother shows him the shame plant, which closes its tiny leaves when touched. She finds a parallel in Anne, who intrudes on his dream when she arrives bearing healing herbs the morning after his wounding. Her voice is "as calm as a stream or one of those tranquil brooks his mother was repeatedly taking him to in his dreams" (Danticat 2004, 236–37). The cleansing waters flow towards him and the recovery of the shame plant points to his potential to overcome guilt, alienation, unworthiness. This shame is complex. It is related to the shame of allowing himself as an ace torturer to be wounded by his victim in the torture chamber, and it is related to the shame of bearing the mark of the beast. His enduring sense of being overexposed is signalled by Monsieur Bienaimé's lifelong gesture of covering his scarred face with his hand. The lesson is that, although the shame plant closes when touched, it opens again.

The order of the narrative is significant. We encounter first the reformed, socially useful and guilt-ridden Monsieur Bienaimé through the eyes of his nearest and dearest. "The Book of the Dead" conveys his daughter's artistic struggle as she grapples with her creative obsession, the task of creating sculptural images of her father, whom she believes to have been scarred as a torture victim in a Haitian prison. The daughter's passion for representing her father can be read as grasping after some mysterious elusive essence of the father's, which turns out to be tacitly related to the fact that he was the torturer and not the tortured. The cracked sculpture is demonstrative both of his scarred imperfections and of the flawed nature of the representation. The daughter's act of sculpting is an attempt to attract the gaze of the father, who has drawn her from infancy into his obsession with Egyptian mythology, with a particular focus on marred statues and the Book of the Dead – spells intended to guide the dead through the labyrinth of the afterlife. Monsieur Bienaimé is haunted by ancient Egyptian mythology as he seeks an answer to his quest: how are those laden with transgression to expiate their guilt and safely negotiate judgement in the afterlife?

Ironically, the visual representation reflects a submerged reality which was transmitting itself to the sculptor. The father is captured in a pose of supplication, "kneeling on a half-foot-square base, his back arched like the curve of a crescent moon, his downcast eyes fixed on his very long fingers and the large palms of his hands" (Danticat 2004, 6). The kneeling posture and downcast eyes speak of prayer and entreaty, while the gaze is fixed on all that is left of the gross physicality of the corpulent Dew Breaker: disproportionately large hands and long fingers which speak of agency and culpability. These are the hands with which he swore allegiance to the dictator, enacted extreme torture, habitually shields his scarred face and captures his daughter in a bone-crushing grip, all the while pleading, "I did not want to hurt you. I did not want to hurt anyone" (20). The sculptural representation arguably points to the potential of the creative imagination to capture submerged and silenced realties which are not accessible to the conscious mind.

The Dew Breaker's bid for redemption is wrapped up in his belief in his *ka*, or double, which comes to be personified in his daughter, whom he names

Ka. In ancient Egyptian mythology, the *ka* is the symbol of life essence which infuses the body. The presence of the *ka*, or spiritual double of the body, therefore, distinguishes between the living and the dead. Egyptians mummified their dead to give the *ka* a place in which to live and therefore to maximize the potential of the dead to achieve eternal life. This spiritual self was also perceived as the higher and more noble self, generating "spiritual and material well being" as well as acting as "conscience and guide", urging "kindness, quietude, honor and compassion". Given the symbolic weight accorded to the Dew Breaker's hands as representing human agency, it is significant that the *ka* is symbolized in Egyptian art as a pair of upraised arms bent at the elbow and balancing on the head (McDevitt 2012). By denoting her his *ka*, or life essence, the father places on his child the heavy burden of ensuring that he remains alive. Hence she compromises, tolerates and forgives much, and even as an adult she is petrified by the notion of his mortality and the possibility of his impending death.

Redemptive potential resides here in family and progeny. The life force resident in his wife and daughter as his good angels transforms the Dew Breaker into a quiet, dependable family man who rarely becomes angry. But this is not an easy resolution. Even the reformed Dew Breaker in subtle ways yokes his daughter inappropriately into his redemptive process, ensuring that subliminally she is visited with a measure of the consequences of the sins of her father. He reads her bedtime stories of morbid and macabre mortuary spells, thereby imparting her own parcel of nightmares. In other words, he colonizes her inner being and her gaze and defiles her innocence through his pursuit of absolution. Without his admission of guilt and culpability as the hunter and not the prey, he inadvertently sets her on a creative journey of discovery in quest of the story that has not been told. Her life's work becomes crafting sculpture which will fill his gaze and capture his essence. The father destroys the statue ostensibly because he is unable to accept its tribute – the burden of supposed heroic scars in the fight against great injustice. In fact he cannot risk exposure, as the statue is destined for Haitian film stars, who would parade the representation before the rich and famous. The narrative remains unclear as to whether the destruction of the work of art is an aspect of his ongoing attempt at evading recognition and thereby exposure.

Love may be a most powerful source of recuperation and transformation for a heinous criminal, but how can one love such a monster, even a reformed one? The filters of love, gratitude, dependency and habit beglamour the Dew Breaker in the eyes of his wife. "The Book of Miracles" portrays him as a loving and caring husband and father – a miraculously transformed man who carries his family to midnight Mass on Christmas Eve. The wife, who is addicted to the miraculous, would deem its transforming power to be sufficient, even while acknowledging its evasion of social responsibility. Against the elaborate celebration of the nativity of Christ, Anne is rendered particularly pious because of her husband's great sin and his great need for forgiveness and redemption. She envisions an apotheosis as she contemplates the mystery of his miraculous transformation: an open heaven in which the physical environment and supernatural world stand at attention to greet the Christ Child: "birds were supposed to begin chirping their all-night songs to greet the holy birth, when other animals were to genuflect and trees bow in reverence . . . water in secret wells and far-off rivers and streams was turning into wine" (Danticat 2004, 77). The vision echoes the Dew Breaker's dream at his point of conversion, of being with his mother in a verdant, idyllic, paradisiacal environment. This highly subjective overarching transcendence does not coexist smoothly with ethical, social and legal requirements, as Anne is forced to admit after her daughter's supposed sighting of Emmanuel Constant, a wanted post-Duvalier political torturer, in the same church, sharing the same magical commemorative moment. Putting undeniable moral and social imperatives aside, the personal issue is how she can credibly stand against other perpetrators of violence while fervently longing that her husband escape detection and punishment. Notwithstanding the power of love to recuperate individuals within families, the issue of collusion with state criminals who have wrought crimes against humanity remains to be resolved.

The diverse perspectives of these stories each add a snippet to the range of highly subjective realities. The implied author quilts fragmented and incoherent narratives, each of which is a subset of larger personal, communal, national and diasporic histories. Dany, the youthful bearer of a transgenerational wound and impulse towards revenge, represents children of unjustly murdered parents who are forced to migrate because of their fearsome histories. Salvation for him comes through confrontation with a criminal deportee of a younger generation who managed to find his way back home, returning to his family in rural Haiti after shooting his father in a drug-induced rage. Whereas place functions as a significant locus of loss for the Dew Breaker, who cannot allow himself coherent memories of locatedness even in the past, place proves to be the salvation for Claude, one of the new generation of criminals. This perpetrator of patricide is exiled to his parental homeland, only to find himself a community prepared to extend forgiveness and belonging. In laying claim to the village environment and belonging in the heart of the community, Claude admits that these people, whom he would have held in deep contempt had he remained in New York, have created a peaceful communal home in which he can find a measure of peace. It is this newfound appreciation of community which exorcises the vengeful spirit and prevents Dany from slaughtering the Dew Breaker, lest he kill an innocent man and deprive the wrong family.

Danticat proffers a range of possibilities but settles on no facile resolution to the complex of issues raised by state criminality. Although the perpetrator hides from public detection and prosecution, he cannot find redemption under the shadow of deception. He must acknowledge culpability for wrong done. He cannot allow torturous activity to masquerade as anything other than transgression against self and community. Love and family make the former criminal vulnerable and resurrect a conscience which becomes heightened as he moves closer to social reintegration. Although he shares with his victims inscriptions of torture on body and mind, the imperative to destroy the iconic statue speaks to the inappropriateness of representing the perpetrator as victim, notwithstanding the fact that both are deeply scarred by their shared experiences.

Danticat speaks too of the particular power of women to live redemptively and to infuse this potential into the social order. In terms of fictional enquiry, she returns full circle to the perpetrator – this after repeated emphasis on the victim of criminal and state violence; strong assertion of the palliative impact of narratives, the necessity that the victims tell the tale, no matter how horrific; and stress on the responsibility of society to receive the telling and thereby affirm belonging for damaged persons whose experiences have thrown them literally and metaphorically beyond the pale of human society. Danticat is arguing here that the perpetrator has not been thrown by his act beyond the boundaries of decent mutuality. For him to be integrated into community, he too must own his story, allow it to surface and acknowledge responsibility to a loved one. The narrative does, however, defer the issue of his debt to society and the workings of the justice system, with its agency to punish the guilty.

This study undermines any attempt to pin the crime exclusively on the criminal, while it also recognizes that any attempt to exonerate the criminal from blame would be too disempowering. To abdicate blame is to abdicate responsibility and potential for change. Yet there is an extent to which this study would seek to contextualize the criminal as produced by broader sociopolitical forces. It interrogates any notion that criminals who are not brought to justice benefit while only victims suffer. The reality which is reflected in these narratives is that a crime does not bring benefit to anyone – not to the criminals, not to the subcultures which they create, not to the families and nations from which they come, not to the persons or institutions which may appear to benefit from their criminal acts. Danticat argues that alleviation of criminal activity and its consequences requires collective social action. Moreover, transgenerational intervention is required to expiate historical transgression and to disrupt its violent present-day outworkings.

6

"WHEN MEMORY IS A BRUISE STILL TENDER"
Ageing and Alzheimer's in *Cascade* and *Soucouyant*

BARBARA LALLA'S *CASCADE* (2010) and David Chariandy's *Soucouyant* (2007) are poignant evocations of the challenges posed to victims and caregivers by Alzheimer's disease, which steals memories, dignity and relationships and leaves its afflicted poised between "a vanishing past and contracting future" (Lalla 2010). This chapter presents a comparative gender-sensitive reading of the implications of treating with mothers afflicted with Alzheimer's. It focuses on the correlation between historical and social trauma and the early onset of dementia, the resultant personal and familial crises, and the narrativization of failing memory, impaired cognitive functions and threatened ontologies. The study traces correlations between the disorder and the narrative strategies deployed to capture its nuances and complexities, to clear away the clutter and trivia of everyday life in order to arrive at a deeper meaning of lived experience which transcends the banal dreadfulness attendant on living with and extending care to persons with Alzheimer's disease.

Alzheimer's is a progressive terminal disease that involves loss of brain function, initially indicated by memory impairment, followed by impairment in thought and speech and leading to incapacity to perform basic daily tasks. The 1984 criteria for Alzheimer's proposed by the National Institute of Neurological and Communicative Disorders and Stroke and the Alzheimer's Disease and Related Disorders Association are the primary standards used in diagnosis of the disease. The criteria include dementia, established by clinical exams, and progressive deterioration of specific cognitive functions such as use of language (aphasia), motor skills (apraxia) and perception (agnosia).

Victims of Alzheimer's disease experience symptoms of depression, insomnia, incontinence, delusions and hallucinations, verbal, emotional or physical outbursts, sexual disorders and weight loss; as the disease advances, people can also suffer from gait disorders. In the Caribbean, Alzheimer's disease is often not clearly diagnosed. It is often associated with senile dementia and subsumed under numerous subtly nuanced Creole expressions such as *dotish* and *beh beh*, which register as pejoratives rather than as illness terms.[1]

Clinical criteria in no way prepare Alzheimer's sufferers, their families and caregivers for the pain of living with the disease. The implied authors of both these narratives take on the challenge of speaking on behalf of loved ones who have been rendered voiceless and in myriad other ways left bereft of the power of communication by this disease. In so doing, they grapple with a fundamental issue – how to understand what the sufferer is experiencing, or, more precisely, the nature of the spatiotemporal orientation and corporeal embodiment of the sufferer. Chariandy's narrator delivers a stern rebuke to sterile medical classifications and diagnoses, indicting Western medicine for its technologically narrowed tunnel vision. He says, in an email interview with Kit Dobson, "the task of adequately representing dementia was an enormous challenge for me, something that profoundly humbled me, something that touched my deepest terrors and curiosities about mortality and unbecoming. Those who deal with this illness, whether directly or indirectly, are exploring the most profound mysteries of existence" (Dobson 2007, 812).

My interest in this topic was sparked by the requirement to give home care to my adoptive mother, who succumbed to Alzheimer's when she was in her late sixties. I was then a young wife and mother of small children. I was constrained to witness close at hand the process of deterioration and to experience the deep sense of impotence, loss and grief that I believe is common to the majority of caregivers of mothers with this dread disease. I particularly recall a day on which she teased me playfully about revealing a photograph she had cradled to her bosom, eventually holding it up and triumphantly explaining that it was her mother. It was a photograph of me in my late teens. At that point I could not see beyond the devastation and the pain. I later experienced a less pain-glazed interaction with a neighbour in her early seventies, "Grace", who in the early stages of the disease regaled me with stories of her absolute refusal to ever cook another meal or sew another garment, because she had done enough of those tasks to last her a lifetime. She had recast her incapacity and her family's resultant safeguards (they controlled her access to appliances with a hidden master switch) as a narrative of individual choice and self-assertion. I also observed that Grace had become freer in her speech, more playful, emotionally expressive and assertive in her oppositional opinions and preferences. These scenarios pose two issues: Where do we find the loved one within the wreckage left by ontological collapse? And what is the role of narrative in making sense, for both victim and caregiver, of the devastation which Alzheimer's brings? The fictional representations speak to both of these issues.

In Barbara Lalla's *Cascade*, the razor-sharp intellect of the versatile Ellie is under attack by a looming entity which remains for the majority of the narrative a thing without a name. Alzheimer's ravages her mind, playing havoc with her emotions and rendering her full of rage, regret, fear, resignation and sorrow – all in quick, unpredictable succession. A multiplicity of voices and perspectives is necessary to piece together the floating spatiotemporal fragments of Ellie's consciousness. Jamaica and Trinidad, distant memory, immediate past and present – actual, fantasized, dreamt, televised – all crowd a mind seeking desperately to bring some semblance of order. *Cascade* gazes frankly into the process of ontological collapse, probing, as it were, for some rationale for what is lost and what remains. Ellie and her courageous husband, Dan, stand as the pivots of a narrative which is also peopled by their daughter, Rachel, and her husband, Rabin, Dan's sister Rosemarie, and Ellie's dear friend and Rosemarie's sister-in-law, Ivy. Ivy is the owner of the grand old country home which becomes Cascade, a guesthouse for tourists and a home for the aged. This multivocal novel gathers in narratives from all of these perspectives, and additionally from the marginal characters Ashmead, the murderer/criminal; Vie, the caring housekeeper; Basil, the gardener; and Evan, Ivy's adopted son. And holding the tightly crafted narrative together is the implied author's firm grasp on all of its worlds – real and imagined – and on the temporal sequences and spatial markers which hold the whole in place. The multitude of people who populate *Cascade*, in stark contrast to *Soucouyant*, bear witness to and become implicated in the care given and the social location afforded to those who suffer from the dread disease.

David Chariandy's *Soucouyant*, set on the Scarborough Bluffs of Lake

Ontario, Canada, evokes a theme which is unique among male-authored Caribbean novels. Displaying continuities – and even more significant discontinuities – with literary portrayals of the powerful mother-women of the Caribbean, Chariandy offers a sensitive representation of a troubled young man's role as primary caregiver to a mother who is suffering the ravages of Alzheimer's. Whereas the pivotal element of this disease is traditionally perceived as the anguish of forgetting, central to this novel is a traumatic experience which Alzheimer's causes Adele to forget to forget. The narrative lends flesh, blood, pain and vulnerability to a highly publicized occurrence during the American military occupation of Trinidad and Tobago in the 1940s. The demand for sexual services was so high and the lure of the Yankee dollar so compelling that prostitution occasionally drew both mother and daughter into its treacherous net. Canadian-born Chariandy stands as representative of a new generation of writers speaking to a new readership about the grim side of this much rehearsed political and socio-symbolic drama. He locates it within the context of a historical trauma generated by migrations and by wars fought in the interests of neo-imperial conquest, its impact on vulnerable island societies and how it touches down in the lives of impoverished women. The implied author reasons: "Memory is a bruise still tender. History is a rusted pile of blades and manacles. And forgetting can sometimes be the most creative and life-sustaining thing that we can ever hope to accomplish" (Chariandy 2007, 32). Both *Cascade* and *Soucouyant* deal with loss, but the latter is also a novel of migration which deals with oppression, isolation, racism, flouted hopes and dreams deferred.

Both authors evoke a world of floating signifiers – textual shadows, ambiguous metaphorical groundings, past histories, memories and signs – as the Alzheimer's victims and those who speak on their behalf seek a measure of stability and fixity in a world of slippery signifiers which are losing connection with shared systems of meaning. The first portion of *Cascade* is poignant, tugging at the heart because of the devastation wrought by this dread disease within families, the stress endured by caregivers, the threat of bodily harm from fires set inadvertently, the wandering, the potential for abuse at the hands of those hired to give care . . . and the list continues. Alongside the victim's growing impotence are the necessity to grapple with the horrific threat of the disease and the need to receive comfort in the face of deep disturbance.

A case in point is the face-saving communication of Ellie's sick husband, who is unceremoniously toppled from his bed because she objects to the familiarity of nurses' hands on his body. When questioned about the incident, he insists with gentle dignity that he slid off. Communication, even for those who honour truth, in this context of necessity means gaps, silences, evasions, erasures – and comforting touch.

The major issue with which both authors grapple is what remains in the case of ontological collapse. Both narratives construct their Alzheimer's victims as capable of self-reflexivity and intentionality, thereby sending a message to any who would dismiss those suffering from the disease as beyond the pale. This coincides with the finding of Sabat and Harré (1994, 145–60), based on their analyses of personal narratives and diary entries scripted by people with Alzheimer's, whom the researchers argue retain their sense of self, notions of social acceptability, and personal presence and identity. Indeed much of the aggression and resentment they manifest appears to be triggered by depersonalization and loss. Sabat and Harre conclude that Alzheimer's sufferers retain a capacity for self appraisal and reflexivity. Indeed, Chariandy's narrative is clear that much of the aggression which the mother demonstrates stems from pride and anger at the indignity of being exposed and undermined.

Common to both novels is the suspicion that society does not value and has no place for the aged and infirm. Lalla expresses Ellie's voice and vision as she watches her husband succumb to ageing and infirmity while arguably masking her own perception and fear of the encroaching symptoms of Alzheimer's:

> I cannot block out the tremor in his hand, the blankness of his gaze. The part of me that searches ruthlessly for truth intercepts that part that knows the truth to be unbearable. For there is a place in the dark for those who have little-understood diseases and need to become slowly and inevitably invisible. Once a gully or some remote corner of a canepiece, but now, here in the twentieth century there is still some way to be found, some mysterious place for throwing people away when their disorders grow inescapable and embarrassing. It is a mindset that renders them invisible. But submerge even that thought. Hide a shadow with other shadows. (Lalla 2010, 73)

The necessary social impulse to shield the self from excessive public exposure becomes a far more intense form of masking. In Ellie's consciousness, her husband's descent into ageing, illness, frailty and the loss of ontological certitude is associated with social disappearance and retreat into darkness. This is the metaphysical darkness of Achebe's evil forest which swallows those whose human failings; sicknesses and difference become an unwelcome reflection of human vulnerability and consequently elicit an atavistic response from the community. In the case of Chariandy's ageing black migrant roaming the streets of Scarborough, her shaming visibility is iconic of a dark, polluting West Indian presence. She in her dementia becomes a collective embarrassment to the entire migrant community, a scapegoat figure on which to hang the shame and belittlement they face as a result of persistent denigration.

Lalla's narrative strategy is telling. The passage quoted is ostensibly a direct rendering of Ellie's mental discourse. The issue is both how to see and how to mask what she sees, because the reality is too difficult to bear. Because of the lack of tags such as *she thought* or *she mused to herself* and quotation marks to delimit reported thoughts, the narrator is free to slip seamlessly into authorial comments which amplify and demonstrate the veracity of floating fragmentary impressions. The passage moves from an intensely personal, specific and time-bound reality to an unspecified, unlimited symbolic and spatiotemporal frame – "For there is a place in the dark . . . Once a gully or some remote corner of a canepiece, but now, here in the twentieth century . . ." – then cycles back to the specific place and time: "But submerge that thought. Hide a shadow with other shadows." As there has been no marker since the first two sentences to pin down the source of the discourse, it becomes ambiguous whether the final impulse towards submerging the grim reality lies with the character or with the implied author.

The texts and their implied authors, who arbitrate the fictional universe, counteract the social impulse to dump their loved ones in the "evil forest". Indeed, the narratives construct elaborate frameworks for understanding apparently irrational behaviour. In *Cascade*, Ellie's long-term memory remains fairly functional in accordance with skewed intuitive connections which appear less haphazard and more accessible to the reader as the right medicines and dosages are calibrated and as the text progresses. Ellie constantly and appropriately quotes the wisdom of the classics, the truths of her faith and her stringent undergirding value system. For Lalla, the fixity is ultimately rooted in moral and ethical grounding. In a context which does not give currency to postmodern genuflection to unending assemblages of self, the Alzheimer's sufferers and those who undertake to tell their narratives recuperate selves which are under assault, by reconstructing ordered life histories that present underlying spatiotemporal connections and causal factors for demented behaviours – this alongside brutally frank representations of decay and dissolution. These underlying unities of space, time and codes of meaning confer on the mothers a measure of ongoing ontological reflection, if not coherence. Both texts attribute intentionality to the Alzheimer's sufferers and carefully encode these intentions, covertly and mysteriously, into their narratives for the discerning reader to uncover.

The texts undertake then to train their readers in interpreting alternative semiotic systems. The reader's hard-won understanding of shared conventions of making meaning and signalling agreement accounts in fair measure for our sense of being drawn into a carefully encoded world. In *Cascade*, for example, a profound respect for the power of the word runs through the narrative. This is not a text which lies flat on the page. It is infused with the speaking voice, with communality, with the power of agreement, with the living utterance which is nowhere reflected as clearly as the chorus which attends every major decision: "So let it be written . . . So let it be done". Lalla is concerned that the part is not metonymically transferred to the whole; the absent cognitive capacities do not translate into the entire being. It matters not how much Ellie changes, how her mind loses its grasp of reality; in the early stages of the disease her language remains measured, threaded through with the codes of fine manners and social conventions, firmly rooted moral groundings which lend her stock phrases that express her worldview and value system. Hence the impulse that leads her, every time she hears the phrase "man and wife", to intone "one flesh" is the same impulse which causes her to recoil in terror at televised scenes of promiscuous sex:

> "I'M A DECENT WOMAN . . . Watch the screen. You think I want to be in someone else bedroom? . . . Oh no. Spare us. All my life I married to one good, clean, faithful, man. I must be involved in someone else's nasty life? Watch the screen. I know her I see her all the time. That is no she is – one after the other." Then she fling her arm across her face. "Jesu! He hit her. No. NO."
> (Lalla 2010, 116)

The cognitive capacity which distinguishes the real from the unreal and the past from the future may have dissolved, but the undergirding moral sensitivity remains intact and governs outbursts which may appear entirely irrational.

The narratives are above all about memory – the role of memory in the construction of the human subject and arguably, by extension, the insight to be gained from memory loss into what constitutes the subject. The issue is if – as with Lalla's criminal Ashmead – the entirety of the past is rent through with grim memories of abuse, belittlement, lack and deprivation, can the human spirit flourish and prosper? If the adult finds in the wake of traumatic childhood abuse not love and affirmation but ongoing objectification, how can he ever find his way to peace? The novel asserts, on the other hand, that if the memories of the past have been sustaining, endued with empowering values, anchored in faith and nourished by love, then the loss of memory does not constitute complete ontological collapse. Some more essential constituent of being remains to sustain the self and, after the rage and fear are exhausted, to bring peace. Ultimately not withstanding the state of the head, it is the heart that matters: Basil's response to Ellie's constant refrain carries the day: "Basil you can ask me anything, but my head not good", "And I say 'But nothing no wrong with you heart, m'am. Is a good heart' " (Lalla 2010, 273).

The texts also demonstrate that the act of constituting the human subject in relation to memory cannot be divorced from communal and historical memory, and ultimately from the modern Caribbean's originary traumatic encounter between worlds. The tumultuous history of the Caribbean and the ignominies of its beginnings are never far from the surface. Lalla, in one of her percipient turns of phrases, characterizes Jamaica as "laid back and traumatized". On the one hand there is a bright world of stunning natural beauty and verdant landscapes, enduring community and rich social customs, and on the other hand there is the normalization of encroaching savagery and brutish behaviours emanating from brutalized peoples. The latter add greatly to the vulnerability and stresses of the ageing.

The myriad meanings of the central trope of *Soucouyant* are rooted in the interplay among troubling histories of transnational encounter, ancestral and mythic metaphors of being and becoming, quests for nationhood and self-determination, communal histories of loss and displacement, and their eruptions into personal histories inscribed on women's bodies. If the key for decoding Lalla's narrative lies in the ethical realm, the key to Chariandy's lies grimly and painfully in the corporeal domain. In *Foreign Bodies: Trauma, Corporeality, and Textuality in Contemporary American Culture*, Laura Di Prete states, in the attempt to "grapple with phenomena that resist definition in terms of normal parameters of causality, temporality and location", evocation of the body "turned foreign, alien, and unfamiliar as the result of traumatic experience – becomes the vehicle through which trauma is told and, possibly, worked through" (Di Prete 2006, 2). Building on Cathy Caruth's notion of trauma as the wound that speaks and Freud's notion of inassimilable fragmented traumatic memories as "foreign bodies", Di Prete argues, "The memory of trauma materially fills like a 'body' a space in the psyche, yet as the 'forgotten' or never remembered, it marks a gap and signals the lack of the memory of an event that cannot be recalled" (12). This is because, even when rendered voiceless, the body remembers the unspeakable and encodes the unrepresentable.

Adele's early-onset Alzheimer's is triggered by her tragic involvement in the outworking of the American military occupation, which further ruptured the already tumultuous social order of Trinidad in the 1940s. The novel frames Adele's personal history within her birthplace's burgeoning national history, attendant upon its highly significant geopolitical location at the foot of the island archipelago, a stone's throw from the South American mainland and proximate to the Panama Canal. Additionally, the island's economic significance to the British Empire as a major oil producer is foregrounded in the narrative by the librarian's injunction to the youthful narrator to possess one's history with pride and a warning about the perils of forgetting: "Do you realise that in 1917, your mother's birthplace produced and refined a full *three-quarters* of the oil for the entire British Empire? Did you know that her island nation was the home of some of the most important strategic and training bases for the allied forces during the Second World War . . . ?" (Chariandy 2007, 106, emphasis in original).

Neo-imperialist impulses towards military conquest led to the creation of American bases in Trinidad and Tobago during the Second World War. According to the historian Stephen High, in *Base Colonies in the Western Hemisphere, 1940–1967*, the American intrusion into Trinidad was rife with conflict. Labour relations were conflictual: trade unions were up in arms about the low wages paid to Trinidadian workers, whose numbers swelled to as many as twenty-three thousand during base construction. In terms of social relations, there were numerous instances of American soldiers acting abusively, with instances of rape, assault and murder being attributed to "poor discipline and morale, poor leadership, and racism" (High 2009, 103). All of this was exacerbated, according to High, by the positioning of soldiers above the disciplinary ambit of local black police and militia. In the independence period, the first prime minister, Eric Williams, in the struggle for an early end to its ninety-nine-year lease, transformed Chaguaramas into an icon of British and American imperialism, and into what High, after French historian Pierre Nora, terms "a mythic site of national memory" which crystallized into a symbol of heroic resistance in the interests of re-appropriating the collective heritage of the newly independent people.

The actual and socio-symbolic impacts of the outworkings of the American occupation of Trinidad have been immortalized in yet another site of collective memory – the calypso, in its role as social barometer and oral and performative repository. The scenario was lamented by the people's philosophers, the lower-strata calypsonians, wearing the paradoxical guise of supplanted womanizers and protectors of public morals; they decried the women who put aside their dependence on fickle, irascible Trinidadian men for the more lucrative pursuit of offering sexual and escort services to American servicemen. The debacle, which has been immortalized in calypso by Lord Invader[2] in "Rum and Coca-Cola" and the Mighty Sparrow in "Jean and Dinah", generated broad-based social upheaval. Chariandy (2007, 179) spins his Alzheimer's narrative around the calypso:

> Rum and Coca-Cola,
> Go down Point Cumana,
> Both mother and daughter,
> Working for the Yankee Dollar . . .[3]

The notion of women being empowered by selling their bodies is unmasked to reveal the pain, humiliation and deleterious intergenerational impact of prostitution. A persistent underlying theme in the novel is the banal injustice of poverty and its resultant compromises.

Adding yet another level of encoded meanings to Chariandy's evocation of dementia is the governing trope of the soucouyant that gives the novel its name. Drawn from West African folkloric heritage, the soucouyant is a Caribbean version of the legendary female succubus or vampire. The most common legend is of an old woman, witch or *higue* who lives on the margin of the village and sheds her skin and is transformed into a ball of fire at night in order to suck the lifeblood of children and men. She leaves her victims with telltale bruises and wounds, as well as lassitude, apathy and weariness. Deployed in cautionary folktales to curtail nocturnal wanderings, the soucouyant, so the legend goes, can be stopped by salting her discarded skin so that it burns severely when she seeks to re-enter it; hence the woman dies from exposure at daybreak.

All these strands of meaning – historical, political, socio-symbolic, mythic, cultural – are relevant for decoding the re-cognition/repetition of signs which govern Adele's demented behaviours. The underlying traumatic catalyst occurs when the beautiful, dreamy young girl, at the incredible age of seven, takes a few halting steps towards prostituting herself with the American soldiers who have begun to reject her ageing mother's sexual services. The mother, driven to despair and near insanity by her growing inability to feed herself and her daughter, seeks to drag the girl off the base and away from potential contamination. A scene of public ridicule ensues in which a soldier drenches them with oil and filth. "It will never come out, Adele knows instantly. They will forever stink of something shat from the bowels of the earth and cooked in hell. They will never be clean again" (Chariandy 2007, 192). In extreme shame at this defilement, the child strikes a lighter she received from the soldier and sets her mother aflame. This is the submerged narrative which Adele cannot tell except in unrelated fragments – the initial insistence that she had seen the legendary soucouyant, and later, when she forgets to forget, incoherent allusions to fighter jets, the smells of the soldiers who visited her mother's home, the thin blue fire: "She told, but she never explained or deciphered. She never put the stories together. She never could or wanted to do so" (136). This incident, rooted in an excruciating corporeality, becomes the key which unlocks the meaning of the densely interrelated network of demented behaviours in the novel.

The initial assumption to come under assault as Adele seeks a new life in Canada as a domestic is that this overwhelming and engulfing shame can be relegated to the past. Adele migrates in pursuit of a dream of prosperity, to be attained by escaping the systemic which transfixes locations of extreme poverty and locations of economic ascendancy. She tries to lay hold of a narrative with which to appraise her new opportunity: "She is living the dream of countless people in her birthplace, *stuck back there* with the running sores of *their* histories" (Chariandy 2007, 51, my emphases). Grim experience belies her attempt to evade the long tentacles which link her to the catalyst of her trauma. Her eventual irrational practice of eating a "lightning shock" – a wedge of lemon, rind and all – is related to an incident which she endures in her early days as a young domestic in Canada. For months a lemon meringue pie beckons to her in a restaurant window before she finds the courage to enter to purchase a slice. There she is accosted first by a man seeking to buy her sexual services and subsequently by the owner, who explains softly that "no coloureds or prostitutes are allowed to eat here" (50). Memories of distant shame are overlaid on new defilements in the land of hope. Moreover, global inequities, the outworkings of which become viscerally embedded in the flesh and psyche, are not confined to fixed times and seasons; indeed, they pursue one into endless tomorrows.

The earliest manifestation of loss of cognitive functioning speaks to Adele's incapacity to keep that crippling incident at bay. Intrusive memory brings it into the present and shapes her odd habits. For example, turning on taps to let running water overflow kitchen sinks and bathtubs and seep through the ceiling is linked to the villager who cursed her for lingering at the well, as if the water could wash away the stink of her mother's prostitution. The constant flow of water symbolizes relief from crippling poverty, represented by the standpipe as opposed to the luxury of simply turning on a tap indoors to produce the precious flow. It also reflects Adele's endless compulsion to wash away the stink – her guilt and shame over prostitution. And the water is related to the soothing baptismal ritual in which the burned, wizened grandmother blesses the young boy chosen to be the carrier or storyteller of a horror so great that, to use Morrison's ambiguous formulation, it is "not a story to pass on". The alternative semiotic system, which the text trains the reader to interpret, figures these irrational behaviours, experienced overwhelmingly in the corporeal domain, as reflecting both the debased and dehumanizing and the redemptive.

Adele's early embrace of a mythological figure as an initial repository for a telling which she cannot articulate constitutes both an embrace and a distancing gone awry. Her recourse to mythology embraces a timeless ancestral symbology, with its quality of eternal relevance. Arguably, it foregrounds for both the character and the discerning reader the legendary association of the soucouyant with female sexual choice and independence, and age-old practices of exploiting and punishing women for their sexuality.[4] Conversely, the recourse to the legendary serves as a distancing device by intervening symbolically and representationally between the reader and the reality to be explored. The process bears comparison to the use of symbolic representation in literature to "distance the reader from the original psychic pain" and mimic "psychic dynamics of repression and dissociation" (Di Prete 2006, 5). Yet both post-traumatic stress disorder and Alzheimer's disease bring an incapacity to discern reality from fantasy, past from present, legendary from real, by damaging the capacity for symbolization and metaphorization. The symbol thereby loses its metaphorical capacity to obscure and distance the event and takes on the tincture of its own haunting reality. Arguably, this collapse of figuration is a very necessary dimension of the telling.

The central issue with the deployment of symbolization in trauma narratives is that it borrows from a pool of shared meanings which cannot convey what it has come to mean in the mindscape of the traumatized. Applied literally, there is a vast gulf fixed between understanding the legendary figuration as rendered by the narrator – "A soucouyant is something like a female vampire" (Chariandy 2007, 135) – and the existential experience of setting one's mother afire, thus making her look like a soucouyant. The imperative of transcending the metaphorical is so urgent that the unnamed narrator (the youngest son) must himself see his demented mother drooling blood at the front door after attacking her gums vigorously with a toothbrush, must inhale the stink of burning and internalize the ear-splitting screaming: "just a ringing which comes from my own head before growing into a horror barely connected with this woman's gaping mouth" (130). The soucouyant also comes to represent for the narrator – who, like the author, was born in Canada of Trinidadian immigrants – a mixed-race mother and a dark-skinned South Asian father, spectral presences of the past which haunt the tincture, feeling and sensibility of the present without ever coming to articulation. The mother in her dementia becomes a soucouyant that threatens to suck the life energies of her son, yet it is in confronting this most extreme duty of care that he locates and enters into connection with the maternal body, the island body, and ultimately the deep recesses of his own being.

It is crucial then that the metaphorical soucouyant of the narrative should be seen, touched, smelt and known as a flesh-and-blood presence. Hence the young mother takes her four- or five-year-old son home to Trinidad to visit his grandmother:

> She was a monster. Someone with a hide, red-cracked eyes, and blistered hands. Someone who would claw her stiffened thumb across her eyes and try to smile through the ruin of her mouth. Someone who knows very well the terror it could bring to a young boy like me, and who was careful not to brush too closely near, or bring her attention too forcefully towards me. That gesture of consideration somehow the most terrible thing of all. (Chariandy 2007, 116)

This wizened, scarred creature, who signifies for the reader the ravaging of the island body in inequitable transnational concourse, becomes for the boy a far more intimate nightmare. The child records and resonates without having any way of knowing or understanding the horror of the traumatic event which is indelibly inscribed on the scarred body – an ultimately undeniable material record. The monstrosity of this body is intensified when the grandmother demonstrates understanding and compassion, which hinders any attempt to dismiss the spectre as less than human. The visit and the grandmother, which survive as a faded photograph of a small boy perched on the lap of a monster, embody dread meanings which cannot be leached away in a sea of symbols. Although, throughout the entire narrative, the meanings of the experience are never fully articulated by those who experienced it, it inhabits their flesh and is passed on intergenerationally in a multiplicity of ways. Indeed, in the absence of confrontation and assimilation, it becomes crucial that the experience be embodied anew in another generation. The narrator, then a child of four or five, was not able to take in the horror of what he had seen, touched and smelt. He is left with his own haunting fragments of memory – of touching his grandmother's trick tendon, which he has inherited and which makes his lineage indisputable, and of pumping water from the well in a feverish attempt to wash away the unarticulated re-cognition passed on through touch.

The entirety of the re-cognition must await the onset of Alzheimer's. The mother's cues, far from being pointless insanities, become signposts for her location in the land of forgetting to forget, in which she has taken up residence. She selects her son to take with her on the pilgrimage and to become her mouthpiece for telling of a trauma she could not pass on. The knowledge recovered is not simply of personal trauma. It is of the injustice of ejecting villagers and communities from their lands for the sake of the government lease; it is memories of healing herbs and ritual practices, of foods and names and folklore, all of which locate a people in space and time and culture.

The feverish passage of this knowledge from mother to son must be executed before her death, to ensure continuity and self-knowledge in the land of their migration. The effectiveness of the transmission is reflected in subtle shifts in narrative perspective, which convey the notion that long before the full knowledge rises to human consciousness and articulation, the visceral sensations and the crippling shame have been conveyed. Hence the son is not named in the narrative, because the mother has forgotten his name. For the duration of the text he lives the unhomeliness of being poised between her forgetting and her forgetting to forget. When he bathes her and she immediately thereafter defecates on herself, it is he who relives the olfactory stink of the traumatizing catalyst, which in a sense she releases from her body to effect a transfer to his: "When I return upstairs with the cocoa it is to an odour that shouldn't ever emanate from a human body. An evil, metallic assault. She's soiled herself again and she's standing in a corner of her room with liquid clots running down her legs, her face breaking" (Chariandy 2007, 84). And it becomes significant that upon her death he should mourn her bodily absence as a site of memory, passing on the abuse to his own flesh by gorging and discarding mountains of food in bulimic excess. By the end of the narrative, the knowledge must be settled deeply into his bones. Significantly, he finds himself in a matrilineage revealed through a quarrel in the bones – an inherited maiming of the flesh, as deep and inescapable as history. This is the location and the vantage point from which he must speak.

What, then, does the unnamed protagonist achieve? The narrator instructs on the perils of forgetting, despite the initial amnesiac retreat from horror too great to bear; how to bear the collective history of shame; how to rise above the chorus of belittlement and self-concealment, which exacts a terrible cost. The narrator negotiates the grim reality and emerges with a measure of wholeness and sensitivity at the end. He is shadowed by his brother the poet, who runs away and stays swallowed in the vast anonymity of the metropolis, in his own deranged scribbles grappling vaguely with the spectral lurking horror but unable to articulate it and thereby to tame its impact on the psyche. The narrator rescues the traumatic event out of oblivion by filling in the sociohistorical framework behind an apparition which the mother can initially appropriate only through the legendary representation of the soucouyant. One can assume that Adele is incapable of going beyond haunting personal guilt for the great wrong she did her mother. It is left to the narrator to contextualize the traumatizing event within broader transhistorical and transnational contexts: the neo-imperial will to power exerted by proximate superpowers, appropriation of lands, displacements of cultures and ways of life, institutionalized poverty. These all locate the trauma where it rightfully belongs – at the crossroads where the personal intersects with the communal, the cultural and the historical. The telling remains to the end hard-won. The unnamed narrator comes to bear within his body the scars of the unjust labour practices of Canadian manufacturing industries, narrowly escaping the fate of his father, whose insides are being corroded by industrial chemicals when he meets his death, caused by his daredevil antics in an unsafe factory environment.

    Both novels are appeals for a way to be human, for a process which honours the humanity of the person beyond a season of social usefulness, and for a deeper understanding of the frailty, vulnerability and interconnectivity of mankind. Redemptive patterns are woven throughout Chariandy's narrative: the coconut bake and cocoa tea offered by the old woman to the starving mother and child survive as favourite winter foods in the new land, and as exemplary of cultural assertiveness in palates which refuse to be overtaken by foreign tastes. The water, which must flow continually to wash away shame, becomes a baptismal healing, easing the psychic pain of persons scarred for life by fire. Trick tendons, manifestations of quarrels deep in the bones, like history, pass from generation to generation, reflecting corporeal lineage and inheritance which travel in the flesh to serve as methods of re-cognition, even when the mind is marred and the body is disfigured beyond resemblance.

    By the ends of both novels, the internal and external tumults are resolved and there is peace. Lalla asserts overwhelmingly the power of love and being that transcends intentionality and doing, leaving a self that responds to sensual fragments, because indeed, the senses outlive the mind:

> The vanishing past and contracting future have taken with them all resentment, mourning and anxiety... The dimensions of the world are disentangled to a seamless presence of loved ones, that palm against this palm, a lingering wisdom of counsel and forgiveness, a mainstay of humour. Time, shattered and reconfigured to crowd past and future away before the infinite present, leaves only patience, the joy in an aroma of spice a texture of soft fabric a safety of roots a discernment of guavas and the relief of owning nothing, of power surrendered, of presence in beloved company and of simply and intensely being without having to do, yet not a second wasting. A riddle in time, is it – this diffusing, persisting consciousness? (Lalla 2010, 299)

In Chariandy's narrative, transcendence is figured in the simplest of gestures, which the young child files in his memory as an enduring signal of forgiveness and mutuality: the two women, mother and daughter, with hands joined, helping each other over the rocks. It is not an easy resolution because that memory predates the gruelling life journey and ascent into the abyss of Alzheimer's disease, yet it remains the last word. And the last word on the matter speaks peace.

7

"NAKED WITH UNKNOWING"
Childhood Trauma and the Unmaking of Self

> Exiled upon this ledge
> I stand
> Naked with unknowing,
> Facing winds that blow
> hurricanes within me.
>
> Standing as I was held
> (their world beginning where
> mine ended)
> shrivelled, wet and crying –
> Mama why did you expel me,
> Left me abandoned upon this
> ledge of
> beginning?
> – Jennifer Rahim, "Beginning"

CHILDHOOD IS CELEBRATED GLOBALLY as the locus of new beginnings. Its joys, powers and potencies seem boundless, as do its dependencies and vulnerabilities. It is the site at which human civilizations renew themselves, nascent possibilities bloom, lurking violations spread their tentacles anew. Scholarship on the impact of psychic trauma in childhood has lagged behind investigations of adult trauma. It is nevertheless emerging as significant because of the practical need to create interventions for children traumatized by numerous catalysts, including the homicide of a parent, kidnapping, natural disaster, war or divorce. Moreover, there is growing recognition of the potential impact of early childhood trauma and its aftermath on the developmental stages and processes which children must negotiate to arrive at healthy adulthood.

The child has consistently figured in Caribbean fictions of development as a metaphor for the becoming of new nations in the wake of colonization. The emergent subject, emblematic of burgeoning sensibility and personhood, must struggle through a morass of racism, denigration, cultural loss and alienation from ancestral and natal social and physical landscapes, all of which fuse to create a sickness of sensibility which has now come to be widely associated with the colonial condition. Through a reading of Olive Senior's "Bright Thursdays", which deals with the common social practice of child-shifting, this chapter locates a representative Caribbean child as caught up in the outworking of a vortex of historical, communal and personal violations. It poses questions on the process by which the violations that lie at the root of the Caribbean social order evolve, transmute and transmit themselves intergenerationally, and the epistemological significance of psychic trauma in children, given the vulnerabilities of the nascent subject in formation, and its impact on their worldview and sense of being, as well as their meagre attempts to rescue a shattered self and a shattered worldview in the aftermath of trauma.

The current Caribbean social scenario offers an astounding range of trauma narratives from which to draw for a study of this nature. One fascinating source is media discourse on the horrific range of crimes which are being perpetrated against children. Consider this case in point: Whereas in current reportage of crime against women in Trinidad and Tobago there is a clear trend towards lurid representation of beaten and damaged victims in distress, in the case of violence against children it is as if this horror is too great for visual representation (Morgan 2010; Youssef 2011). Accompanying their reports of children unceremoniously gunned down in their innocence because they were living in or near neighbourhoods riddled with gang violence, newspapers consistently display either scenes of excessive grief at funerals juxtaposed with pictures of dead children with angelic faces, surrounded by stuffed toys and flowers, or of happy, smiling, physically healed children being cuddled by – apparently – the most loving of parents and caregivers. Salient questions emerge (or are being masked) about the psychic damage which is being done to children, the nature of these representations and the role of the media in terms of bearing witness.

Fictional examples abound, with diverse nuances and significations: from the physically and verbally abused children of Naipaul's *A House for Mr Biswas* to the sexually abused and gagged Mala Ramchandin (Shani Mootoo's *Cereus Blooms at Night*), Dionne Brand's raped child transmuted into disturbed wife ("Sans Souci") and Harold Sonny Ladoo's severely brutalized children adrift in a hostile post-indentureship social and physical landscape (*No Pain Like This Body*). This study deliberately turns away from numerous examples of heinous acts of abuse against children in favour of a focus on the violence of everyday existence and its deleterious impact as experienced in the (un) making of self. It focuses on a fictional evocation of the common practice of child-shifting, that is, the placing of children in the informal care of relatives or non-relatives, which emerges in this case as a traumatizing catalyst with potentially disastrous outcomes.

Contemporary child-shifting in the Caribbean is an adaptation of the practice of shared and communal childrearing, a fundamental legacy of the ancestral cultures of both Africa and India; it was transmuted in the Caribbean to deal with the exigencies of enforced and bonded labour scenarios. The enslaved and indentured were made to be first and foremost labourers; their children were cogs for imperialist mills. Michelle Cliff, in "The Land of Look Behind" (1990), mourns this condition in retrospect. Spurred by a touristic visit to a tiny watch house – a structure poised on the edge of the cane fields in which older enslaved women, past their prime as field labourers, looked after the babies of nursing younger field workers – Cliff's disoriented and overwhelmed persona seeks to anchor herself by throwing into the pregnant, unspeakable void a series of unanswerable questions which resonate with her sadness, anger and loss:

> What did their voices sound like?
> What tongues? What words for day and night?
> Hunger? Milk?
> What songs devised to ease them?
> Was there time to speak? To sing?
> ...
> To bring down Shàngó's wrath.
> How many gums daubed with rum to soothe the teething or bring on sleep?

> How many breasts bore scars?
> Not the sacred markings of the Carib –
> but the mundane mark of the beast.
> (Cliff 1990, 68–69)

Cliff's lament speaks to the disruption of intimacies, loss of moorings in mothering, paternity, mother tongue, ancestral faiths. Her questions probe shadowy violations and attendant responses – scars and even the progeny of routine, ritualized sexual violence and early recourse to rum as anaesthetic and opiate, impotence, and rage. The unanswered enquiries speak to the unrepresentable nature of their suffering and the challenges of seeking in retrospect to voice the pain of the erased and silenced.

The radical disruption of ancient childbearing practices spawned child-shifting as one of its adaptive responses. The informal arrangement may include the promise – often far more than the practice – of financial support and the establishment of a set duration during which the child may be collected or "sent for from foreign" to be restored to parental care. Traditionally this practice was ideologically undergirded by deeply held convictions about collective responsibility for childrearing and communal well-being which are losing currency today. Child-shifting survives in contemporary times as a reaction to a complex of factors, including early childbearing by single mothers, male psychic and economic inability and/or reluctance to assume conjugal and paternal responsibility, marriage of a woman who was previously a single mother, and migration of one or both parents in the quest for a better life. The historical underpinnings of Caribbean society and its contemporary grim socioeconomic realities combine to create an overdetermined location for migration in the Caribbean imaginary. A 2009 UNICEF study identifies children who have been left behind due to migration as being vulnerable to a range of children's rights violations: "They face risks of abuse, including sexual abuse, and suffer from psychosocial problems and educational accomplishments due to parental migration. Their psychosocial well-being is greatly impacted by feelings of abandonment, low self esteem, anger, depression, material obsession and violence" (Bakker et al. 2009, 8).

A substantial cross-section of Caribbean persons, including Olive Senior, who engages this issue from a range of perspectives, have been brought up under informal child-sharing arrangements. Senior, who speaks of a childhood spent shuttling between a dark-skinned village environment and a light-skinned socially privileged environment, has also engaged the underlying causal factors of child-shifting from a sociological vantage point. In *Working Miracles: Women's Lives in the English-Speaking Caribbean* (1991), Senior indicates that "only one-quarter of the region's children are born into what conforms to the nuclear family". The majority are raised in households defined as "a group of people residing under one roof and sharing at least one meal a day, who may or may not be family" (8). Some 50 per cent of Caribbean households are headed by women. Making reference to Edith Clarke's seminal 1950s study of Jamaican rural communities – titled *My Mother Who Fathered Me* after George Lamming's famous allusion in *In the Castle of My Skin* – Senior concludes: "The paradigm of absent father and omniscient mother is central to the ordering and psyche of the Caribbean family" (1991, 8).

Based on a 1970s survey by G. Roberts and S.A. Sinclair, *Working Miracles* estimates that about 15 per cent of the population under the age of fifteen has been shifted. Senior's story "Country of the One-Eyed God" (1986b) features a young male whose disappointed hopes, year after year, that his parents will send for him "in foreign" are in no small measure responsible for his descent into anger, aggression and criminal activity. He threatens his grandmother with violence and perhaps murder to persuade her to part with her carefully accumulated burial money, emerging as emblematic of a dangerous counter-hegemonic masculinity which recognizes no call of duty to family and community, and certainly no allegiance or duty of care to an ageing, disempowered matriarchy, whose herculean effort and authority have in the past kept together blood and fictive kinship networks in the face of extreme poverty and plague, disaster and, most significantly in this case, migration. (For a fuller discussion, see Morgan 2004).

This is not to imply that child-shifting is always an unmitigated disaster. Senior, making reference to Erna Brodber's research for the Women in the Caribbean Project, cites Brodber's appraisal that the region's child-rearing practices, and especially that of child-shifting, with its " 'lack of fixed emotional centres', do encourage independence since they require adjustments of the emotional self and help to develop flexibility in dealing with the world . . . It develops in women emotional expansiveness as reflected in their ability to make room for children who are not their own" (Senior 1991, 24). Arguably though, Senior posits that said practices can "also create feelings of anomie, of displacement, of anger, of worthlessness, of guilt which can consume a great deal of creative energy as children struggle to rebuild wounded psyches" (24).

The former scenario finds real-life expression in my own upbringing in my maternal grandfather's family, in which the deaths of my mother and grandmother within one week of each other and the conspicuous absence of my father left me enriched, with a great-aunt as primary caregiver, a distant grandfather/provider and no fewer than six other mothers/aunts, each of whom brought value to a rich, though challenging and eclectic, upbringing. The nature of the experience was such that as an adult I was amazed to be referred to as an orphan. Never once had I considered myself to be orphaned. In fictional terms, Merle Hodge's *For the Life of Laetitia* (1994) presents a best-case example of child-shifting, while Senior's "Bright Thursdays" (1986a) does not present such a happy outcome. For the close reading which follows, I deliberately select the relatively mild and innocuous upbringing experienced by Laura, the protagonist of "Bright Thursdays", which exemplifies how complex the overlapping determinants of childhood trauma can be .

The forces which threaten to overwhelm the protagonist of Olive Senior's "Bright Thursdays" (1986a) are embedded in overlapping spatio-geographical, cultural and personal histories. Born as the result of a casual sexual encounter between a black maid and a brown gentleman of means and social standing, Laura is groomed by her mother for elevation to the social stature of her father's world. Socialized by her mother to believe that she is better than her restricted country world and her peers, the child finds herself shifted into the wealth and privilege of her father's house, where she occupies a liminal position, hovering between bastard child of the house and informal unpaid child helper whose business it is to dust the family photos, among which her image cannot be legitimately represented.[1] This script plays out the deeply entrenched historical practices of privileged males routinely using enslaved and other labouring women for sexual services, and the women in turn using the children of such unions as leverage for personal and/or intergenerational upward mobility. In the interests of upward mobility, Laura is shifted from her mother's house into her father's household and the care of her kindly patrician grandparents. This exploration reads this relatively benign scenario as the catalyst of deeply rooted childhood trauma. The brief text stands as emblematic of fictional evocations of child-shifting specifically triggered by notions that the child's socially desirable phenotype is evidence that she is destined for an exalted social position. The golden-skinned Hortense of Andrea Levy's *Small Island* (2004) is another case in point.

Childhood Trauma and the Unmaking of Self

Extreme need and vulnerability can make the world a potentially risky place for children. Medical researcher Bruce D. Perry, in his study "Trauma and Terror in Childhood: The Neuropsychiatric Impact of Childhood Trauma" (2000), indicates that whereas moderate and controlled levels of stress in childhood – when balanced by a safe and secure environment and the presence of loving caregivers – develops healthy resilience in children and readiness for the stresses of adulthood, severe, prolonged and chronic stress is extremely dangerous for children. Defining stress as "any challenge or condition that forces the regulating physiological and neurophysiological systems to move outside of their normal activity", he indicates that "severe, unpredictable, prolonged or chronic stress can cause the compensatory mechanism to become" overactivated, fatigued and incapable of restoring the previous state of balance or equilibrium. An event becomes traumatic when it "overwhelms the organism and dramatically and negatively reorganizes the basal pattern of equilibrium" (Perry 2000, 1–2).

Spencer Eth and Robert S. Phynos, in "Developmental Perspectives on Psychic Trauma in Childhood" (1985), examine forty children – of preschool age, school age and adolescence – who have witnessed the homicide of a parent. They cite the applicability of DSM-III criteria of PTSD to children who have been physically abused, kidnapped and even bitten by a dog. Eth and Phynos conclude that the "symptoms, presentation and content of a post-traumatic stress disorder may vary according to age" (Eth and Phynos 1985, 37). Younger children, because of their helplessness and dependence, are more inclined to dissociative responses such as detachment, numbness and compliance, whereas older children are more inclined to hyperarousal responses such as hypervigilance, anxiety, hyperreactivity, flight and panic.

Presentation of the symptoms and content of post-traumatic stress disorder in children has also been shown to vary based on the duration of exposure to the catalyst. A single occurrence of even a severely traumatizing event is often forgotten by young children because the brain, as it develops, can dispose of the synaptic connections which are responsible for disturbing memory. In the case of multiple recurrences, an increased number of these synapses groove themselves into the brain even if they are not accessible as recoverable memory (Perry 2000). Traumas experienced in childhood set up a haunting presence which can in turn influence attitudes, worldview, perceptions, thoughts, sensitivities and actions. Childhood traumas often intrude through some form of visualization and through cycles of repetition. They shape trauma-specific fears and anxieties and alter worldview and prospects in relation to the future. Traumatic memories, even when they occur in detail, are not reliable. They morph such that an early childhood trauma can overlay fantasies; for example, an operating theatre experience, with its mechanistic stainless-steel paraphernalia, can present as a memory of a spaceship abduction (Perry 2000).

Theorists have identified two distinct legacies of psychic trauma. Trauma destroys not only the individual's sense of well-being, trust, safety, self-esteem and purpose. The traumatized self is unmade, but so is the victim's worldview.[2] According to Karyn Freedman, "These are the twin sides of surviving sexual violence: a shattered self and a shattered world view. Whereas the former is a statement about ourselves, the latter is a statement about the world and our beliefs about it – the cognitive place" (Freedman 2006, 107). The traumatized person's universe becomes hostile and indifferent, a terrifying entity in which the boundaries between a nightmarish waking reality and a horrifically real dreaming reality are blurred. The haunting belatedness of trauma makes nonsense of the socially accepted boundaries, spatiotemporal parameters and security quotient which normatively order the world, as reflected in notions of past and present, here and there, threatening and nonthreatening, waking and dreaming.

The perspectives on childhood trauma summarized above provide an appropriate frame for reading the common and relatively benign childhood experience of Senior's "Bright Thursdays". The third-person narrative voice tells of the child's initial though naive sense of utter safety, security and belonging in her village deep in Cockpit Country, enclosed by towering mountains which represent to the burgeoning child's consciousness a safe and hospitable womb for nurturing the nascent self.³ The traumatizing catalysts are triggered nevertheless, first in her mother's house, where, though habituated to and comfortable with its basic cultural practices, she is displaced early by difference occasioned by her racialized embodiment.

Fundamental to the psychic homelessness of the child is the ongoing centrality of race as a determinant of belonging and upward mobility in Caribbean society. The pain, torture and non-belonging which Laura experiences are rooted in a historically based trauma of racism, as it shapes the social practices of the time period of the narrative and as it is imprinted on a sensitive and vulnerable child. This feature of identity politics in the Caribbean, though clearly articulated in academic and popular culture discourses, remains paramount, though heavily masked, in day-to-day social relations. Race ideology was perpetrated within the colonial value system to secure the privilege of the dominant race and their access to a guaranteed pool of labouring bodies, constructed as destined to occupy menial positions based on racialized embodiment. This entrenched ideology fuels the mother's deep conviction that her daughter's phenotypical features lift her out of the prescribed social location for black women as productive, reproductive and sex labourers and destine her for the pampered position made possible by "browning", that is, "high brown" women in the exalted social echelons of her father's house. For clearly, a child with "such long curly hair, with such a straight nose, with such soft skin (too bad it was so dark) was surely destined for a life of ease and comfort" (Senior 1986a, 39).

Senior's narrative resonates with an ongoing real-world problematic. Notions of race-identified belonging are layered on and often masked as more socially acceptable class aspirations. What mother is not to be commended for seeking to place her child on a pathway to mobility which leads her offspring away from her own disadvantageous social location? There is a similarly narrow line between isolating the child from her community and protecting her from its sexual predators and risky patterns of gender relations, which could place her on the same slippery pathway traversed by the mother – early pregnancy, single parenthood, financial insecurity, underdevelopment and back-breaking labour to support her brood.⁴ Racialized embodiment, with its inherent practices of shaming and its attendant network of systemic inclusions and exclusions, when internalized creates an inescapable skin that does not fit dis-ease. The external displacement and inability to find a space in which to thrive are a mere projection of the internal malaise.

The story sets up the contrastive spatial frameworks. The child, seeking to negotiate a viable and nurturing selfhood, is poised between what is acceptable in her father's house and in her mother's house: "But even though others kept pushing her, and she tried to ease, to work her way into that space too, she sometimes felt that Life had played tricks, and there was, after all, no space allotted for her. For how else could she explain this discomfort, this pain it caused her *in this her father's house* to confront even the slightest event. Such as sitting at table and eating a meal. *In her mother's house* . . . A meal was something as natural as breathing" (Senior 1986a, 37, emphases added). Spatial dichotomy between the father's and mother's houses is emblematic of the divergent worlds the child is expected to negotiate. She is to migrate from the casualness of a country upbringing, which is devoid of the extensive range of social prescriptions that grip the Jamaican upper strata – legacies of stringent colonial rituals – with threats of discipline and judgement hanging over one's head should one lapse at "table manners", which are vital if one is "going to get somewhere" (38).

The spatial dichotomy of the mother's and father's houses, with their divergent cultural traditions, readily collapses at the level of ideals. Although the practices, social graces and income levels may be different, the values of the respective houses are not. Both the mother and the paternal grandmother are intent that Laura should become upwardly mobile, and they collude to impose a series of socializing practices that prove to be yet another traumatizing catalyst for the protagonist. Laura is psychically abused, first by her well-meaning mother's insistence on her difference, which becomes a basis for isolating her from the commonness of her environment. Subsequently she is abused by her paternal grandmother's efforts to clothe this difference in the appropriate social guise and to change her behaviours in order to ensure her access to a privileged social position. The task which the child confronts is an ongoing and contradictory (un)making of selves. Both caregivers – mother and grandmother – tacitly agree that the child's racial embodiment, which positions her as privileged to the former and disadvantaged to the latter, establishes a platform for social engineering based on their divergent perceptions of her raced body. As the child is constrained to assume and strip off multiple modes of being, she experiences an increasing cognitive dissonance between her interior experiencing self and her emerging social selves in interface with her multiple world. Her natural exuberance and spontaneity are initially stamped out by her mother's assertion that she is different and, hence, not to be what her immediate social environment would produce. Laura's early response to the daily onslaught is silencing and numbing dissociation, which the mother misreads as even greater evidence of her "natural" refinement.

In her father's house, Laura faces an even more stringent range of regulatory discourses and the requirement to adopt yet another range of dissimulating practices – societal norms, codes and injunctions to stage herself as an upwardly mobile socially situated body which is migrating away from lower-class habits and mentalities, towards the fringe of a social class to which she can never fully belong. This requirement laid on the child, to interpellate herself into an alternative mode of being by appropriating layers of alienating social accretions, generates deep-rooted anxieties. The reality is that performing an upwardly mobile, "non-niggery" identity both opens psychic fissures in the already damaged self and moves her farther away from a socially located nurturing world and worldview which could conceivably generate healing and coherence. Rendered increasingly incapable of speech by intense shyness and desire for erasure of her unwholesome accent, her skin colour and even her presence, Laura becomes a mousy, silent, haunting ghost in her father's house.

Labelled as "Bertram's stray shot" by family members in the know, traumatized by her inability to find a place and an acceptable presence, Laura in turn embodies trauma's belated intrusive, ghastly presence, which disorients and disturbs the consciousness of those around her. To her kindly old patrician grandparents, she represents the intrusion of insidious and shaming blackness in bloodlines which the family has laboured for generations to nullify and erase. She represents the shadowy lineages of miscegenation which lurk in the background of practically every Caribbean family and are particularly problematic for those who self-identify as Euro-creoles and whose self-valuation and societal standing hinge on an assumed "purity of bloodlines", garnered through proximity to uplifting white ancestors and distance from denigrating black ones. The reader is disallowed access to Laura's father's consciousness, but one can only assume that she haunts him too, as tangible evidence of his subset of entrenched patterns of unquenchable interracial desires, shady acts and shameless parental neglect. Most of all, Laura haunts herself, as an unwholesome, unwelcome dark, shaming presence which she would rather not have to come to terms with and of which she cannot rid herself.

Laura's quest, then, is for a narrative – a story to tell herself about the selves she is becoming. She longs to speak her pain and to call forth a language which would facilitate healing, and this within a social context which does not readily facilitate frank discussion of painful emotional issues. In keeping with Eth and Phynos's finding of children's age-specific responses to trauma, Laura resorts to fantasies which alter the outcome of the trauma, which is precisely the response the researchers attribute to school-age children. Fantasy becomes the psychic flight response for young children whose physical vulnerability, small size and impotence militate against fight. When her father returns to the family home with his American wife, Laura reverts to the fairytale paradigm imbibed from the mother, that tough, resilient, self-reliant woman who paradoxically retains an enduring faith in the culturally sanctioned fantasy fiction of rescue: namely, a knight in shining armour will turn up and rescue his damsels in distress from the ignominy of poverty, drudgery, low self-esteem and rejection. Above all, the child longs to be recognized by her father. "For all the woman's attentions, it was the man that she wanted to attend her, acknowledge her, love her" (Senior 1986a, 52). The quest for a place in the father's house is supplanted by a quest for a place in the father's heart, which would settle once and for all questions of ancestry, lineage and patriarchal favour and protection. In response to the father's coldness and evasion, she fabricates a romantic plot, an elaborate secret plan for a sudden meeting and melting into love and acceptance within a perfect setting and a perfect moment. The brusque, decisive rejection of the father – he calls her a "bloody little bastard" – puts a stop to all such fantasies.

Senior's narrative is linked to yet another narrative of homecoming, welcome, rescue and salvation. The network of dominant motifs in "Bright Thursdays" links it to the promise of Jesus Christ: "In my father's house are many mansions. . . . I go to prepare a place for you. And if I go and prepare a place for you I will come again and receive you to myself that where I am there you may be also" (NKJV John 14:2–3). Laura's longing for her father is paralleled by the promise of the divine embrace. If he received her unto himself, he would thereby deliver her and secure her place eternally in her father's house. Laura's traumatized state comes to the fore in a mild form of agoraphobia – in this case a fear of open spaces which leads to her fear of bright Thursdays. Even prior to the return of the earthly father, Laura develops a fear of clouds which rises to fever pitch on bright Thursdays, when her customary school transport – a bus groaning under the weight of market vendors – regularly breaks down. Here too the depths of her fear are related to submerged historical violations. A child of Cockpit Country, Laura has grown up sheltered, protected, cradled by towering mountains. These are the "mossy coverts, dim and cool" which Erna Brodber has numbered among her many kumblas – safe and protective environments which nevertheless have the potential to become stultifying. And these mountains originally sheltered the Maroons – aggressive autonomous communities of runaway slaves. To travel to her father's house, Laura must leave this nurturing womb of space and traverse through the primary site of enforced labour and cultural denigration to a house set high on a hill, a fitting location for those who fancy themselves gatekeepers for hegemonic ideologies and masters of all they survey:

> They were hemmed in by the mountains on all sides and Laura liked it, because all her life was spent in space that was enclosed and infinite, protecting her from what dangers she did even not know.
>
> And then, from the moment she had journeyed to the railway station some ten miles away and got on the train it had begun to travel through the endless canefields, she had begun to feel afraid. For suddenly the skies opened up so wide all around her; the sun beat down and there was the endless noisy clacking of the train wheels. She felt naked and anxious, as if suddenly exposed, and there was nowhere to hide. (Senior 1986a, 45)

The fear that creeps into her, for reasons which she cannot access, is a visceral response to oppressions she has never experienced, meted out in a place which she has never seen. The fear is stirred by submerged fragments of ancestral memory, which latch on to her as she leaves the site of resistance in the sheltering Cockpit Country and traverses the site of oppression: cane fields watered with the sweat, tears and blood of her ancestors. She takes up residence in a site of ascendancy into which she cannot fit and which serves to foreground her liminality straddling two worlds, both of which have been rendered alien and alienating. Psychically naked on the open plain and exposed to the fat cumulus clouds, she fantasizes that God himself is looking upon her in judgement while riding on the clouds, which she has always associated with the second coming of Jesus.

Laura's traumatized sensibility delivers her into the grip of an emotional response which is related to neither her cognitive state nor the external reality. The external reality is that she is safe. She is accustomed to walking long distances. She feels envious of the freedom and camaraderie enjoyed by children who dawdle and play in the dust as they walk to school daily. Indeed, her coping strategies impair her development of social functionality among her peers, presaging long-term ill adjustment. Her irrational fear response is related to a fragile and tenuous sense of being in a hostile universe which is frowning in judgement at her dark and shameful embodiment. Freedman argues that in dealing with traumatized persons it is not germane to seek to persuade them of the irrationality of their response: "It is as though there is a traumatized part of our body that stores the experience of the trauma, and when something triggers that part, because it is not *itself* a cognitive place, no form of *rational* persuasion can effectively mitigate it" (Freedman 2006, 110).

What, then, is the nature of the resolution implied in the final passage of the narrative, after the father erupts?

> "Oh for chrissake. Why don't you stop fussing so much about the bloody little bastard" . . . Laura heard no more for after one long moment when her heart somersaulted once there was no more time for hearing anything else for her feet of their own volition had set off at a run down the road and by the time she got to the school gate she had made herself an orphan and there were no more clouds. (Senior 1986a, 53)

Despite the presence of parents and grandparents, we are told that she has in that run made herself an orphan and her fear of clouds has been resolved. Laura's dawdling was associated with flight and fantasy responses. Her sudden bolt into "no more clouds" reflects a shift into hyperarousal and fight responses. Hyperarousal, devoid of recognizable cognitive stimuli, can haunt victims of trauma for decades. On one level, the final line of the narrative does bring resolution. The cognitive dissonance is resolved: the clouds of illusion, shadows and fantasy have lifted. Laura no longer believes in or expects to find a nurturing, sheltering, protective world and family within which she will be loved into wholeness and security. Her cognitive perception is now aligned with her experiential existence. The lack of dissonance brings her closer to the truth of her reality but does not in any way relieve her psychic distress. Orphaned, she is thrown back on her flimsy, underdeveloped impotence to make her way in the world. In fact it creates another dissonance, given the great fortune of her grandparents' patronage, which would ensure her upward mobility. Externally she is an intelligent, well-educated child brimming over with "broughtupcy", which is her passport to higher social echelons. Internally she is bruised, broken, rejected, terrorized, fearful and – barring drastic intervention – bound for a long future of psychic unease and unbelonging. Before the coming of the father, Laura began with a shattered self, but in the wake of the father's coming and rejection, she is also burdened with a shattered worldview.

Senior's "Bright Thursdays" does a significant service in her sustained focus on the impact of the absentee father on the making of the nascent female self. This is the flipside of the cultural significance of the widely acclaimed and ideologically saturated Caribbean mother-woman, and the corresponding imperative for women writers of the Caribbean to offer literary genuflection to the mammoth works of maternal sacrifice that were necessary to deliver the new nations of the Caribbean to where they are today. The required tribute is reflected in the towering representations of Merle Hodge's *Crick Crack, Monkey* (1970) and *For the Life of Laetitia* (1994), as well as Lorna Goodison's "I Am Becoming My Mother" (1986). The conversely terrible mother emerges as the murderer of her homosexual son in Patricia Powell's *A Small Gathering of Bones* (1994), and both the nurturing earth mother and the terrible mother manage an uneasy marriage in Kincaid's fiction.[5] Female-authored fictions are only now beginning to deal with the impact of the denial of paternity and/or the absentee father on the sensibility of the young girl. Stacyann Chin's *The Other Side of Paradise* (2009) is a case in point.

This chapter identifies "Bright Thursdays" as a trauma narrative in the full knowledge that trauma narratives by definition speak to experiential states which cannot be fully mediated through discourses. The ending, which is typical of Senior's narratives, is open-ended and inconclusive. We search for clues as to where we leave Laura at the end of the text. What narrative can she conceivably invent in order to survive? What resources can she draw upon in order to construct a coherent mode of being in order to face a now recognizably hostile and inimical world?

Of significance to this enquiry into the material and psychic location of children in the Caribbean are the following assertions. The child depends on family, community and society for projecting a valid sense of being in the world. The psychological fitness and well-being of the child pivot on the health, balance and well-being of the community from which she emerges and in relation to which she is being socialized. The historical traumas rooted at the inception of modern Caribbean society have imparted transgenerational legacies which impact the wholeness and well-being of children down to the present time; epistemic violence generated by race, gender and class politics as the triangulated locus for fixing the value of the human person has not been adequately addressed. Indeed, these forces remain firmly entrenched in the value systems, hopes and aspirations of many families and communities. Race plays a pivotal role in this regard. At the cognitive level, the assumption of valuing the human person based on race has been effectively exposed for the irrational and foolish fiction that it is. At the psychic level, it is so deeply ingrained in the collective psyche that it retains a compelling grip on the social order. Like a collective haunting it lurks, often unnamed, to crop up repeatedly, shattering the self and the worldview of young persons from generation to generation. Trauma, notwithstanding the tangibility and enormity of its external catalyst, assaults and undermines the subjectivity of the child from within. This reading demonstrates how the child in the Caribbean can be routinely assaulted by ungraspable violations from within which undermine at a tender age his potential to construct an internally consistent narrative of self.

8

"RUM TILL I DIE"
Discourses of Alcoholism and Death

> They never teach me rum control,
> So put as long me glass could hol'
> They say a hungry man's a angry man,
> Well, a drunken man's a happy man
> Good Friday, could fall on Ash Wednesday,
> As long as it's rum-day, I ain't goin nowhere, until I get
> Drunk and disorderly...
> – Mighty Sparrow, "Drunk and Disorderly"

THE PIVOTAL LOCATION OF RUM within Caribbean societies and economies has made it a powerful literary trope of the joys, intoxications and perils of the colonial encounter and its aftermath. Emblematic of creole excess and the lush and decadent life of plantation society, rum was not only central for medicinal, ritual and celebration purposes, it became the fuel for the labouring masses on the plantation, with severe consequences which remain with us until today. Excessive affection for alcohol arguably emerges as yet another legacy of a plantation system energized by mass enforced labour movements, with its heavy burden of dislocation, loss and anomie.

This chapter focuses on associations between alcohol addiction and death, using a range of primary material: popular culture, particularly calypso and chutney rum lyrics; interviews with members of Alcoholics Anonymous; and fictional discourses. It interrogates the primary material using phenomenological approaches to probe what the diverse narratives have to say about the lived experience of alcohol addiction, the manner in which the respective characters and key players make meaning out of this state, and the process by which alcoholism becomes linked to death. On the basis of the assumption that alcohol addiction is a disease which is deleterious to individuals, communities and societies, and hence requires intervention, the exploration probes the needs and impulses which seduce persons into excessive alcohol consumption, the pleasures it affords for a season, the disruptions it generates and the slippery pathway which leads to death impulses. It culminates with a narrative of recovery: the testimony of a person whose alcohol addiction drew him to the brink of the abyss but who emerged to tell the tale.

My interest in the topic is rooted in my own experience of growing up in an extended family household in which my Indo-Trinidadian grandfather – a sensitive, diligent, loving, hard-working man and a good provider – was also a weekend alcoholic, a maudlin drunk who, under the influence, would drone on for hours about his experiences of childhood rejection and disrespect and the lack of love he felt within his own household. The household was, in my perception and in keeping with the custom of the time, centred around him as patriarch and provider.

I selected a phenomenological approach as a tool to probe the underlying significance of an ordinary everyday happening. This approach facilitates investigation which goes beyond a commonsensical understanding of an experience, in search of insight into the essence of the phenomenon through a process of "reflectively appropriating, of clarifying, and of making explicit the structure of meaning of the lived experience" (Van Manen 1990, 77). It interrogates the respective texts – oral and scribal, real-life and fictional, performative and spontaneous – to engage in a process of disclosure of their meanings and phenomenological themes, that is, the experiential structures that make up the named experience. According to Max Van Manen, in *Researching Lived Experience: Human Science for an Action Sensitive Pedagogy*, writing of phenomenological themes, "metaphorically speaking they are more like knots in the webs of our experiences, around which certain lived experiences are spun and thus lived through as meaningful wholes" (90). The reading also incorporates Mikhail Bakhtin's notion of a "chronotope" – literally, "time space" – which functions as "the primary means for materializing time in space" and "emerges as a centre for concretizing representation" in narrative (Bakhtin 1981, 150).[1] He further indicates, "The chronotope is the place where the knots of narrative are tied and untied. It can be said without qualification that to them belongs the meaning that shapes narrative" (250). Bakhtin theorized the notion of chronotope to measure the interface between real historical time and socially situated narrative genres, with their specific artistically expressed conventions of space–time relations. The study structures the exploration around four existentials of lived experience: corporeality, spatiality, temporality and relationality/communality.

In *Caribbean Rum: A Social and Economic History*, Frederick Smith documents the Caribbean's lengthy relationship with rum in a diverse range of literal and symbolic associations whose dynamics were in place by the 1800s, such that it became iconic as a driver for the plantation economy. This lucrative by-product of sugar production resolved the issue of what to do with the vast quantities of syrup left over from the sugar-making process. Caribbean rum became a pivotal ingredient in the Caucasian effort to subjugate Native Americans. After some slave ships delivered their cargo of Africans to the Caribbean, their next leg was a journey to the New England states, and their cargo included copious supplies of rum.

Allowances of rum were variously deployed by slave masters to pacify slaves, to reward skilled slave workers for their willingness to do difficult tasks, and even to replace portions of their legally stipulated dietary provisions. Moreover, rum was seen to have health benefits in terms of relieving chills and warding off colds and flu (Smith 2005, 25). In African spiritual cosmology and ritual practices, then and now, rum was used to enhance community and to facilitate access to the spirit realm; hence it became instrumental in creating connections for displaced Africans with their lost homeland.[2] Smith notes that excesses of consumption were correlated to enormities of anxiety and pain, and that drunkenness in the enslaved served as a shield to allow them to protest with impunity (125–26). Alcohol facilitated symbolic escape from the bondage of enslavement, as a facet of bacchanalian celebrations and temporary role reversals, which according to Smith the planters found more acceptable than "marronage, revolt and other forms of resistance" (157). After emancipation, the workers' wages were partially paid in rum.

Similarly, when the Indian indentees came to the promised "Chini-dad" ("land of sugar") in the 1800s, rum became for many their life's work, their recreational drug of choice as well as a readily available anaesthetic for pain, hopelessness and despair. The imperial overlords, recognizing the power of addiction, once again sealed their workers' propensities by paying wages and bonuses in rum allowances. Smith contends: "Reading rum attentively can demonstrate how items of everyday use continue to activate old oppressions in new ways that complicate contemporary efforts to undo or ameliorate those inequities" (2005, 313). Up until today, rum has been seen as a cultural symbol of the spirit of the Caribbean. Its abuse has been implicated in a range of attendant social practices, flouted aspirations, parental neglect and family discord, chronic wife beating and murder, and high suicide rates. Alcohol addiction is problematic for all subgroups of Trinidad and Tobago's contemporary multiethnic society, and within the Indo-Caribbean population, alcohol addiction has garnered its most consistent overt association with death.

The title of this chapter is drawn from a popular chutney song by Adesh Samaroo, "Rum Till I Die" (2002), the major context of which is an Indo-Trinidadian ethno-cultural location. Smith points to a particularly high level of alcohol consumption within the East Indian community of Trinidad, despite proscriptions against alcohol use in their three major religions, Hinduism, Islam and Presbyterian Christianity. He cites downtime in the agricultural work regime as a possible cause and also references anthropologist Carole Yawney's contention: "According to Yawney, the higher incidence of alcoholism among the East Indian men in Trinidad is the result of the East Indian male's desire to escape intense personal conflict with wives, parents, children and in-laws. These conflicts, including intergenerational tensions between young men and their fathers, stem from rigid Hindu attitudes about proper male roles, which force young East Indian men to seek sanctuary in all-male drinking clubs" (Smith 2005, 241).

This is not to associate rum lyrics exclusively with the Indo-Trinidad community. Whereas "Rum Till I Die" deals with the cause of addiction, the extremely popular calypso "Drunk and Disorderly", by the Mighty Sparrow, economically points to the centrality of alcohol consumption within the cultural fabric, as well as its pivotal location at the heart of the society's annual cycle of religious festivals and its life-cycle markers: birthdays, anniversaries, christenings and weddings.

> Drink and drunk yes that's me name
> Always make me family shame
> Like Mary Anne all day all night
> I start whoring high like a kite
> Is Christmas everyday is Christmas
> I could drink me rum trust
> Even in the Mass. I like to be
>
> Drunk and disorderly
> Always in custody
> Me friends and me family
> All man fed up with me, cause I
> Drunk and disorderly
> Every weekend I in the jail
> Drunk and disorderly
> Nobody to stand me bail
> (Mighty Sparrow 1972)

The popular calypso describes a scenario in which every cultural and existential identity marker through which the persona experiences self in space, time, corporeality and community has been overtaken by a compulsive desire for alcohol. The persona declares from the outset, "Drink and drunk yes that's me name." And with this new designation comes distance from the host of other meanings traditionally associated with naming which situate an individual within family, community, ethno-culture and a series of social expectations. The pursuit of alcohol at the expense of all else invites an enquiry into the alcoholic's lived experience of time. The persona violates the spatiotemporal boundaries set up to delimit appropriate use.

It is generally perceived as socially acceptable to imbibe more freely during the festive seasons in the nation's diverse cultural and religious calendars. The socio-religious cycle also determines cycles of feasting and fasting, both of which are perceived as beneficial to communal well-being. Indeed, the periods of restraint make those of indulgence all the sweeter and safeguard against uncontrolled excess, which is damaging to both the individual and the social order. "Drink and drunk" has breached these temporal boundaries, declaring, "It's Christmas every day is Christmas / I could drink me rum trust / Even in the Mass." Despite this sly allusion to sacramental consumption of alcohol during spiritual observances, the persona has entered into a topsy-turvy interface with the communal ritual calendar, such that "Good Friday [the end of the Lenten season] could fall on Ash Wednesday [the beginning of the Lent] / As long as it's rum-day". These ritual fasting days delimit a sacred season of restraint in preparation for the Easter celebration of the risen Christ. The phrase positions the persona as moving backwards in time and away from the benefits to be derived from judiciously observing the communal religious cycle.

The drunkard, having lost his way in time, is spatially excluded from home, with its customary associations of love, acceptance, shelter and protection. He has so shamed, embarrassed and harassed the family that he has been ostracized and conversely has ceased to experience himself relationally within family and community. Because of his increasingly aggressive and disorderly behaviour, "Drink and drunk" has been left to the custodial care of the criminal justice system. He refuses to take responsibility for the problematic nature of this existential location and focal point of desire, alluding indirectly to contributing factors underlying his pursuit of happiness: "They say a hungry man's a angry man / Well a drunken man's a happy man." Moreover, the line "They never teach me rum control" uses ambiguous pronominal reference to shift any personal requirement for taking responsibility onto an unnamed unidentified *they*. The incisive calypso implicitly poses rum control as an alternative to the control exerted by the criminal justice system. As devastating as the scenario which rolls out in this popular song may be, and despite the strong implication that this person may well be existentially – in terms of time, space, body and community – drinking himself to death, it nevertheless stops short of a direct association with death.

"Rum Till I Die", written and performed by young chutney artist Adesh Samaroo, shot to the top of the charts in 2002. Chutney is exemplary of innovative modalities of bridging ancestral rituals with contemporary cultural practices. From the indentureship period up to about the 1970s, chutney was seen as exemplary of Hindu low culture, properly belonging exclusively to the matikor ritual – a female prenuptial ceremony which uses tassa drumming, song, dance and ribald humour to instruct young brides on the sexual obligations of the marital state. In the 1980s chutney, and with it a cross-section of its female singers, transitioned onto the national public stage and in the process raised stringent protest from conservative Hindus with an interest in policing the public display of women. It has since blended with numerous other popular forms to become chutney-soca, ragga chutney, chutney hip-hop and chutney-bhangra. Today chutney functions variously as a common Indo-Caribbean marker of ethnic solidarity in the multicultural terrain and as a site of contestation over Brahminical versus lower-caste cultural forms that serve as ethnic boundary markers within the broader social fabric.

Adesh Samaroo's popular release "Rum Till I Die" stirred controversy because, given the ethno-cultural location of chutney, the song appeared to be glorifying alcoholism within a community in which it is a major source of social distress. There have been countless instances when disappointment in love in combination with excessive alcohol consumption became a trigger for violent death, whether homicide, suicide or murder/suicide pacts. The popular song sits at the troubling interface of cultural expression as mimetic, reflecting a common, well-recognized scenario, and paradigmatic, proffering models of unwholesome response to one of life's common distresses.

The lyrics focus on the most common association of alcohol with death – as a result of tabanca. *Tabanca* is defined by Winer in the *Dictionary of Trinidad and Tobago English*: "A painful feeling of unrequited love, from loving someone who does not love in return, esp. someone who was once a lover or spouse." Tabanca is also associated with social ridicule, particularly of a man who makes a fool of himself because of love. It elicits hilarity because of the "bazoodee" state in which it leaves the sufferer – "you take it on, keep studying it". It is demonstrated viscerally by "a heavy heart, by lassitude, loss of appetite, stomach cramps, insomnia and loss of interest in work or social life". The consequences of tabanca can include "death from accidents whilst drunk or loss of work . . . if unresolved it can lead to murder or suicide" (Winer 2008, 871).[3] Tabanca is a condition usually associated with males, as those traditionally empowered to be aggressors and inclined to claim the right of possession in male–female relationships. It stands to reason then that the male loses face the most when rejected. Alcohol here is perceived as giving the tabanca sufferer the capacity to drown sorrows and anaesthetize psychic pain.

The lyrics are as follows:

> Rum till I die. Is rum till I die.
> She tell me she don't love me and that's the reason why.

> Because she see me talking to anedderr woman
> She gone without telling and she take a nex man
> De woman I was talkin to ah doh even know she
> She was asking me for direction and yuh gone and leave me.
> Each day pass without you is getting better and better
> Ah doh know why yuh couldn't leave a little sooner
> When yuh leaving something always leave for better
> That is why I leave she and ah take she sister

The salient point of access into this popular expression of lived experience of alcoholism is relational and corporeal rather than temporal and spatial. The persona, in deep grief over the lover's rejection and departure, foregrounds alcohol consumption as his coping strategy for dealing with rejection. He also signals that without his lover, life does not seem worth living, hence his intention to eradicate himself, using rum as his weapon of self-destruction. These chutney lyrics home in on a commonly held assumption that alcoholism will eventually lead to death, through a related complex of illnesses, job loss leading to loss of income and incapacity to care for oneself, diminished capacity to assess risk, acts of aggression and violence, or despair leading to suicide.[4] The focal point of the litany is also telling. The alcoholic seems incapable of grasping a cause-and-effect sequence predating the lover's offensive act which aggrieves him into taking this self-destructive course of action. Rather than take any responsibility, he blames the lover for the breakup and offers a range of conflicting and paradoxical ego-retrieving excuses: there was no infidelity, as he was merely talking to a woman who was asking him directions; the quality of his life has improved because of the lover's absence; he initiated the breakup in order to change this lover for a better one – her sister – thereby adding sibling rivalry to the relational mix. All these hilarious excuses and rationalizations are undercut by the chorus, which speaks to the need to drink himself to death – the ultimate separation – because of the pain of desertion. Death would also arguably draw sympathy to the persona and condemnation onto the lover.

Numerous fictional evocations correlate alcoholism and domestic abuse and murder. The most common association is with drunken and murderous husbands and fathers whose alcohol abuse brings them to the thin edge of sanity, with the consequential murderous impulse directed against those closest to them. The fiction is replete with evocations of men who, in drunken irrationality, beat and slaughter their wives and children. Harold Sonny Ladoo's *No Pain Like This Body* and Shani Mootoo's *Cereus Blooms at Night*, which I have discussed at length elsewhere (Morgan and Youssef 2006), both focus on the insane murderous violence which the alcoholic father visits on his family. In the latter, released inhibition created by drunkenness is in part responsible for Chandin Ramchandin's initiation of long-term incestuous relations with his daughters and the brutal rape with which he asserts right of possession when "his Pohpoh" shows an interest in a young suitor.

The associations between alcoholism and death in female-authored fictions tend to be cemented in a long history of domestic abuse which produces battered women who kill. The equation goes like this: boy marries girl, encounters challenges with employment and experiences frustration and lack of opportunity, which leads to high levels of male aggression that targets the closest and most vulnerable person – his wife, who loves and serves him notwithstanding. This pattern is so deeply entrenched that not even the wife's independence is sufficient to reconfigure it. In Rosanne Kanhai's "Rum Sweet Rum", Dolly, herself a heavy drinker, works, provides a living and owns the house in which the family resides. Yet the familial and social expectations are that she should take the vicious beatings which are regularly meted out to her. Left to her own resources, she comes up with a formula: "I will have to kill him before he kill me. I studying my head good. It wouldn't be always the same, you know. The longest rope have an end" (Kanhai 199, 9). The narrative hints at the possibility of radical, murderous acts of resistance successfully executed by desperate women whose chronic abuse is sanctioned by social mores and who are bereft of familial and state protection and milder forms of self-defence.

In keeping with the focus on banal violence in the Caribbean, the text chosen for close analysis places emphasis on a less common scenario: a son whose problematic social location in relation to his drunken father leads him to commit patricide. Michael Anthony's "Drunkard of the River" (1973) is a terse and deceptively simple three-part short narrative which examines the impact of alcoholism. The narrative unfolds in three places: the private domain of the home (Parts 1 and 3) and the public domains of the rum shop and the river (Part 2). The title of the story implies that its focal point is Mano, the "drunkard of the river". The reality is that, although Mano is a catalyst for all the major events, the narrative focuses more on the impact of the alcoholic's conduct and practice within his home and his ethnic, social and cultural contexts. This reading focuses on the familial and social location of the alcoholic, as father, husband, villager and consumer, and the impact of his drinking habit as creating acceptable and unacceptable behaviours, equilibrium and disequilibrium, in those respective spheres. It deals also with the conflictual responsibilities, aspirations and attitudinal locations of the key players: the drunkard Mano; his son, Sona; Sona's mother (who is unnamed); Assing, the Chinese shopkeeper; the villagers; and (by implication only) the law enforcement authorities, that is, the police. The naming as well as the typological dimensions of the scenario impart an archetypal quality to the narrative. Mano and Sona are both common Indo-Trinidadian names, but they also promise a story of a quintessential Man(o) seeking to interact with his Son(a). The archetypal self-sacrificing partner is named not as Man(o)'s wife but as Son(a)'s mother.

The story is told by a first-person narrator but focalized and pivoted through the young son, who emerges as both violated and violator. The boy is the only character who is constrained to move between the private space of the home and the public space of the shop. The river represents a place of inbetweenness which facilitates concourse between these domains. As a young male, he must face the contradictory values, assumptions, equilibriums and disequilibriums of both places, which interface with his personal dis-ease as a heavily burdened, conflicted youth emerging from an abusive environment. The plot is simple. The boy comes home from the shop with groceries but without his father, who, as is his custom, is drinking himself into a stupor at the shop. His mother, through a combination of command and shaming rebuke, compels him to return to the shop for his father. The father in turn subjects him to public physical and verbal abuse. The young man, seeing his father as the locus of his problems, takes vengeance on him by some veiled and unnamed shameful act on the river. The story ends at home with the mother calling for the father, who she assumes is drunk in the boat, while their son flees into the mangroves, fearing the intervention of the police.

The conflicting aspirations, equilibriums and disequilibriums in the story differ in the respective places. In the communal space, the drunkard becomes a public nuisance. The rum shop is a significant location in village life. In the post-indentureship period, small shops started by Chinese immigrants who settled in remote rural areas were pivotal to settlement patterns. The "Chinee" shop became the centre of the village and the daily meeting place for all strata of the society, particularly for low-income persons, whose purchases of food and daily necessities occurred on a daily or weekly basis. The shop was roughly divided into two parts: the food-selling portion and – through a small, often symbolic rather than physical partition – the rum shop, where patrons would buy drinks and sit at ramshackle tables to socialize. Traditionally the rum shop was seen as a space frequented by men, who were occasionally accompanied by female companions of ill repute. Decent women who came to the shop would limit their activities to the food-selling section.

The Chinese village shop was the hub of the community, the locus of commercial and social interchange. Without access to the formal financial sector to buffer them from payday to payday, some villagers' ability to eat daily depended on "trusting" food from the shopkeeper, who would occasionally also advance small loans against projected income.[5] It was the message and gossip centre and the platform from which the communal voice resonated. The shop is also the space within which the overlapping spatiotemporal frames of the story derive their meanings. The events occur at the end of the weekly cycle, when the villagers seek provision and recreation, and at the end of the diurnal cycle, when day and twilight give way to the deep darkness of night.

The shopkeeper Assing, arguably representing the sector of society which stood to benefit financially from the sale of alcohol, is fundamentally quite satisfied with Mano's excessive alcohol consumption. For him, the drunkard's nuisance value is more than compensated for by the substantial sums of money which he spends on drink. Even the ensuing antics and abuses, democratically extended to all, bring disequilibrium in the public space only when they interfere with the main agenda – other customers' ability to buy "in peace". Assing and the sector he represents are content if alcohol-obsessed Manos buy prolifically to feed their addictions but manage to contain their antisocial behaviours so as not to hamper commercial interchange. For him and the harassed Saturday-night customers, Sona's arrival to cart away his father represents "sweet relief" (Anthony 1973, 57). The villagers are by implication tolerant of the man's drunken conduct; indeed, he may even possess a measure of amusement value until he draws them into violent confrontations.

It is in relation to the private space of the home that Anthony explores the complex psychosocial interactions which variously cushion alcoholics at the expense of their families and erupt in acts of violence. The father's alcoholism brings into the home shame, powerlessness and resentment. Although the wife is enraged by the husband's drunkenness, her response to him – as mediated through the gaze of an Afro-Trinidadian male author – is tempered by a love that transcends all abuses. Within the home she cushions him, absorbs abuse, worries herself sick: "To her he was as mighty as the very river that flowed outside. She remembered that in his young days there was nothing any living man could do that he could not" (Anthony 1973, 55). His abusive drunkenness remains a thing apart from the love, honour and respect which she gives to him as a matter of course. The quintessential mother-woman, she longs first and foremost to draw him home, where he can be safe and sheltered, because she is powerless to spread this protective cloak of love over him in the public space – the shop where by his own abuses he invites violent reprisals. Since she cannot erase the long-standing habits and patterns of drunkenness, the satisfactory immediate outcome is to bring him home, where she can keep him safe by absorbing his abuse to the detriment of her own well-being – notwithstanding the fact that she is prematurely aged by her husband's drunken abuse and emaciated and half-starved because of his lack of provision. When he comes home, momentarily she experiences rest: "She knew when he staggered back how she would shake with rage and curse him, but even so, how inside she would shake with the joy of having him safe and home" (55–56).

The son finds himself caught between the requirements of the public and the private place. Societal gender assumptions dictate that if a woman went to the shop to collect her intoxicated husband, that would emasculate him further and draw him into greater public disfavour because of the inevitable abuse he would release on her, there and then. The devilish nature of his behaviour is reflected in the observation "It would be fire and brimstone if she went" (54). Instead she shames her son into going to collect his father, on the basis of her assumptions about his unconditional filial responsibility. In her eyes, Sona – whose identity is doubly foregrounded by the focalizer as Son(a) and by the label "the drunkard's son" – is an appropriate mediator between the worlds, or rather the only mediator that she can deploy in her helplessness. Hence she lays on the young lad a multiplicity of painful and arduous responsibilities: rescue his father, face his public abuse, defend him against those who would harm him in reciprocity for his acts of drunken aggression, bring him to the safety of his home – in short, defend him against all the consequences of his drunkenness.

The son stands at the problematic interface of the private and public worlds. In the private space he must deal with expectations of appropriate filial responsibility, notwithstanding his internal response, which is to label his father a "beast" and to wish to eject him from the home. In the public space he must deal with the shame attendant upon the public abuse he receives from the father whom he is trying to protect from himself. The resolution is shadowy but the implication is that the son resolves the issue by committing patricide, returning the drunkard to the river, the luminal transitional place between the public and private domain. The irony is that, having done this, the son finds a paradoxical affinity with the father. He has now become the beast, a raging lion bent on revenge at the river. But upon return home he becomes a lamb, beset by dread of the consequences of his action. "His bones, too, seemed to be turning liquid. Not from drunkenness, but from fear" (59). The greatest irony is that though his father had a proper assigned place in the public and private domains, the son seems by his action to have relegated himself to the river – the space of inbetweenness, outside the social regulations of time and space.

The spatiotemporal location of this story invites us to attribute the archetypal nature of the narrative to its cyclical quality. The representative characters are caught in a cycle of unending impoverishment, abuse, violence and struggle to keep food on the table and flesh on the bones, in opposition to grotesque and demeaning alcohol consumption. These factors militate against belonging and entrap the characters in a state of abjection. They are constrained to take their space in unending cycles of futility, such that Mano could easily be the Sona of another season, and Sona an early manifestation of a Mano of the future, in training to terrorize a mother of yet another generation. Timelessness is crystallized by the river, which despite its constant movement merely facilitates transition between fixed spaces, states and ontologies. Indeed, to Sona's mother it represents the non-passage of time, allowing her to paradoxically read her husband as ageless: "In her eyes he was still young. He did not grow old. It was she who had aged. He had only turned out badly" (55).

The representation of Sona's mother resonates with the submissive image of the Indo-Trinidadian wife in the personal narrative which is the final sample of primary material selected for analysis. These women have grown to accept a culture of alcoholism which in certain social contexts tends to be associated with becoming a man. They become enablers who endure heinous abuse yet continue to love and provide, arguably until they are pushed over the brink to become battered women who kill.

The House of Terror

> The house was full of terror . . . full of evil because of me . . . I would be a very kind person – loving, caring. . . . from the time I open the gate and go inside, I became abusive. (Personal interview with Alcoholics Anonymous member)

The final segment of this enquiry sounds a positive note, with a selection drawn from personal narratives gathered through interviews with members of Alcoholics Anonymous, popularly known as AA. This global organization was established to allow recovering alcoholics to nurture and encourage each other and to intervene in the lives of those who have newly determined to break their addictions. It uses a simple twelve-step process.[6] Its major strategy is to implement a talking cure, intended to lead its members to face the reality of their condition, confront and take responsibility for its consequences, seek forgiveness from those they have wronged, and envision and seek a pathway for their recovery, thereby exchanging a life of tumult and chaos for "serenity".[7] AA intervention depends heavily on storytelling, in which an embodied voice expresses a self-fashioning narrative before a group. It involves ritualized performative forms, so much so that in *Storytelling in Alcoholics Anonymous: A Rhetorical Analysis,* George Jensen argues that appropriating the form of the tale is a crucial dimension of the success of the procedure. It is teaching the alcoholic to shift his or her gaze away from personal guilt and the specificity of individual wrongdoing and latch on to the potential for the God of his or her understanding to operate redemptively, even in the grimmest of life situations. Pivotal to the process is empathetic communal identification with fellow travellers on a rocky road.

The organization recognizes excessive alcohol consumption as symptomatic of more deeply rooted problems; hence it holds that it is possible for a person to cease drinking and yet remain poisoned by and capable of poisoning others because of the underlying cause of the destructive habit. It conceives of both the alcoholic individual and the family of the alcoholic as diseased; therefore, entire families stand in need of intervention if they are to recover. And the objectives extend beyond the cessation of drinking. In keeping with the focus of this analysis, Jensen recounts numerous instances in which speakers credit AA with saving their lives. They associate cessation of the drinking habit with pre-empting early death. He indicates that for those who arrive at what the programme defines as serenity, "They did not so much regain what they had lost through years of drinking; they found something new – a sane life, a place within a community, an acceptance of life on its own terms" (Jensen 2002, 129).

This final sample of primary material is drawn from a semi-structured interview with a person encountered at an AA meeting. The analysis surveys the interview for phenomenological themes, identifies the dominant point of access into the lived experiences explored in the story and highlights correlations between this real-life narrative and the fictional and popular culture texts. The themes identified as the major foci of the persona are heuristic devices to demonstrate the manner in which the speaker makes meaning of his experience of alcoholism. As indicated by Van Manen, "The thematic meanings of human experience are self-constituted. They reflect the ways that we tend to make sense of life as human beings – as human beings who are embedded within certain linguistic, historical and cultural contexts. That is why we can say that human meanings are discovered but also self-disclosing, constructed by us but also constructed of us" (http://www.phenomenologyonline.com/inquiry/methods-procedures/reflective-methods/thematic-reflection/)

This interview was held with Ravi (name changed), a forty-nine-year-old

Indo-Trinidadian male. The initial contact was made at an AA meeting. The narrative which is analysed below is based on a face-to-face interview rather than an open-session testimony, but the AA culture can be expected to inform the process of self-fashioning which emerges. During the interview, Ravi was relatively relaxed and willing to speak about his journey. The analysis which follows takes cognizance of what the interview reveals as well as what it does not reveal, what he can or cannot tell or has erased, what he knows and what is allocated to the realm of the unknowing, the not-knowing, or the gradual revealing in the act of telling. It will also take cognizance of whether the interviewee presented as being closed or open to a process of knowing as part of the process of telling.

Theme 1: Alcohol consumption was engrained in the communal cultural and religious life cycle and pivotal to a good life and a good time.

> As a child growing up . . . there would always be an occasion . . . There were particular times when alcohol was served. Yes, I grew up in St James and there it was the best of both cultures. My own East Indian culture plus calypso, pan, everything, you name it. And, um, I always liked that, I always liked the free flow of life, the enjoyment of life . . . I could not imagine that anyone could enjoy life without alcohol.

The role models one receives as a child are pivotal to one's narrative and pathways of being and becoming. In this particular instance, seasons and cycles of cultural locatedness marked by alcohol consumption were pivotal to the child's sense of being in the world. Children are socialized from infancy to participate in ritual feasting through imbibing what is considered appropriately small quantities of alcohol. This democratic social practice extends from adults dipping their finger in alcohol to place some on a baby's tongue to the pouring of libations on the ground to allow dead ancestors to enjoy their share. Within this context, consumption would be experienced as conferring belonging to community and culture and enjoyment of the good life. This process is intensified in a multicultural nation in which all ethnicities participate in each other's festivities and holy days. Trinidad and Tobago is unique in having a diverse range of holidays throughout the year, ranging from Indian Arrival Day to Shouter Baptist Liberation Day and a multitude in between.

His early exposure to alcohol felt good to Ravi. Temporally, it located him within the festive season – it was Christmas time: "You know, thirteen or fourteen years old and we would go by a neighbour and they would give us a drink and that was the norm" (Interview 1). The children would also revel in the amused attention which their tipsy antics would win from the adults. For the abused child that Ravi was – his paternal grandparents raised him from infancy in part to shield him from the abuses of his alcoholic father – drink made him feel powerful: "It gave me confidence. It made me feel better." He went on to state that his first serious experience with drunkenness also took place at Christmas, at home. He was about fifteen years old then, maybe younger. This bout attracted censure only because of its excess and the fact that he used up the alcohol intended for Christmas visitors. The shift in tense – "I could not imagine that anyone could have a good time without alcohol" – indicates that by the time of the interview, the tight mental association between celebratory times and alcohol consumption had been loosened.

Theme 2: Paternal abuse generated low self-esteem, low achievement, social awkwardness and verbal inadequacy, which could be overcome by drinking.

> That low self-esteem was not there when I drank. It put me above . . . [The low self-esteem was] because of the upbringing I had with him. Because of his abuse, physical as well as verbal. Right. It was terrible. I mean, I am a big man. I am forty-nine years old now and I still have fears.

Deep anger and contempt characterized Ravi's feelings towards his father, who drank heavily and abused his wife and children mercilessly. Although he felt pleased and comfortable speaking about how much he despised his father, Ravi was reluctant, even when probed, to speak about his mother, only indicating in passing, "She couldn't help me because she would hand down the same abuse she got to us." The denial or erasure of blame for implied maternal complicity in acts of abuse and the absence or nondisclosure of anger against the mother are telling. Significantly, Ravi saw himself as poised within a male lineage between his caring, balanced grandfather, who was a disciplined social drinker and who would never beat, only talk, and his raging father, who would pursue him even in his grandfather's home in order to abuse him. The trauma induced by the abuse produced in him visceral responses which, up until the time of the interview, could not be relegated to the past. He yearned to follow the role model of his grandfather but was fixated on his father's wrongdoing; he could not forgive him, and eventually he became impotent to prevent himself from becoming his father.

Ravi's shame and embarrassment about his poor academic performance, social awkwardness and low self-esteem were associated with the way paternal abuse made him feel about himself. This was the case even though in retrospect he claimed that he did not want to blame his father – a response which can arguably be attributed to the AA intervention that instructs its members to assume responsibility for their condition. At this stage Ravi was demonstrating both understanding of the contributing causative factors and a willingness and commitment to assuming liability for his condition.

Theme 3: Released inhibition due to alcohol consumption facilitated consistent fabrication of a more socially pleasing self-construction.

> Well, to be honest with you, I never thought that my life would have come to anything. I never believed that I would have had a wife, children and even a job, a permanent job like this. So when I came and met this girl, I wondered if . . . and I had to lie. I had always believed all my life that I had to paint a picture. I had to make up these stories . . . so selfish, so self-centred, so egocentric . . . I always had to be in the limelight.

Given the correlation between low self-esteem and dishonourable actions, drink was a panacea because it not only gave him confidence but also allowed him to "paint a picture", to make up grand stories about himself that would make him acceptable and loved and wanted. Burdened as he was with a sense of his unworthiness and inability to be loved for himself, the fabrication and storytelling were an extrapolation of the performance of drunken antics which served the same function in his teenage years. Paradoxically, the underlying inadequacy later combined with the storytelling impulse to motivate him to make up stories about his wife's supposed infidelities because of his assumed unlovability, and to punish her severely for the same.

Theme 4: Entrapment by home and family led to transformation of the home into a place of terror which had to be escaped.

> To be honest with you . . . and I am not sure how to explain this, nah. I tried to understand myself, to put it into words, to analyse myself, why I behaved as I behaved. All I know, all I could say for a fact is that I didn't want my family. Committing suicide, I tried many . . . I used to think about it, but I had

> a Christian upbringing . . . not an upbringing, but I believed in Christianity. Since I was small I went to a Catholic school . . . so I was scared to commit suicide. I was afraid to die. I was wishing to die. Because my family wouldn't go, my wife wouldn't go. She wouldn't take the children and go. And then every time she said that she was leaving, I got scared [laughter]. And I got scared because I did not know how to start my life all over again.

The abuse completed its self-perpetuating cycle when Ravi ended up creating the very horror from which he had run as a youth. Having trained his wife to be an enabler, to provide money to support his drinking habit, to expect minimal contribution to the running of the home and to submit to his drunken abuses, he longed to be free of all responsibility for home and family. Although he was able to acknowledge freely that it was his drunken abuses which turned the home into a house of terror, he paradoxically believed he could escape from the terror by chasing his wife from the home, as opposed to removing himself. Incapable of availing himself of its comfort and satisfaction, unable to meet its demands, he set out to destroy the family which served as a reflector of his inadequacies. Simultaneously he recognized that their departure would signal an end to his life. The predominant emotions at this stage were fear, impotence and hopelessness. The notion of his creating a living hell for his family included concepts of possession by a malignant force: "Satan waiting for me at the gate."

Theme 5: Alcohol consumption is symptomatic of deeper underlying causal factors, which are unmasked after the alcoholic stops drinking.

> I got to like the meetings. I started to enjoy the people, the atmosphere. I liked to hear the stories . . . And I started to like, you know, that I could play with my daughter if she was awake when I got home. My son and I, after a few months, we started to talk and I liked that . . . Although I was sober, a lot of the problems were still there. I was dealing with me, dealing with family members. I still had that arrogant way about me. I still had my low self-esteem. I was still selfish, self-centred, you know. And I still had my fears. I still wanted to be the dominant factor in the home. I still wanted everybody to do things my way.

Cessation of alcohol consumption is not an end in itself; it is merely the initiation of a process of healing and reconciliation. The cessation facilitates the recognition that alcoholism is a mask for more deeply rooted psychological and relational issues which must be dealt with instead of being anaesthetized by alcohol. Pivotal to healing in this narrative is the requirement for self-knowledge and assuming responsibility for negative mindsets and feelings. Ravi arrived at a high level of self-reflexivity. He came to a determination to put aside fear, self-centredness and arrogance, which were masks for his insecurities and low self-esteem. For Ravi, the impetus to resolve his issues came from the joy he garnered from relationships. In other words, he learned in a deliberate and measured fashion to substitute alienation, masking and ego retrieval with genuine and open relationships. Ravi also testified to a deep sense of pride and satisfaction in his burgeoning self-awareness, self-control and sense of responsibility.

Theme 6: Faith in and reliance on God can break futile intergenerational cycles and create access to inner peace.

> And they told me to find the God of my understanding. And I had always believed that God had turned his back on me. I believed that old saying that the sins of the father would fall on the children. And as the eldest son, I believed that I was paying for my father's sins and behaviour. I believed that God didn't like me, wanted no part of me. So I used to call myself Satan. I always ask God forgiveness for my sins. I know now that He is a loving God and a merciful God and that He would work in my life if I ask Him to. God has granted me more than I ever thought possible. He has taken me out of a dark hole that I never thought that I would have come out of. He has put me on the bank of a river with beautiful running water on the side. It is something else. Something that words cannot describe.

Ravi spoke clearly and joyfully of coming to inner peace by finding the God of his understanding. Significantly, this was not a vague, nebulous benign spiritual force but a God with a specific nature and orientation: loving, compassionate, merciful, responsive, empowering, compensatory in the face of human weakness. He came to an encounter with this God, who accepted him in his sorry state and forgave his shortcomings and transgressions. The implication is that he found the grace to forgive and to love himself because he came to accept God's forgiveness and love for him. The acceptance of a loving, caring father God was also pivotal in releasing him from the negative cycle which he described as paying for the sins of his father by repeating the father's wrongdoings. Using an image which resonates with the central motif of "Drunkard of the River", Ravi spoke about his new spiritual and psychic location as his being lifted out of a dark hole into which he had plummeted downward, as if into a murky, threatening, confining place, and ascending into a domain of openness, light, vistas and potentialities at the side of a river which flowed with streams of refreshment – an indescribable place of safety, blessedness and peace.

Analysis

This real-life narrative echoes a cross-section of the themes evoked in the fictional constructions. In all the narratives, the psychosocial explanations for alcoholism – the cultural as well as the psychological and personal – figure prominently. The social and communal function of alcohol consumption, and the manner in which it functions as a cultural symbol, dovetails neatly with consumption as providing escape from low self-esteem and frustration, and as facilitating fantasies of power. In the cross-section of popular culture, fictional and personal narratives, people were seduced into drinking because it alleviated their sense of non-belonging and social awkwardness and made them feel empowered. They came to recognize the enormity of their problem only when those whose company and support they valued began to shun and ostracize them. In the most extreme cases, even drinking buddies begin to avoid the alcoholic because of his propensity for unprovoked aggression.

The gender differential is significant and deserving of further attention elsewhere. Arguably, men and women inhabit the identical sociocultural domain, and a substantial number of women succumb to alcoholism. Yet overwhelmingly, excessive alcohol consumption is constructed as a male-centred activity associated with a good time and with the annual cycle of religious and cultural festivals. In Sparrow's "Drunk and Disorderly" and for Ravi, the narrative chronotope is instructive. Because alcohol abuse is tied to festive and special events, the process of entrapment and/or enlightenment is marked by the seasonal and festive calendars. The relational issues are also related to issues of spatiality. The protagonist of the calypso is excluded from the domestic domain and left to the ministrations of the criminal justice system. In the personal narrative, the person who demonstrates love and kindness outside the home turns into a beast as soon as he reaches its gate. Indeed, Ravi uses the metaphor of satanic influence or possession to explain how he became transformed into an abusive beater at home. Despite shame, without a sustained intervention he seemed incapable of halting the cycle of abuse which he had despised in his father and had run from. The narrative also testifies to experiencing simultaneously a strong compulsion to distance himself from the loved one, who represents unwelcome responsibility, and a deep-rooted fear that the loved one – who also represents caring and stability – would actually leave.

A major coping strategy for low self-esteem lies in fabrications and face-saving storytelling. The incredible tall tales of the protagonist of Samaroo's "Rum Till I Die" are fleshed out in Ravi's fabrications. Significantly, Alcoholics Anonymous creates an alternative community and an opportunity to testify and to use narrative to impose a measure of order on a chaotic life. On the basis of his three years of research on storytelling within the AA context, Jensen identifies a process during which the shame, guilt and fragmentation of the narrative of the newcomer are translated over time into the sermonic, at times humorous, tales of the old-timers, testifying of a heroic journey with confidence, considerable skill and even pride. Jensen concludes that the old-timers are not only speaking for themselves, they are also speaking for and on behalf of the values of an entire culture, a way of being in the world.

The narratives examined here point to the potentiality for storytelling as mask and ego-retrieving device to be replaced by testimony as an aid to understanding and an ordering device. The "Rum Till I Die" lyrics and Ravi's personal narrative speak of the challenges of finding reasons for actions, ordering life according to a credible narrative and cause-and-effect sequences, authentic characters as opposed to projections of a drunken imagination, a quest for truth to take the place of fabrication. Significantly, numerous times during Ravi's interview he repeated the phrase "to be honest with you". The major fabricator of lies – of the ilk reflected in the lyrics of "Rum Till I Die" – is transformed into someone who humbly seeks the truth about himself and about others as a basis for constructing an authentic self and valid place in the world. And this feeds directly into viable relationships, which are significant for the process of recovery.

All the narratives examined indicate that alcoholism is a disease which inflicts suffering on families and loved ones, not just the addicted individual exclusively. The impetus which pushed Ravi into alcoholism was the constant verbal and physical abuse meted out by his alcoholic father, which he sought with all his might to escape but to no avail. His incapacity to forgive his father did not allow the corrosive buildup of anger, hatred, mistrust and low self-esteem to dissipate so as to provide a generative environment for healing. The practical implication of this is that it is insufficient to treat with the alcoholism exclusively; the underlying determinant must also be addressed. Moreover, cycles of repetition which perpetuate the transgenerational transmission of abuse must be recognized and broken. In the narrative of transcendence, faith in a loving, compassionate, forgiving God has proven to be instrumental in such a journey.

9

"NO MONEY, NO LOVE"
Representations of the Social Impact of Poverty

WITHIN A GLOBAL SCENARIO THAT increasingly measures the worth and accomplishment of people, communities and nations in material terms, Caribbean societies continue to grapple with legacies of entrenched poverty and its intergenerational transmission. The challenge remains of how to transcend a brutal history of enforced and unjust labour systems, racialized inequities, secondary migrations, natural disasters, structural adjustment and globalizing impulses. Moreover, traditional avenues of poverty alleviation and upward mobility, including education leading to professional careers, which undergirded the birthing of the new nations of the archipelago, are today proving increasingly distant or even unattainable for a widening cross-section of youth.

The issue of defining poverty is as complex as designing and implementing measures for its alleviation. The statistical evidence provides a useful though severely limited way of knowing. The imperative to know poverty in greater measure in order to design appropriate interventions has been heightened given global interconnectedness in trade, finance, health, migration, drugs, crime and war. The 2008 riots triggered around the globe by increases in food and fuel prices are a case in point, demonstrating the connection between poverty and peace. President of the World Bank Group James Wolfensohn, addressing the 2000 Conference on World Poverty and Development: A Challenge for the Private Sector, argues as follows:

> the issue of poverty is no longer an issue that you can consider either within the developing world where there is poverty or the developed world looking out to the developing world. You have to consider it as an integral issue. And it is an issue not just of equity and social justice and morality. It really is an issue of

> peace, because it is unlikely that you will have stability in a world of inequity. People who have nothing, or have little, or no place to go or no opportunity, react like you or I would react. You want to protect your kids. You want to create a life . . . The issue is not just money. The issue is self-esteem. The issue is wanting a better life for your kids; a household free of domestic violence, protection against crime, security and opportunity. (Wolfensohn 2000)

The Caribbean is no stranger to this complex of issues. The island societies spawned by the forces of early capitalism and globalization demonstrate the unhappy outcome of commoditization of the human. The Caribbean's formative labour migrations have been entrenched in racism and structural inequities. Indeed, to ensure the plantation societies' operation with a minimum of disruption, it proved necessary not only to draw the blood, sweat and tears of the labouring populations but also to erode their histories, cultural moorings and self-esteem. Despite the success of Caribbean societies in creating viable social orders in the aftermath of this originary trauma, the legacies of these inauspicious beginnings undermine attempts at poverty alleviation even today.

The first part of this chapter explores extracts of popular and media discourses to garner insights into the far-reaching social consequences of poverty and their correlation to gender-based abuse. The second examines literary selections which represent the social impact of poverty in broad structural terms. The exploration points to poverty's differential impact as dependent on the age, gender and social locations of its victim, its intergenerational impact and its prospects for alleviation. It is to literary expressions that the exploration turns to examine the subjective experience – the sights, sounds, mood and tincture of poverty; it traces intersections of gender and poverty. In other words, do men and women experience and interface with poverty differently? What are the correlations between impoverished social relations and material poverty's close henchmen, hunger, drug abuse, crime, underdevelopment and despair? The analyses identify the points at which Caribbean writing and popular expressions, in the process of defining a place and a way to be human, are working towards more affirmative measures of the worth of both persons and societies.

Poverty and Gender-Based Violence in Contemporary Media Discourse

The initial focus of this section will be on the manner in which poverty cycles overlap with gender norms and assumptions to produce the all-too-common domestic disasters that are featured in newspaper reports almost daily. This is significant, given the extent to which attitudes and orientations to these issues are in turn constructed in discourse. Media discourse is both mimetic and paradigmatic as it simultaneously shapes and reflects world knowledge. Societal and institutional perspectives exist in dynamic interplay with the reporter's individual perspective. Readers in turn filter the reports through their own worldview and social and psychological perspectives, which are shaped by the body of knowledge, attitude and feeling they bring to the table. Analysis of media discourse yields significant insights into representational and ideological politics. As indicated in *Writing Rage: Unmasking Violence in Caribbean Discourse*, the complex representation of events and circumstance by different media and government agencies can often shroud events and motivations in the perspective of their agents, complicating and distorting an already complex picture (Morgan and Youssef 2006, 22).

Print, radio and television media also provide fora in which the nation and transnation are being constantly shaped and reshaped. There is a high level of citizen participation in discourses of self-fashioning and notions of how we appropriated our common collective identities.

The *Trinidad Guardian*, the nation's oldest newspaper, which has the finest reputation as a quality press, carried a report in its 16 September 2008 edition about what has now become a typical case of gender-based violence. The case was given front-page billing. In recent years there has been a growing trend in the *Guardian* towards the tabloid format, in terms of both the size of what was previously a broadsheet and in its style of reporting. The 16 September report follows what has now become a generic style: lurid photos of female victims of abuse, direct quotations from victims, family and neighbour eyewitnesses giving details of the crimes committed, and a strong focus on the cause of frustration in the assailant. The report pictures two battered women in hospital garb. The headline reads: "Hungry Man Runs Amok. Stabs Lover, Family. Torches House. Kills Self" (*Trinidad Guardian*, 16 September 2008, 1).

The front-page headline is reflective of the most significant news item of the day. It focalizes the event and creates a filter through which it will be read. Headlines and large photographs are displayed prominently to catch the eye of early commuters trapped daily in extensive traffic jams. In this instance, despite the pain and anguish inscribed on the faces of the women, overlaying their severe injuries, the headline – which plays on the adage "A hungry man is an angry man" – implies a measure of justification for this extreme act of violence. No censure or blame is attributed to the apparently justifiably angry man, who threw a concrete sink at his common-law wife and a brick at her mother and subsequently set the home on fire (*Trinidad Guardian*, 16 September 2008, 3). The grouping of the elements in the front-page headline implies his ownership of the property; however, given the fact that there is no mention of the lover or her mother and sisters leaving the premises in order to get away from him, the strong possibility is that the house belonged to one of the women of the family.

The stories inside the paper, written by two female journalists, strengthen this range of assumptions. The page 3 story, headlined "Man found dead after burning Valencia home", continues to imply a measure of justification for the assailant: "Determined to hold on, 24-year-old Jamel Sebastian refused to end his relationship with his common-law-wife Alisha Wellington. But when the 21-year-old woman tried to make a clean break, Sebastian became enraged and went on a stabbing spree." The stabbing spree included the lover, her sister and her mother. The account casts the assailant as a man full of determination, steadfastness, even fidelity and commitment to a long-term love relationship. His admirable determination to hold on is placed in opposition to his common-law wife's desire for a clean break. Diction and sentence structure work to impute blame and to alleviate responsibility. The assailant is nowhere reported as someone who attempted mass murder and succeeded in inflicting grievous bodily harm on three women and two children, all of whom had to be hospitalized for their injuries.

Even more bizarre elements appear in the reported interview with the mother. Rendered immobile in a hospital bed by her severe injuries, she offers apparent justification for the assailant, based on commonly held assumptions about a man's rights in his home, even while stating of her severely burnt daughter, "She is in the ICU right now. She is real bloated. She is unable to speak." The mother nevertheless reportedly directs all her implied and stated criticism at her own daughter, in extremely simplistic terms which are supportive of the hungry man/angry man connection: "I heard him complain that he wasn't getting any food cooked . . . How could a man feel when he comes home from work and nothing is there to eat? When I had a man, I used to come home and cook and clean and do things for him" (*Trinidad Guardian* 2008, 2). The report implies the mother's distant, superficial knowledge of a disastrous scenario that was unfolding in the home in which she was co-resident with the daughter and her lover. Moreover, the mother, who proffers her own behaviour (when she had a man) as exemplary, appears well schooled in the expectations and mores of common-law unions. She has imbibed, and to imply judgement of her own daughter she uses a range of tacit though widely held assumptions about the privileges a man should enjoy in his home, and his right to do violence should he not receive his due.

On what basis can we tie this all-too-common case to the social impact of poverty? If the causative impact of poverty on the acts of violence in this scenario is difficult to discern from the flattened account which is inherent to newspaper reporting, the post-disaster outcome of poverty is clearly displayed on the same page, so to speak. The indicators are all present: the squalor of the incomplete, windowless, unpainted home pictured in the newspaper and the dependency of the victims on state services, which do not work and which compound the suffering and neglect. In a small, oil-rich nation in which state authorities are indulging an obsessive focus on large-scale ostentatious projects in the pursuit of developed-country status, the poor are not only abused and disadvantaged within their domestic circumstances, but in seeking to cope with familial crises, they are oppressed and abused by the system. The newspaper reports a layering and multiplication of traumas. A neighbour who walked to the police station to report the crime is quoted as saying, "But the police tell me to go home and sleep, because they said they have no vehicle" (*Trinidad Guardian* 2008, 3). Who can tell whether this was pure callousness or the frustration of officers who lacked the resources to do a high-risk job? The Sangre Grande Fire Station was without a truck to send to the blaze. The Sangre Grande District Hospital kept the injured women waiting long hours for medical attention. Thankfully, at the end of the extended period, the Port of Spain Hospital had beds to receive them.

Too many cases of gender-based violence become significant only after the most heinous acts of brutality against the self and the other are perpetrated. When they do come to public attention, invariably through media reporting, these reports – written by two female journalists in this instance – speak reams about what is not said. There is no mention of the violent tendencies of the young male, only of his faithful persistence; the former is not perceived as a salient issue. There is no attempt at explaining the woman's desire to separate from her potentially violent mate. There is no attempt to delve beyond the most superficial of explanations for the crisis. No connection is made between the plight of the abused women and their ongoing abuse suffered at the hands of the state representatives from whom they had a right, as citizens, to expect support and service – the police, the fire service, the hospital. Neither is there any mention of the undervaluing of community, the impotence of the neighbour who sought to assist by walking to the police station to get help (the implication being that telephone service was not available). The impoverished national becomes in effect a second-class citizen who is constrained to live with – or in extreme cases to die because of – the outworking of inequitable distribution of the resources in the national coffers.

> When you try to caress her, she will tell you stop
> "I can't carry love in the grocery shop."
> (Growling Tiger, "Money Is King", 1935)

This contemporary crisis can be measured against countless similar tragedies that have played themselves out on the national stage since the beginning of the previous century. Indeed, male–female violent conflict of every imaginable shape and form has occupied a prominent place in the Trinidadian imaginary. Since the 1930s such conflict has been a constant theme of calypsos, whose bards are seen as the people's philosophers, offering profound insights into social conditions while speaking the language and reflecting the worldview of the common man. The values presented in calypsos represent the views of the songwriters and performers, but they present to the broader population an opportunity to negotiate a stance and formulate a value system in relation to what validly constitutes a positive quality of life and society.

And these notions are constantly being constructed and reinvented. Gender critic Patricia Mohammed argues for the power of calypso critique to unwrap a complex process by which identities – national, cultural, ethnic, class and particularly gender – are cumulatively being fashioned (Mohammed 2003, 130). V.S. Naipaul, who has indicated that it is only in calypso that the Trinidadian touches reality (Naipaul [1962] 1969, 58), structures his urban vignettes on the mock epic search for significance on Miguel Street, Port of Spain, around a series of popular calypsos of the 1940s, the majority of which focus on chaotic gender relations (Naipaul [1959] 1974). And Gordon Rohlehr, in "Images of Men and Women in the 1930s Calypsos", argues that "We are never far away from the context of hunger, unemployment, economic depression, worker militancy, desperation, struggle and sheer survivalism, out of which the fictions of the thirties were shaped." According to Rohlehr (1988, 238), the notion that "one's domestic and marital relationship depends on money" emerges as a cardinal truth for calypsonians, and the theme of "no money, no love" has been recurrent in calypsos "from the thirties to fairly recent times".

The social context is that the Eurocentric Victorian ideology of family, with its male breadwinner and female homemaker model, though patently unsuited to Caribbean gender relations, nevertheless sets up the expectation that men should provide for their women whether or not they are capable of so doing. This ideology was based on the ideal of conjugal union, defined according to Christine Barrow as marriage legally and religiously sanctioned, co-resident, permanent and based on love and togetherness, "with distinct but complementary male and female roles". The man inhabited the public domain as wage earner and discipliner and trainer of the children, while the woman's place was in the home (Barrow 1999, 459). Violence was one outcome of the spectacular failure of this model for Caribbean gender relations. Burdened by unrealistic expectations and bereft of skills, education, jobs and money, men were forced to face the humiliation of desertion by their women, who opted for prosperous partners: "Relationships were based on the necessity for food, and hunger was a reality graphically portrayed in several songs. Hunger was evidence that the male provider could not adequately provide; that the bourgeois ideal of the household or family wage earned exclusively by him had not been attained. Hunger brought deep shame and was wherever possible concealed and denied" (Rohlehr 1988, 242).

The 1930s calypsos identified by Rohlehr focused on the male dilemma – his pain, anguish, sense of being used, despair and hopelessness at his incapacity to provide. Rohlehr's exhaustive study of the output of the 1930s considers some two-hundred-odd calypsos. It supports the conclusion but not the cause posited by J.D. Elder in relation to more than fifty years' worth of calypsos: "Many calypsos were male rationalizations of felt inadequacies, or served as therapy via wish-fulfilment." Conversely, Rohlehr points to male–female conflict as being rooted not in the Oedipus complex but in the "logical product of the context of survivalism in which both men and women were placed" (Rohlehr 1988, 306).

The most famous calypso on the theme was sung by the Mighty Sparrow.[1] The conflicting vantage points expressed in this and others of its genre clearly articulate the differential gender perspectives in the far from subtle negotiations in relation to food, money, sex and romantic and marital unions. Given the context of a long history of male self-aggrandizement and ego retrieval in the calypsos on this topic, Sparrow offers a relatively straightforward composition in "No Money, No Love", with an implied focus on the perspective, action and agency of the female and the impotence of the male that leads him to resort to violence.[2] Significantly, the calypso holds love to be a constant. Down-and-out Johnny loves Ivy and Ivy loves Johnny greatly, but since he is without resources to supply her with the basic necessities of food and housing, she has made arrangements to leave him for a better provider, arguing:

> We cyar love without money
> We cyar make love on hungry belly
> Johnny, you'll be the only one I'm dreaming of
> You're my turtle dove
> But no money, no love

The issue here is currency. Love and sex are the currency that Ivy brings to the relationship. In exchange, Johnny is expected to provide her with shelter, food and other material provisions. In the ruthlessly pragmatic scenario, there is no room for him to renege on his part of the exchange, so much so that she threatens police intervention if he seeks to detain her. Through the male calypsonian's perspective, the woman is portrayed as possessing agency to fight back against debilitating constraints, decision-making capacity, and a voice to speak. Fourteen lines of the calypso are in the voice of the narrator, while twenty-five lines, including the catchy chorus, are dedicated to Ivy's direct speech. The chorus is her definitive and memorable statement on the matter, while we are told indirectly and mockingly in relation to Johnny: "If you hear how he plead with she to get she to understand." Outside of personal power, Ivy is also portrayed as having power to access the intervention of state authorities. It is as if the poverty of the male has also robbed him of all of the emblems of agency and power. Robbed of voice and the capacity to reason persuasively, his avenue of first resort is to beg and his second and final resort is to beat.

> Johnny nearly killed she with blows
> Poor Ivy bawl like a cow
> Rip up she wig and he tear down she clothes
> The South man ain't want she now
> Oh, Lord, what a fight
> They roll until broad daylight
> Charlotte Street was hot that night
> She get some good lick but she let go kick and some bite

The violence that ensues is constructed as rooted in Johnny's extreme need and desperation. Surveying the scene and imparting filters for its interpretation is the calypsonian, acting as the voyeur and interpreter of the interaction and as the commentator who voices the collectivity's judgement on the values of this social interaction. What are these values? Love is commoditized. There is no assumption in the calypso of the woman's capacity to go out and earn a living except in this risky form of commodity exchange. The long history of women working – making do and often single-handedly successfully supporting the family – is not honoured in calypsos of this thematic focus, and neither is the imperative to feed, clothe and educate their offspring. A stark focus is maintained on the couple. The male response to female agency and self-worth is to damage the woman's value in the commodity exchange. Johnny unmasks the basis of Ivy's beauty as false accretions of wig and clothing. Ivy is stripped naked. Blows and bruises further rob her of desirability and render her as impotent as he is to effect change in her circumstances.

A lengthy tradition of calypsos of this nature and the widespread popularization of these and similar sentiments are the constitutive ubiquitous, circling discourses which surface in the 2008 media reports, and they continue with all the power of discourse to shape lengthy, meandering trajectories of violence. Little wonder that when female calypsonians enter into voice, they sound a very different note. The innocuous call is to flee. In 1979 Singing Francine counselled women to respond to violence with flight; the refrain goes:

> Dog does run away
> Cat does run away
> Child does runaway when you treating them bad
> Woman put two wheels on your heels
> You should run away too.
> ("Dog Does Run Way", http://guanaguanaresingsat.blogspot.com/2011/02/run-away-song.html)

This evolves a decade and a half later into a strident call for vigilante justice and castration in response to violence, rape and incest. As Rohlehr explains in his critical commentary on the sociocultural conditions within which Singing Sandra offered the composition "The Equalizer" in 1993, gender-based and other forms of violence had by then become so gross and gratuitous that the female calypsonian offers a far more terrifying alternative – for women to come out to equalize.[3]

Poverty and Hunger

While media reportage and popular cultural expressions yield insight into the outworkings of poverty within diverse social contexts, it is to literary expressions that this enquiry will turn to understand the mood, taste, feel and tincture of poverty. Significantly, media and popular cultural expressions focus on the practicalities of unemployment, food acquisition and gender-based violence, while the literary expressions produced by the male and female writers explored below address questions of the universality of poverty, as ubiquitous and as a consequence of the sudden intervention of natural disaster.

Martin Carter's *University of Hunger* (1954) subsumes the specificity of the Caribbean social and political conditions into an elegiac exploration of poverty and hunger as endemic to the human condition. Carter, in descriptions of the traumatizing impact of poverty on individuals and communities, is testing the boundaries of language by layering an array of rhetorical devices to give voice to the indescribable. In this sense, the narrative strategy mirrors the grim reality of poverty itself, which layers impact upon impact until its victims teeter on the brink of loss of meaning. In this exploration Carter does not emphasize social and historical contexts. Note the elliptical nature of his allusion near the end of the poem to the journey of enslaved Africans, which reads "is they who heard the shell blow and the iron clang" (Carter 2006, 223). It connects the impoverished travellers to the enforced migration in chains, from the villages where they were forcibly conscripted, to the coastal slave-holding bays, and from thence to the New World and beyond.

Carter's poem is rich in conveying the subjective experiences of poverty which propel a quest – the long, long march of man in search of a better life. The University of Hunger – the dominant metaphor – speaks of a stringent institution of higher learning which schools men in the gnawing adversities of the human condition: starvation, lack, vulnerability and frailty. The densely packed proliferation of meanings is illustrated in the phrase "twin bars of hunger mark their metal brows" (Carter 2006, 222). The metal brows represent the countenance of persons whose adversity has etched itself on their permanently toughened and lined visages. The bars on the faces also convey the agony of souls imprisoned within bodies that are hungry for food and, more fundamentally, for rest, order, beauty, creativity, purpose and self-esteem. All these aspirations are held captive to that most basic but not most significant of human needs.

The poor are characterized by a series of images of diminishment and debasement. Their stature in the landscape is compromised:

> is the dark one
> the half sunken in the land
> is they who had no voice in the emptiness
> in the unbelievable
> in the shadowless.
> (Carter 2006, 222)

The poor have no voice in the land, no stature and no social presence.[4] Their ultimate lack of presence and substantiality is reflected in their shadowlessness. The misery and impotence become the impetus for migrations. But the multiple migrations do not necessarily bring relief. Migration in time positions them between the mocking twin seasons of parching drought and flood, which represent threat to food supply, shelter and livelihood. Migration in space lifts them from the rural desolation of "broken chimneys, brown trash huts and jagged mounds of iron" to the urban landscape, with its promise represented by the "moon like the big coin in the sky". Yet the urban ghetto brings its own brand of woe: impoverished living conditions, overcrowding and lack of privacy such that "men's huts are fused in misery" (222). Here again Carter deploys the metonymic transfer between the physical state of the living quarters and the socio-psychological and psychic states of persons huddled within such abject living conditions. Pushing the boundaries of meaning, he deploys metalepsis, that is, the combination of multiple figures of speech: "The long street of night move up and down / baring the thighs of a woman / and the cavern of generation" (222).

Gender relations in this male-authored evocation are not explicitly adversarial, because universalized victims of poverty are not gendered. Males and females are equally victimized by poverty, although not equally susceptible. The commodification of sexuality brings enhanced vulnerability to the women and their offspring. Darkness, personified as the long street of night, is itself moving in search of empty release in loveless intimacies. The thighs of women, by virtue of their contiguity to the sexual organs, are a metonym for sexual intercourse. The cavern, which connotes a hollow, cradling darkness, becomes the birthing chamber of a new generation. The woman herself becomes a terrain that the streets of night penetrate to produce children of darkness, who are condemned in their own generations to the long march of man, "the terror and the time" (Carter 2006, 222). Arguably the woman, as opposed to the man, carries the anguish of her children's migrations, poverties and failed quests within the bloodstream of genealogy.

The elegiac sweep of the poem is emphasized by the use of initial rhyme, and particularly the persistent repetition of "is" as if in response to a question: What is the university of hunger?

> is the university of hunger the wide waste
> is the pilgrimage of man the long march . . .
> is air dust and the long distance of memory
> is the hour of rain when sleepless toads are silent
> is broken chimneys smokeless in the wind
> is brown trash huts and jagged mounds of rain.

Of the fifty-four lines of the poem, seventeen begin with "is". The experience of extreme poverty tinges one's inhabitance of space-time and even "the long distance of memory". The poet implies not only that it is impossible to escape poverty by travelling from one place to the other, it is impossible for the family of man to escape poverty by travelling from one time to another, from one generation to another. Barbara Lalla, in her careful reading of conceptual perspectives on time in this poem, argues that *The University of Hunger* rewrites "history as incomplete, progressive and current – unbounded action that perpetuates the past in the present, and iterative action . . . that unlocks closure . . . This is the big picture – vast landscape and seascape, vast movements of people over geographical space, irrational suffering of cosmic dimensions" (Lalla 2000, 113). Poverty takes on the quality of a haunting trauma because, notwithstanding its ubiquitous meandering imprint throughout the land, it remains elusive, horrific and amorphous. Hence there is a dense layering and intermingling of its causes and effects – poverty and hunger head the list, and then drought, famine, dust, flooding, migrancy, urbanization, ghettoization, overcrowding, unwanted and impoverished children – and so the long march begins again.

Poverty and Natural Disaster

Olive Senior's sociohistorically situated "Hurricane Story, 1903" and "Hurricane Story, 1944" delve into the poverty generated or exacerbated by natural disaster. Together they form insightful vignettes on coping strategies deployed over time and their interface with gender relations. For the Caribbean nations, hurricanes are constant impending disasters and are becoming more so in this age of global climate volatility. The sudden potentially devastating natural disaster can sweep away a nation's development efforts in a flash and leave behind the threat of yet another onslaught next year. A current case in point is severely impoverished Haiti, which was battered by four hurricanes within an eight-week period early in 2008, creating in the hardest-hit areas starvation, disease, anarchy and mayhem such that international aid workers have termed the scenario hell on earth. This improbable occurrence was followed by yet another unprecedented event in January 2010: a devastating earthquake of magnitude 7.0 struck the Haitian capital and its environs, creating an unparalleled humanitarian crisis which will test global goodwill and aid resources for years to come. According to government estimates, some 220,000 people are thought to have died, an estimated 300,000-plus were injured, and about 1.5 million people were rendered homeless. The cost of damage exceeded the nation's gross domestic product. The irony is that poverty also militates against risk management for those who need it most.

"Hurricane Story, 1903" and "Hurricane Story, 1944" test a range of coping strategies over the decades and exemplify how the definition and significance of poverty can substantially alter from generation to generation, place to place and time to time. "Hurricane Story, 1903" recalls through the eyes of a young child strategies deployed by her grandparents to deal with a hurricane. This is the rural, land-based peasantry who in the post-emancipation period engaged in the practical outworking of breaking free – clinging to the land, depending on subsistence agriculture, building villages, markets, schools and communities. Senior attributes the effective riding out of the storm to simple rooting in supernatural ethos, place and environment. The capacity to effectively deal with natural disaster hinges on faith, closeness to nature and the capacity to tap into intuitive ways of knowing: "but he was the seventh son / of a seventh son and could read signs / and interpret wonders" (Senior 1994, 20). This is the early warning system which instructs when to board up against the coming storm.[5]

The dominant metaphor is that of Noah's ark, that quintessential symbol of a structure built to withstand unprecedented disaster. The ark, though crowded with people and animals, rides to safety as its inhabitants are calmed and comforted by mournful Protestant hymns (led by the grandmother, schooled in the Sankeys[6]), which themselves call upon the help of God:

> ... In our frail bark
> in total darkness we passed through the eye
> and out on the other side, till all was still.
> When Grandfather opened the window the sun
> was shining.
> (Senior 1994, 20)

The simple cadences and sentiments of the poem echo those of the hymn to which it alludes:

> And it holds, my anchor holds:
> Blow your wildest, then, O gale,

> On my bark so small and frail;
> By His grace I shall not fail . . .
> For my anchor holds, my anchor holds.

The biblical Noah's ark was also a gene conservation bank, and this element surfaces in the poem, as indicated by the child's fascination as she eagerly awaits the offspring of the sensay fowl and the leghorn rooster who survive the hurricane together in the cleft of a silk cotton tree. There is no sense in this poem of poverty; despite the family's survival on subsistence agriculture and the absence of all the trappings of modernity, the family is rich in coping strategies. The careful listing of what the grandmother, as opposed to the grandfather, does to ensure the safety of all speaks to intergenerational, intra-generational and gender concord and complementarity as much as it speaks to harmony with natural and supernatural realms.

By the time of "Hurricane Story, 1944", the coping strategies have changed to yield a counterproductive social dynamic. By this time the rigid system of class stratification, with education as the passport to upward mobility, has begun to take root. The nascent sense of self which emerges from this process is buttressed by stereotypes and assumptions which entrap persons in postures that are potentially deleterious to themselves, their families and communities. The father of this hurricane story has indeed become the literate, upwardly mobile dandy on whose shoulders the social standing of his entire family lies. The capacity to read the signs and wonders has been replaced by literacy and graduation away from land to white-collar work – clerking in Solomon's Dry Goods and Haberdashery. The significance of status is reflected in the spatial and kinetic imagery which is the dominant motif of the poem:

> and when he left
> freewheeling downhill
> his barefoot country brothers
> ran long distances behind
> falling back from exhaustion
> while their pride
> their hope
> kept riding
> on that frail back.
> (Senior 1994, 24)

The father's aspiration towards upward mobility is reflected in his laborious pedalling uphill to visit his barefoot country brothers. Moreover, he carries the weight of their communal expectations of upward mobility, as the one who transcends the hardship and debasement of land-based poverty. The story demonstrates the extreme self-centredness and visibility of the upwardly mobile family member whose accomplishment becomes a source of pride for the entire family and emblematic somehow of its worth.

For the father, class aspirations prove to be noxious. The impulse towards upward mobility proves to be his downfall, for when the hurricane forces closure of the dry goods store, the father is left without work. His incapacity to dirty his hands renders him impotent in crisis and ashamed of the "low class" occupation of his wife. Conversely, his wife invokes the traditional though effective coping strategies of the past: coaxing the land to produce bountifully through hard work, faith and mournful hymns. In the midst of harsh, abusive circumstances, she becomes emblematic of wholeness, enjoying oneness with nature, peace and productivity within her body, and peace with her God. Her reproductive function and harmony with God both infuse her agricultural production, producing high levels of synthesis and integration.

> My mother who hardly ever spoke
> crooned hymns in the garden
> to her skellion tomatis pumpkin melon
> which thrived (as everybody knows)
> from her constant labouring
> (nothing like a pregnant woman to encourage
> pumpkin and melon)
> she sang mournful hymns as she reaped

As in the Ivy–Johnny debacle of "No Money, No Love", the woman finds a coping strategy while the man, to cover the shame of his dependence on his wife, who becomes a higgler, resorts to violence.

> Meantime
> he coasted downhill
> and we settled onto our new routine:
> Monday Tuesday Wednesday our mother worked in the fields
> Thursday Friday she went to market

> Saturday she left him money on the dresser
> He took it and went to Unity Bar and Grocery got drunk
> came home and beat her
> Sunday she went to church and sang
> (Senior 1994, 27)

The closing stanza zeroes in on the dull, routine cyclic nature which informs the correlation between poverty and domestic abuse and the tacit institutional complicities that sustain its cycle. The male, floundering under personal and societal expectations that he cannot meet, is disappointed by his incapacity and imbibes alcohol to soothe his shame and insufficiency and dull his pain. With inhibitions lowered by consumption, he turns his self-hatred, disappointment and aggression on his wife, on whom he is reliant for his daily bread. The wife, beaten and accepting of her God-given lot, submits to her abusive husband and then sublimates her discontent with her lot through worship. Senior alludes indirectly to the complicity of religious organizations and belief systems in keeping women subordinated to patriarchal structures and strictures and tolerant of abuse.

These extracts from popular, media and literary discourse selected for analysis of the social impact of poverty are exemplary of a far broader corpus of material on the subject. They turn the spotlight on poverty but are not in any way intended to convey the notion that domestic violence is limited to the poor. The primary material explored demonstrates the significance of gender differentials in terms of coping strategies for dealing with poverty and its wide-ranging consequences. All of the discourses – fictional and real-life – demonstrate the pain and shame of the men grappling with poverty, which they seem powerless to alleviate. Similarly, they demonstrate the women deploying more effective coping strategies in terms of dealing with the stranglehold of poverty; simultaneously they bear in their bodies the lacerations that their husbands or partners mete out as they lash out against those who are closest and most vulnerable. Faith figures prominently both as an avenue which empowers the women to function and lends them spiritual sustenance and as an opiate which dulls their pain and facilitates their ongoing participation in violent male–female relationships. These evocations imply that the issue is not being alleviated with time. Indeed, contemporary real-life enactments bear a tired resemblance to decades-old scenarios. The possibility is, as suggested by Morgan and Gopaul, that the gains for women in terms of upward mobility, enhanced education and increasing resources may not have panned out as reduced vulnerability to violent interpersonal relations (Morgan and Gopaul 1997, 16).

AFTERWORD

THIS EXPLORATION OF CARIBBEAN trauma narratives draws its raw material from literature, personal narratives, print media and popular culture. The first segment of the text deals with ontological traumas of being and becoming, while the second segment turns attention to social suffering resulting from state torture, ageing and Alzheimer's, child-shifting, alcoholism and poverty. Its focus is on tracing contemporary legacies of originary historical violations – traumas of violent rupture; enforced and voluntary migration; subjugation of language, custom and being; violation of ancestry and community, nation and ethnicity, family and sexuality. Trauma is democratic. It does not knock to seek admission. It equally afflicts those who have lost hold of the fragmenting umbilical cord of ancestral cultural forms and those who are constantly and repeatedly reconstructing it, testing the strength of its sinews, reinventing and replaiting and reshaping it, testing its ability to deliver nutrients. While this study in no way seeks to erase the differential impact on and responsibility of perpetrators and victims of trauma-inducing violence and violation, I assert that trauma's tentacles, its intrusive belatedness and rhizomatic roots entrap victim and perpetrator alike. Spatiotemporal distance dulls pain but historical traumas do not simply disappear over time. The grim reality is that globally, unresolved historical and/or intergenerational wounds and offences are a major cause of individual and communal dis-ease, factions and wars, civil and international unrest. They are major determinants of national and transnational politics, socioeconomic policies and migratory flows.

The narratives explored figure slavery and indentureship as primal scenes which prove traumatic in retrospect to diverse ethnic populations of the

Caribbean. The problematic and ambivalent response to the African presence in the Caribbean remains entrenched despite black governance, and more or less overt racism remains entrenched within the social order. As a traumatizing catalyst, this originary violation has proven to be both known – apparently locked down by dates, times and historical and archival records – and, as Michelle Cliff laments in "The Land of Look Behind", quintessentially unknowable – who can tell the depths of human suffering, anguish, rage and despair? The stranglehold of shame has been loosened. The season has come for strategic practical and judicial intervention.

In 2001 the call for reparations for slavery was hotly debated at the United Nations Conference against Racism held in Durham, South Africa. Economic historian and UWI pro vice-chancellor Hilary Beckles, in his feature address to that gathering, made an impassioned plea for Europe's "enrichment project called colonialism" to be recognized as a "denial of justice, liberty and human rights, the tentacles of which extended into post-slavery apartheid and beyond". Beckles, speaking to the deep and enduring lacerations of colonialism, identified this recognition as the bedrock of "racial and cultural atonement . . . The call for reparations is the call for collective healing and closure" (Beckles 2013, xvii). He frames the case as pivotal to the well-being of the entire human family. Cleavages are so deep that there is no possibility of "reconciliation without atonement" (12). A systematic case has subsequently been laid out by Beckles in *Britain's Black Debt*, which charts the extent to which Britain's agents – the state, Church and financial sectors – were complicit and remain complicit in New World genocides and the immoral abuses of slavery and its aftermath. Beckles identifies Caribbean plantation societies as the hub of empire and the driving force behind Britain's emergence as the primary global superpower. He argues that Caribbean indigenous communities remain two hundred years later in the grip of Britain's "genocidal policies" while a substantial cross-section of the Afro-Caribbean population remains "economically disenfranchised and racially targeted as a subordinate ethnicity" (15). Based on the findings of this study, I lend support to the burgeoning call for reparation as pivotal to the crafting of a more just and equitable global social order. This judicial and economic intervention, when successfully executed, will constitute but one plank in the restorative process.

How else are we to lay to rest the malign unpropitiated duppy of history?

Cultural and creative workers, explored in this text among countless others, have intuitively plumbed the deep-rooted, often irrational traumatizing forces at work within the contemporary social order. Analyses and re-cognition of the root of dis-ease provide opportunities for the nation-body to seek out the locus of its hurt and to yearn after and work towards healing. Much of the damage has been done though cultural denigration; much of the healing can be and is being effected through the myriad works of the spirit and of the creative imagination. It is being undertaken by cultural and knowledge workers in the broadest sense – the people's philosophers, its calypsonians, its mas men, its classical singers and musicians, its storytellers. Collectively their representations and performances enact the glories and ruptures of our histories, the joys and griefs of our present, the pitfalls and potentialities of our future. As surely as ancestral hurts and legacies of extreme violence are being staged in grim corporeal re-enactments of exceptional violence, healing rites and rituals are also being embodied and enacted. They are being staged in both sacred and mundane rituals. They are being danced through bodies in motion which act as bridges between distant pasts and futures yet to come, whose gestures unlock ancient memories because the body remembers what the conscious mind erases. The potential for transcendence is being transmitted anew in simple incremental acts each time a child joins a troop of moko jumbies and experiences for the first time the dexterity, balance and sheer joy of rising above. The knowledge and cultural workers in their numerous configurations will continue to work through the necessary processes.

The process is exemplary of nations and communities in crisis, which are constrained to invent on an ongoing basis acceptable representations and narratives of self and self-fashioning. This is the particular purview of the creative writers, who speak in and on behalf of the distinctive voice of vernacular modernity, characterized by Stuart Hall as "the sound of marginal people staking a claim to the New World" (1995, 12). The greater the originary trauma and resultant amnesia, the greater the need to embrace symbols of resistance, wholeness, creativity and beauty and to project the dark, unwelcome and unclean onto the Other. Narratives of self-fashioning, which tell what we have and how we have come to assume our collective identities, are pivotal for centring community and self, and for establishing boundaries between self and Other. And the media workers, particularly those who superintend the ubiquitous talk-shows and letters to the editor, are also facilitating a vociferous grassroots self-fashioning and self-affirming dialogic process within the national and transnational family. This mass-mediated communal talk, which is by no means consistently positive, nevertheless goes beyond the crisis-generation and dread instilled by the average daily lead story. It is also a facet of the restorative process.

The hope remains that leaders in every facet of the social order of resilient Caribbean nation-states and their diasporic communities, as survivors and progeny of an earlier empire-building effort, will find the cumulative wisdom and resolve to shape an empowering future in the face of new globalizing empires. The region's ongoing cultural certitude, works of faith, engagement and creativity speak positively in this regard, despite the grim socioeconomic realities and messages conveyed in many a contemporary media headline.

APPENDIX
Selected Song Lyrics

"Bed Bug"

Mighty Spoiler

Yes, I heard when you die after burial
You have to come back as some insect or animal (x 2)
Well if is so, I don't want to be a monkey
Neither a goat, a sheep or donkey
My brother say he want to come back a hog
But not Spoiler, I want to be a bedbug
Just because . . .

Chorus

Ah want to bite them young ladies, partner
Like a hot dog or a hamburger
And if you know you're thin, don't be in a fright
Is only big fat woman that ah going to bite
What would you like to be, I ask Mr. Ross
He say he'll beg the Devil to turn him a horse
Ah ask another fellow they call Lawrence
He say he want to be a big black wood ant.
Dey too foolish. When you turn a horse
You have to carry people load, get licks from your boss
And as a wood ant, is old wood you have to eat

But as a bedbug, ah biting the human meat
That is why . . .

Chorus

Yes, I want you believe it, so help me bless
I'll be a different kind of bedbug from all the rest
I ain't biting no ordinary people
You have to be quite social and respectable
Such as female doctors and barristers
Duchesses, princesses with nice figures
An' when ah bite them, friends, ah goin' and boast
And ah callin' meself King Bedbug the First
That is why . . .

Chorus

Yes, I know some husbands, how they fast and fresh
They will be waiting for the Spoiler to bite their flesh
But I wouldn't bite a man if they kill me dead
Not as long as the opposite sex on the bed
Biting a man, ah might break mih teeth
To a bedbug, man skin harder than concrete
So if a bug bite a man the result is bad
Man foot ha' too much hair an' dey leg too hard
That is why . . .

Chorus

"Rum and Coca-Cola"

Lord Invader

If you ever go down Trinidad
They make you feel so very glad
Calypso sing and make up rhyme
Guarantee you one real good fine time

Drinkin' rum and Coca-Cola
Go down Point Cumana
Both mother and daughter

Workin' for the Yankee dollar

Oh, beat it, man, beat it

If a Yankee comes to Trinidad
They got the young girls all goin' mad
Young girls say they treat 'em nice
Make Trinidad like paradise

From Chicachicaree to Mona's Isle
Native girls all dance and smile
Help soldier celebrate his leave
Makes every day like New Year's Eve

It's a fact, man, it's a fact

In old Trinidad, I also fear
The situation is mighty queer
Like the Yankee girls, the natives swoon
When she hear der Bingle croon

Out on Manzanilla Beach
G.I. romance with native peach
All night long, make tropic love
The next day, sit in hot sun and cool off

Oh it's a fact, man, it's a fact

"No Money, No Love"

Mighty Sparrow

Ivy pack up she clothes to leave
Because John was down and out
All alone he was left to grieve
She had a next man in South
She said openly I really love you Johnny
But you ain't have no money
So what will my future be
Even though you love me?
Chorus

We cyar love without money
We cyar make love on hungry belly
Johnny you'll be the only one I'm dreaming of
You're my turtle dove
But no money no love

If you hear how he plead with she
to get she to understand
Listen, mister, she tell Johnny
Leggo me blasted hand
And make up your mind
We got to break up this lime
She said poverty is a crime
You got no money
Still you tanglin' me all the blinkin' time

Gentleman let me tell you plain, she say
I don't want to make a scene
But if you only touch me again
The police will intervene
You ain't got a cent
I couldn't even pay me rent
I had to give up me apartment

You give me nothing to eat
Now you want me to sleep on the pavement
Johnny nearly killed she with blows
Poor Ivy bawl like a cow
Rip up she wig and he tear down she clothes
The South man ain't want she now
Oh, Lord, what a fight
They roll until broad daylight
Charlotte street was hot that night
She get some good licks but she let go kick and some bite

"The Equalizer"

Singing Sandra

Man get so callous man get so cold
no remorse no humanity
they moving brassface they moving bold
imagine they light in UWI
this little black gyul listen to Gypsy
she went up dey to study she get rape instead
that dread!
She thought she woulda find de key
but is a Pandora box of misery
some might even say she better off dead

but when they hold that son of a Satan
don't tell me bout no Constitution
with me he don't have a prayer
hang him high in Woodford Square
tie he drawers around he neck
leave it for corbeaux to peck
all who find that harsh them too civilize
ah come out to equalize
me ent had no time to philosophize
ah come out to equalize
send he brain to doctor to analyse – not me!
The equalizer, the equalizer
Equal rights equal pain
that is my franchise
Ah come out to equalize

All you faddas who like to rape
you dogs committin incest
from my wrath there is no escape
you just raise the hornet's nest
when you stoop so low to molest
your daughter no amount a holy water
could ever save you now –

no how is more than just flesh you bust
you destroy that young girl's trust
ah go stamp 666 on your brow
all ah dem abusing they daughter
put them with a horny gorilla
they can't control they appetite?
More than the lion go roar tonight
they won't stop their bacchanal
let King Kong roam their root canal
them who like to threaten and terrorize
them wolf in sheep clothing in disguise
whether we castrate or desensitize
ah come out to equalize

NOTES

Introduction

1. Lamming differentiates between the colonial situation and colonial experience, identifying a continuing psychic experience that has to be dealt with long after the actual colonial situation formally ends (interview with Kent, 1993).
2. The title *The Terror and the Time* echoes a visual metaphor which has been used internationally to crystallize the sense of apocalyptic dread. The Doomsday Clock has embellished the *Bulletin of the Atomic Scientists* since 1947. It was designed to convey "how close humanity is to catastrophic destruction – the figurative midnight – and monitors the means humankind could use to obliterate itself. First and foremost, these include nuclear weapons, but they also encompass climate-changing technologies and new developments in the life sciences that could inflict irrevocable harm" (http://www.thebulletin.org/content/doomsday clock/overview). When accessed on 14 January 2014, the clock read five minutes to midnight. Molly Wallace indicated that this clock stood at a perilous two minutes to midnight following the detonation of the Soviet hydrogen bomb in 1953 and a relatively comforting seventeen minutes to midnight in 1991. Arguably a device such as this is a metaphoric barometer with as much potential to produce anxiety as to produce interventions (Wallace 2011, 15). Although the referents and symbolic valence change with the time, the sense of impending apocalypse remains unabated.

Chapter 1

1. Wilson Harris argues that traditional monolithic societies ossify in terms of their social structures, values and worldviews. He terms the imperial encounter a "happy catastrophe" because the clash of ethnicities, epistemologies and worldviews breaks fixed structures and liberates new creative potentialities.
2. The journey which has brought diverse people-groups to the New World has been

explored fictionally by numerous authors, including but not limited to George Lamming (*Natives of My Person*), Derek Walcott (*Pantomime*), John Hearne (*The Sure Salvation*) and David Dabydeen (*Turner*). It is the foundational trope of Paule Marshall's *Praise Song for the Widow*. The poets have also engaged this theme, for example, Mahadeo Das ("They Came in Ships"), Olive Senior ("Meditation on Yellow") and Edward Braithwaite ("Discoverer").

3. It is the African American Toni Morrison (1987) who, in the process of resurrecting the beloved victim of infanticide to communal awareness and a long-awaited, ritualistically empowered laying to rest, speaks of the anomaly of a people of oral tradition emerging from the excesses of the Middle Passage without a story to "pass on".

4. In *Capitalism and Slavery*, historian Eric Williams gives a dismal overview of losses aboard five slave ships: "The losses sustained by these five vessels amounted to 617 out of a total cargo of 1,933, that is 32 percent. Three out of every ten slaves perished in the Middle Passage" (1991, 122).

5. Historian Hilary Beckles reproduces a tabulation of life and death at Lowther Plantation, 1825–32, which demonstrates the indiscriminate accounting of the enslaved as livestock, attributing profit-and-loss dollar value to each birth and death (2013, 69).

6. John Ruskin was a famous British art critic and author of the book *Modern Painters*. Four years after it was painted, *Slave Ship* was given to young John Ruskin by his father. In his book *Modern Painters*, Ruskin called *Slave Ship* "the noblest sea that Turner ever painted . . . and if so, the noblest certainly ever painted by man". "If I were reduced to rest Turner's immortality upon any single work," he declared, "I should choose this." Ruskin owned the painting for twenty-eight years and then, succumbing to the morbidity of its subject despite the sublime sky, he sold it to a collector in New York in 1872. "I think as highly of it as a work of art as I ever did," he explained. "I part with the picture because, as I grow old, I grow sad, and cannot endure anything near me either melancholy or violently passionate." The painting was purchased by the Museum of Fine Arts, Boston, in 1899. (Adapted from http://www.thefreelibrary.com/Turner%27s+Slave+Ship.-a065014679.)

7. J.M.W. Turner painted *Slave Ship* in 1840 after reading about the 1781 *Zong* massacre. He exhibited this work during a meeting of the British Anti-Slavery Society, juxtaposed with a verse from his own untitled poem written in 1812: "Aloft all hands, strike the top-masts and belay; / Yon angry setting sun and fierce-edged clouds / Declare the Typhon's coming. / Before it sweeps your decks, throw overboard / The dead and dying – ne'er heed their chains / Hope, Hope, fallacious Hope! / Where is thy market now?"

8. Ruskin's description reads: "Purple and blue, the lurid shadows of the hollow breakers are cast upon the mist of night, which gathers cold and low, advancing like the shadow of death upon the guilty ship as it labours amidst the lightning of the sea, its thin masts written upon the sky in lines of blood, girded with condemnation in that fearful hue which signs the sky with horror, and mixes its flaming flood with the sunlight, and, cast far along the desolate heave of the sepulchral waves, incarnadines the multitudinous sea" (http://www.thefreelibrary.com/Turner%27s+Slave+Ship.-a065014679).
9. This statement resonates with words of the African-American spiritual: "Sometimes I feel like a motherless child, a long way from home".
10. Martin Dockray subsequently discovered a written testimony by James Kelsall, the *Zong*'s first mate, given in a parallel hearing in Equity Court. The discovery led to a conference, the deliberations of which were documented in the 2007 issue of the *Journal of Legal History*.
11. Erna Brodber actually came to creative expression as she sought for a tool to communicate to the "children of the people who were put on ships on the African beaches and woke up from this nightmare to find themselves on the shores of the New World" (Cudjoe 1990, 164).
12. Burrows critiques Jean Rhys's *Wide Sargasso Sea* as implicated in the process of "colonial cover up" (Burrows 2004, 34), for the manner in which Rhys appropriates a submerged trope of marronage to describe the historical abandonment and dispossessing of other white Creoles, and also elides specificities of black historical trauma and resistance: "White individualized family trauma thereby replaces the collective subaltern history, and the many ways in which slaves fought back against the white ruling class" (p. 33). The reading invites us to view both blacks and whites as "victimized alike by imperialists" (p. 35). While I agree that it is essentially dishonest to erase the specificities and radical differences in the suffering encountered by blacks and whites during slavery and emancipation, creative writers are consistently making the point that traumatic impacts of this cataclysmic nature cannot be reserved for the victim. The perpetrator is equally trapped and therefore compelled to embark on cycles of remembering, forgiveness and atonement.
13. Despite opposition from a variety of people with vested interests, the abolitionists and their supporters persisted. In 1806 Lord Grenville made a passionate speech arguing that the trade was "contrary to the principles of justice, humanity and sound policy". When the bill to abolish the slave trade was finally voted on, there was a majority of 41 votes to 20 in the House of Lords and a majority of 114 to 15 in the House of Commons.

Chapter 2

1. These include "(1) A movement away from origin and the difficulty of reconstructing a path back to the source(s) suggested in the etymology of the term. (2) The inescapability of difference . . . . (3) With the historical experience of colonialism . . . the primacy of the cross-cultural encounter and the location of Creoleness at an intersection, negotiating between identities and forces, and defined by its relations. (4) The consequence . . . of a modification of type involving rejection, adaptation, accommodation, imitation, invention. (5) The value of nativisation or indigenization . . . . (6) . . . a dynamic process of interaction with new influences. (7) The multiplicity of Creole forms and types making context and point of view crucial to understanding" (Allen 2002, 57).
2. In Marshall's fictional universe, the men, whether or not they prosper materially, tend to remain disconnected. *Praisesong for the Widow*'s Lebert Joseph, an androgynous incarnation of the maimed god Legba and the "hub and polestar" of the annual excursion and ritual to beg pardon of the ancestor, is the notable exception. On the other hand, the women tend to seek valid communities, a task which becomes increasingly difficult within the adopted metropolitan space.
3. For a fuller discussion of this role of the Afro-Caribbean matriarch, see Paula Morgan, "Fashioning Women for Brave New Worlds" (2006). This is yet another evocation of the stereotypical mythic matriarch named by Lamming (1953) as "my mother who fathered me". The problematic of her location has received close scrutiny from Edith Clarke in *My Mother Who Fathered Me* ([1957] 1999), Lucille Mathurin Mair in "Reluctant Matriarchs" (1977) and Olive Senior in *Working Miracles* (1991).
4. Senior's memorable "Colonial Girls School" (1985) reflects the extent to which stamping and schooling of the body into appropriate gestures and stance were pivotal to educating good colonials.
5. Selina's lifestyle dance in *Brown Girl, Brownstones* speaks to the power of community to celebrate its capacity for unity, pride and self-affirmation and to move as a single body with the attendant power to include or exclude. In *Praisesong for the Widow* (1983) Marshall also evokes dance as enabling humans to use the body as a channel of the divine, through dances of possession.
6. Mr Watford, the only surviving child of his mother, who lost nine others shortly after their birth, is haunted by a fear of death, personified as the proverbial "terror which lurks in the darkness". The irony is that this persistent fear of death has contributed to a death-in-life existence in which he seeks to fend off mortality through a punishing schedule of work which denies the body's natural life cycles. This night terror is named in the immensely popular biblical Psalm

91: "(1) Whoever dwells in the shelter of the Most High will rest in the shadow of the Almighty. (2) I will say of the Lord, 'He is my refuge and my fortress, my God, in whom I trust.' (3) Surely he will save you from the fowler's snare and from the deadly pestilence. (4) He will cover you with his feathers, and under his wings you will find refuge; his faithfulness will be your shield and rampart. (5) You will not fear the terror of night, nor the arrow that flies by day, (6) nor the pestilence that stalks in the darkness, nor the plague that destroys at midday."

Chapter 3

1. This chapter was initially presented as a conference paper titled "East Indian West Indians: Nationhood and Unhomeliness in the work of V.S. Naipaul", presented at the thirty-first anniversary conference on West Indian literature held at the University of Miami, on the theme "Imagined Nations 50 Years Later: Reflections on Independence and Federation in the Caribbean". I am grateful for the comments which informed the final version of this chapter and to Bridget Brereton, who kindly read it and also contributed insights.
2. Naipaul's dismissal of the term *new politics* seems prophetic. This was the buzzword of the Congress of the People, which emerged in Trinidad in 2006. It quickly rose to prominence by riding on mass disillusionment with the ruling People's National Movement and the United National Congress, capturing an impressive 148,000 swing votes in the 2007 election but no electoral seats. The party's image, and with it the promise of new politics, became severely tarnished after it became a member of the governing coalition headed by the United National Congress leader and first female prime minister of Trinidad and Tobago.
3. I am grateful to University of the West Indies librarian Professor Margaret Rouse Jones for directing my attention to this letter.
4. The spatial frames of all of the short narratives in the volume *In a Free State* (Naipaul 1967b) deal with migrants who move away from restrictive, oppressive land-spaces – cupboards, huts, compounds – into wider spaces, only to encounter thwarted potential for accomplishment and personal freedom.

Chapter 4

1. For a fuller discussion of the ongoing impact of the carnival arts on the national psyche, see Morgan 2012.
2. See appendix for lyrics.
3. According to Stuempfle, "It is unlikely that there was any 'first' steelband which

inspired all others. Rather, the evidence suggests that during the late 1930s young men in a number of different neighborhoods were experimenting with the plenitude of metal containers and other objects that an urban environment like Port of Spain provided. . . . By the mid-1940s panmen began to take advantage of the abundance of large oil drums that Trinidad's industries offered. It was through the combining and manipulating of this diverse assortment of metal objects that the steelband began to take shape" (1995, 37).

Chapter 5

1. The International Civilian Mission in Haiti, for example, has been dedicated to establishing respect for human rights since its inception in February 1993. After Haiti's return to constitutional order in October 1994, the Mission expanded its work to include promotion of human rights, civic education, electoral assistance and institution-building. It supports the National Truth and Justice Commission and assists in strengthening the Haitian judicial and penal system. See http://www.un.org/rights/HRToday/hrconfl.htm (accessed May 2012).
2. In an interview with Robert Birnbaum (2004), Danticat explains: "It comes from the Creole. It's an expression *choukèt laroze*; it really means somebody who breaks or shakes the dew. That's where that comes from. Creole is very forgiving of things like that. There is also an expression on the other side, *gouverneurs de la rosée*, people who govern the dew, who are kinder people, people of the land who nurture the land and try to control their destiny through the land. But that was the first one I wrote and I was very intrigued by the father so I started writing the very last story, which talked about his past and the last time he was in Haiti."
3. Crime and fiction make fine bedfellows. Criminality has always occupied a pivotal location in literary and cultural imaginaries. On the one hand, literary representations can be productively analysed for cultural, social and psychological insights into cultures of criminality and their interplay with justice systems. On the other hand, for many law-abiding citizens seeking to negotiate the labyrinth of social interaction in increasingly crime-prone societies, crime strains the boundaries of credibility and readily approximates fiction. The details of specific criminal acts register in the collective consciousness of the body politic as a fictive narrative; the bewildered grapple with what happened (event), in what sequence (plot), who did it (character) and for what conceivable reason (motive). For potential victims, criminal activity becomes the subject of obsessive, repetitive storytelling by way of rationalizing the erection of elaborate defences against the "enemy".

Stereotype, exaggeration, generalization and prejudice are all effectively yoked into this service. Moreover, the consequences of real-life criminal activity are never restricted within neat borders; they constitute a neverending mystery with a border-crossing tenacity which circulates transnationally through space and cross-generationally through time. All of these are the oeuvre of fiction – the epic sprawling over page and mind, the suspenseful crime narrative skilfully woven for infotainment, and the psychological thriller/investigative article probing the macabre criminal mind.

Chapter 6

1. According to Winer's *Dictionary of Trinidad and Tobago English* (2008), *beh-beh* means "mentally handicapped". The term is drawn from the Hausa and Kikongo word *bebe*, which means "deaf and dumb" and "of limited intelligence". It also refers to a "foolish or stupid person, someone who talks or behaves in a foolish or nonsensical way" (67). Winer defines *dotish* as "stupid, slow-thinking, incompetent . . . silly, imbecile, stupid, childish" (308).
2. The impact of prostitution with American servicemen surfaces in Seepersad Naipaul's portrayal of Daisy Seetohal in *Gurudeva and Other Tales*. It is immortalized in Mighty Sparrow's "Jean and Dinah", in which the calypsonian crows with glee at the opportunity to exhibit phallic prowess: "And if yu ketch them broken you could get all for nothing / De Yankees gone and Sparrow take over now." It is also a running theme in V.S. Naipaul's *Miguel Street*, which focuses on the humiliations Trinidadian lower-strata males had to bear in their competition with American servicemen for women's affection and allegiance. The fatherless child left behind after sexual concourse with American servicemen finds voice in the character of Joyce in Walcott's *Steel*. (See appendix for Lord Invader's "Rum and Coca-Cola" lyrics.)
3. The song, which was popularized by the Andrews Sisters in the 1940s, became the target of an intellectual property suit against the alleged composer, Morey Amsterdam, and Leo Feist, Inc. The plaintiff was Maurice Baron, who claimed that the song was plagiarized from a book he had published called *Calypso Songs of the West Indies*. Based on a folksong, "L'Année Passée", the song was composed by Lionel Belasco in 1906. Baron argued in court that the folksong was based on the true story of a young woman from a prominent family named Mathilda Soye, who fell in love with a man who made her work on the street as a prostitute. The courts judged that the song had been plagiarized.
4. Giselle Anatol (2000) and Meredith Gadsby (2006) explore numerous associa-

tions between the soucouyant and female sexual independence. They argue that the soucouyant is punished through the poisoning of her skin for challenging patriarchal controls over female sexuality.

Chapter 7

1. This complex short narrative finds its echo in a range of Caribbean women's texts in which traumatizing catalysts, rooted in racism and the vestiges of a denigrating colonial values system, propel the ejection of young girls out of the nurturing womb of their childhood environment into spaces unaccommodating.
2. Worldview is the cognitive location from which the person seeks to address fundamental life questions: Who am I? Why am I here? What is the purpose of my life? What gives me significance?
3. This natal place, the Cockpit Country of Jamaica, is characterized by Erna Brodber in *Jane and Louisa* as "mossy coverts, dim and cool" – one of a multiplicity of womblike kumblas which variously lend protection and nurturance to the young girls, but should they remain in it for too long, it suffocates their potential for growth.
4. In Jamaica Kincaid's *Annie John* (1983), this looming threat propels Annie Senior to socialize her daughter into a restrictive "young ladyness" and to protect her at all cost from the attention of "wharf rat" boys.
5. In "Fashioning Women for Brave New Worlds" (2006) I argue: "Hodge is representative of the emergent Afrocentric Caribbean female writers of the 1970s, who in the battle against erasure and in the response to the imperative of recuperation of so-called 'reluctant matriarchs' asserted the visibility and vocality of a powerful matrilineage rooted in a distinctly Caribbean Afrocentrism rather than Africa. Hodge's representation of the Caribbean mother/woman is fundamentally an idealized, near deified, though often contradictory, external portrayal of foremothers – a literary genuflection in tribute to the amazing survival strategies exerted by lower strata Afro-Caribbean mothers. . . . Yet this literary phenomenon is a distinctly New World creation, related to the nationalist quest for a Caribbean motherland to honour, within which to root and sprout a Caribbean female subjectivity. The excavation/recovery/recuperation/inscription of a matrilineage ensures, in turn, the inheritance of a true name for the literary daughters." See http://www.feministafrica.org/2level.html (accessed July 2011).

Chapter 8

1. I am indebted to George Jensen (2002) for the incorporation of Baktin's chronotopes. His application of this concept to storytelling as a genre within AA sensitized me to its potential for illuminating accounts of lived experiences of spatiotemporal embodiment.
2. Smith indicates that Africans were accustomed to producing a range of fermented drinks. He surmises that they rather than the Europeans may have been responsible for the initial rum-making experiments (2005, 17).
3. This term is variously spelled *tabanca, tabanka, tabankca* or *tobanca*. It is a constant source of public amusement and even ridicule because of the perceived foolishness and loss of face of the sufferer (Winer 2008, 871).
4. In *Storytelling in Alcoholics Anonymous: A Rhetorical Analysis*, George Jensen comments on this common assertion in testimonies that "AA saved my life": "They do feel that they have changed, and they truly believe that AA has preempted an early death. As I attended open meetings for over three years I watched newcomers enter the program with horribly shattered lives, barely able to speak at their first meetings, and I witnessed their progress towards what the programme calls serenity. They did not so much regain what they had lost through years of drinking; they found something new – a sane life, a peace within a community, an acceptance of life on its own terms. I also watched some newcomers repeatedly relapse and eventually die" (Jensen 2002, 129).
5. Alfred Mendes's "Pablo's Fandango" sketches economically illustrate the process by which rural Chinese shopkeepers functioned as informal moneylenders and thereby gained access to the lands of impoverished small estate owners.
6. The twelve steps of Alcoholics Anonymous: "(1) We admitted we were powerless over alcohol – that our lives had become unmanageable. (2) Came to believe that a Power greater than ourselves could restore us to sanity. (3) Made a decision to turn our will and our lives over to the care of God *as we understood Him*. (4) Made a searching and fearless moral inventory of ourselves. (5) Admitted to God, to ourselves, and to another human being the exact nature of our wrongs. (6) Were entirely ready to have God remove all these defects of character. (7) Humbly asked Him to remove our shortcomings. (8) Made a list of all persons we had harmed, and became willing to make amends to them all. (9) Made direct amends to such people wherever possible, except when to do so would injure them or others. (10) Continued to take personal inventory and when we were wrong promptly admitted it. (11) Sought through prayer and meditation to improve our conscious contact with God, *as we understood Him*, praying only for knowledge of His will for us and the power to carry that out. (12) Having had a spiritual awakening

as the result of these Steps, we tried to carry this message to alcoholics, and to practice these principles in all our affairs" (Alcoholics Anonymous 2002, http://www.aa.org/en_pdfs/smf-121_en.pdf, emphasis in original).

7. AA guides its members through the twelve-step process, which is both an utterance often repeated by rote and a text read at every meeting. It gains the authority of a definitive communal utterance, a word which is seeking to be made flesh. The meeting scenario embodies the word through the presence within the group of persons at every stage of the process. Those who have arrived at serenity represent potential, order and promise of fulfilment; those who have stayed away from alcohol for an extended period see embodied in the tortured words and fragmented speaking of the newcomer the pitfalls inherent in any relapse into the drinking habit.

Chapter 9

1. This is the work of the king of the sexist double entendre, who delivered this piercing lament on the fall of patriarchy when Britain, the colonial motherland, was governed by Margaret Thatcher, with Queen Elizabeth as ceremonial head: "In a land that used to be strong / There's a woman wearing the crown / And another one running de town / London bridge is falling down" ("London Bridge Is Falling Down").
2. See appendix for lyrics of "No Money, No Love".
3. See appendix for excerpts from the lyrics of "The Equalizer".
4. The poem echoes Carter's indictment of the Burnham regime, under which he suffered and witnessed severe atrocities. Carter deems this regime "assassins of the voice".
5. This would have appeared spurious as a coping strategy, had not the same skills saved indigenous tribes in the disastrous 2007 Asian tsunami.
6. Ira David Sankey (1804–1908), author, evangelist and songwriter, teamed up with Dwight L. Moody in 1871 to form a world-famous evangelistic team. Mr Sankey was the author of one of the most popular hymnbooks in the English language, titled *Sacred Songs and Solos*. Together with the celebrated *Gospel Hymns*, of which he was one of the authors, it has had the largest circulation perhaps of any evangelical hymnbook ever published.

REFERENCES

Allen, Carolyn. 2002. "Creole: The Problem of Definition". In *Questioning Creole: Creolization Discourses in Caribbean Literature*, edited by Verene Shepherd and Glen Richards, 47–66. Kingston: Ian Randle.
Anatol, Giselle. 2000. "Transforming the Skin-Shedding Soucouyant: Using Folklore to Reclaim Female Agency in the Caribbean". *Small Axe* 7 (March): 44–59.
Anthony, Michael. 1973. "Drunkard of the River". In *Cricket in the Road*, 54–50. London: Heinemann Educational.
Bakhtin, Mikhail. 1981. "Form of Time and Chronotope in the Novel". In *The Dialogic Imagination: Four Essays*, edited by Michael Holquist, 84–258. Austin: University of Texas Press.
Bakker, Caroline, Martina Elings-Pels and Michele Reis. 2009. "The Impact of Migration on Children in the Caribbean". Paper no. 4 (August). Bridgetown: UNICEF Office for Barbados and the Eastern Caribbean.
Balaev, Michelle. 2008. "Trends in Literary Trauma Theory". *Mosaic* 41, no. 2 (June): 149–66.
Barron, Maurice, Massie Patterson, Lionel Belasco and Olga Paul. 1943. *Calypso Songs of the West Indies*. Port of Spain: M. Baron.
Barrow, Christine. 1999. *Family in the Caribbean: Themes and Perspectives*. Kingston: Ian Randle.
Beckles, Hilary. 2013. *Britain's Black Debt: Reparations for Caribbean Slavery and Native Genocide*. Kingston: University of the West Indies Press.
Benítez-Rojo, Antonio. 1998. "Three Words towards Creolization". In *Caribbean Creolization*, edited by Kathleen M. Balutansky and Marie-Agnès Sourieau, 53–61. Kingston: University of the West Indies Press.
Bhabha, Homi. 1994. *The Location of Culture*. London: Routledge.
———. 1992. "The World and the Home". *Social Text* 31–32: 141–53.

Birnbaum, Robert. 2004. Interview with Edwidge Danticat. *Morning News*, 20 April. http://www.themorningnews.org/article/birnbaum-v.-edwidge-danticat.

Boulter, Jonathan. 2011. *Melancholy and the Archive: Trauma, History and Memory in the Contemporary Novel*. London: Continuum.

Brand, Dionne. 1989. *San Souci and Other Stories*. Stratford, ON: Williams-Wallace.

Brathwaite, Edward Kamau. 1971. *The Development of Creole Society of Jamaica, 1770–1820*. Oxford: Oxford University Press.

———. 1972. "The Discoverer". In *West Indian Poetry: An Anthology for Schools*, edited by Kenneth Ramchand and Cecil Gray, 4–5. Port of Spain: Longman.

Brodber, Erna. 1980. *Jane and Louisa Will Soon Come Home*. London: New Beacon.

———. 1988. *Myal*. London: New Beacon.

———. 1990. "Fiction in the Scientific Process". In *Caribbean Women Writers: Essays from the First International Conference*, edited by Selwyn Cudjoe, 164–68. Wellesley, MA: Calaloux.

———. 1994. *Louisiana*. London: New Beacon.

———. 1998. "Where Are All the Others?" In *Caribbean Creolization*, edited by Kathleen M. Balutansky and Marie-Agnès Sourieau, 68–75. Kingston: University of the West Indies Press.

———. 2007. *The Rainmaker's Mistake*. London: New Beacon.

Burrows, Victoria. 2004. *Whiteness and Trauma*. New York: Palgrave Macmillan.

Carter, Martin. 2006. *University of Hunger: Collected Poems and Selected Prose*, edited by Gemma Robinson. Hexham, UK: Bloodaxe.

Caruth, Cathy. 1996. *Unclaimed Experience: Trauma Narrative and History*. Baltimore, MD: Johns Hopkins University Press.

Chariandy, David John. 2007. *Soucouyant*. Vancouver: Arsenal Pulp.

Chin, Stacyann. 2009. *The Other Side of Paradise: A Memoir*. New York: Scribner.

Clarke, Edith. (1957) 1999. *My Mother Who Fathered Me: A Study of the Families in Three Selected Communities of Jamaica*. Kingston: University of the West Indies Press.

Cliff, Michelle. 1987. *No Telephone to Heaven*. New York: E.P. Dutton.

———. 1990. "The Land of Look Behind". In *Creation Fire: A CAFRA Anthology of Caribbean Women's Poetry*, edited by Ramabai Espinet, 68–69. Toronto: Sister Vision.

Colley, Rupert. 2011. "The Zong Massacre: A Summary". *History in an Hour*. http://www.historyinanhour.com/2011/11/29/the-zong-massacre-a-summary.

Conrad, Joseph. 1973. *Heart of Darkness*. Harmondsworth: Penguin.

Craps, Stef. 2013. *Post-Colonial Witnessing: Trauma Out of Bounds*. Basingstoke: Palgrave Macmillan

Craps, Stef, and Gert Buelen. 2008. "Introduction: Postcolonial Trauma Novels". *Studies in the Novel* 40: 1–12.
Crosthwaite, Paul. 2011. *Criticism, Crisis and Contemporary Narrative: Textual Horizons in an Age of Global Risk*. New York: Routledge.
Cudjoe, Selwyn, ed. 1990. *Caribbean Women Writers: Essays from the First International Conference*. Wellesley, MA: Calaloux.
Dabydeen, David. 2002. *Turner: New and Selected Poems*. Leeds: Peepal Tree.
D'Aguiar, Fred. 1997. *Feeding the Ghosts*. London: Chatto and Windus.
Danticat, Edwidge. 1994. *Breath, Eyes, Memory*. New York: Vintage Books.
———. 1998. *The Farming of Bones*. New York: Penguin.
———. 2004. *The Dew Breaker*. New York: Knopf.
Das, Veena. 2007. *Life and Words: Violence and Descent into the Ordinary*. Berkeley: University of California Press.
Dauge-Roth, Alexandre. 2010. *Writing and Filming the Genocide of the Tutsis in Rwanda: Dismembering and Remembering Traumatic History*. Lanham, MD: Lexington.
Dawes, Kwame. 1997. "Interview with David Dabydeen by Kwame Dawes". In *The Art of David Dabydeen*, edited by Kevin Grant. Leeds: Peepal Tree.
Diedrich, Bernard, and Al Burt. 2005. *Papa Doc and the Tontons Macoutes*. Princeton, NJ: Marcus Wiener.
Di Prete, Laura. 2006. *"Foreign Bodies": Trauma, Corporeality, and Textuality in Contemporary American Literature*. New York: Routledge.
Dobson, Kit. 2007. "Spirits of Elsewhere Past: A Dialogue on Soucouyant" [interview with David Chariandy]. *Callaloo* 30, no. 3: 808–17.
Eichorn, Kate. 2011. "Multiple Registers of Silence in M. Nourbese Philip's *Zong!*" http://kateeichhorn.files.wordpress.com/2011/07/zongarticle1.pdf.
Eth, Spencer, and Robert S. Phynos. 1985. "Developmental Perspectives on Psychic Trauma in Childhood". In *Trauma and Its Wake: The Study and Treatment of Post-traumatic Stress Disorder*, edited by Charles Figley, 36–55. Bristol, PA: Brunner/Mazel.
Eyerman, Ron. 2001. *Cultural Trauma: Slavery and the Formation of African American Identity*. Cambridge: Cambridge University Press.
Ferguson, James. 1987. *Papa Doc, Baby Doc: Haiti and the Duvaliers*. Oxford: Basil Blackwell.
Freedman, Karyn L. 2006. "The Epistemological Significance of Childhood Trauma". *Hypatia* 2, no. 1: 104–25.
Gadsby, Meredith. 2006. *Sucking Salt: Caribbean Women Writers, Migration and Survival*. Columbia: University of Missouri Press.
Gibbons, Rawle. 1999. "Room to Pass: Carnival and Caribbean Aesthetics". In

The Enterprise of the Indies, edited by George Lamming, 140–52. Port of Spain: Trinidad and Tobago Institute of the West Indies.

Gilroy, Paul. 1993. *The Black Atlantic: Modernity and Double Consciousness*. Cambridge, MA: Harvard University Press.

Goodison, Lorna. 1986. *I Am Becoming My Mother*. London: New Beacon.

Guilbault, Jocelyne. 2005. "Making and Selling Culture: Calypso Music during Carnival". In *Globalisation, Diaspora and Caribbean Popular Culture*, edited by Christine G.T. Ho and Keith Nurse, 141–61. Kingston: Ian Randle.

Hall, Stuart. 1995. "Negotiating Caribbean Identities". *New Left Review* 1, no. 209 (January–February): 3–14.

Harris, Wilson. 1998. "Creoleness: The Crossroads of Civilization?" In *Caribbean Creolization: Reflections on the Cultural Dynamics of Language, Literature and Identity*, edited by Kathleen M. Balutansky and Marie-Agnès Sourieau, 23–35. Kingston: University of the West Indies Press.

Hartman, Sadiya V. 1997. *Scenes of Subjection: Terror, Slavery and Self-Making in Nineteenth-Century America*. New York: Oxford University Press.

Hearne, John. 1981. *The Sure Salvation*. London: Faber and Faber.

Hermon, Judith. 1997. *Trauma and Recovery: The Aftermath of Violence – From Domestic Violence Abuse to Political Terror*. New York: Basic Books.

High, Stephen. 2009. *Base Colonies in the Western Hemisphere, 1940–1967*. New York: Palgrave Macmillan.

Ho, Christine G.T., and Keith Nurse, eds. 2005. *Globalisation, Diaspora and Caribbean Popular Culture*. Kingston: Ian Randle.

Hodge, Merle. 1970. *Crick Crack, Monkey*. London: André Deutsch.

———. 1994. *For the Life of Laetitia*. New York: Farrar, Straus and Giroux.

Hurston, Zora Neale. (1937) 1990. *Their Eyes Were Watching God*. New York: Harper and Row.

Hyppolite, Joanne. 2004. Interview with Fred D'Aguiar. *Anthurium* 2, no. 1.

Ismond, Patricia. 2001. *Abandoning Dead Metaphors: The Caribbean Phase of Derek Walcott's Poetry*. Kingston: University of the West Indies Press.

Jensen, George. 2002. *Storytelling in Alcoholics Anonymous: A Rhetorical Analysis*. Carbondale: Southern Illinois University Press.

Kanhai, Rosanne. 1999. "Rum Sweet Rum". In *Matikor: The Politics of Identity for Indo-Caribbean Women*, 3–17. St Augustine, Trinidad and Tobago: University of the West Indies School of Continuing Studies.

Kent, George E. 1973. "A Conversation with George Lamming". *Black World* 22, no. 5: 4–14, 88–97.

Kincaid, Jamaica. 1983. *Annie John*. New York: Farrar, Straus and Giroux.

LaCapra, Dominic. 2001. *Writing History, Writing Trauma*. Baltimore: Johns Hopkins University Press.

Ladoo, Harold Sonny. 1972. *No Pain Like This Body*. Toronto: House of Anansi.

———. 1994. *Yesterdays*. Toronto: House of Anansi.

Lalla, Barbara. 1989. *Arch of Fire*. Kingston: Kingston Publishers.

———. 2000. "Conceptual Perspectives on Time and Timelessness in Martin Carter's 'University of Hunger' ". In *All Are Involved: The Art of Martin Carter*, edited by Stewart Brown, 106–14. Leeds: Peepal Tree.

———. 2010. *Cascade*. Kingston: University of the West Indies Press.

Lamming, George. (1953) 1970. *In the Castle of My Skin*. London: Longman Caribbean.

———. 1971. *Water with Berries*. London: Longman Caribbean.

———. 1994. *Natives of My Person*. London: Pan.

Levy, Andrea. 2004. *Small Island*. London: Headline.

Mathurin Mair, Lucille. 1977. "Reluctant Matriarchs". *Savacou* 13: 1–6.

Marshall, Paule. (1959) 1981. *Brown Girl, Brownstones*. New York: Feminist Press.

———. 1961. "Barbados". In *Soul Clap Hands and Sing*. Chatham, NJ: Chatham Bookseller.

———. 1983. *Praisesong for the Widow*. New York: Putman.

McDevitt, April. 2012. "Ka". In *Ancient Egypt: The Mythology*. http://www.egyptianmyths.net/ka.htm.

Meeks, Brian. 2007. *Envisioning Caribbean Futures: Jamaican Perspectives*. Kingston: University of the West Indies Press.

Mohammed, Patricia. 2003. "A Blueprint for Gender in Creole Trinidad: Exploring Gender Mythology through Calypsos of the 1920s and 1930s". In *The Culture of Gender and Sexuality in the Caribbean*, edited by L. Lewis, 129–68. Gainesville: University Press of Florida.

Mootoo, Shani. 1996. *Cereus Blooms at Night*. London: Granta.

Morgan, Paula. 2003. "Homecomings without Home: An Intertextual Reading of *Wide Sargasso Sea* and *No Telephone to Heaven*". *Journal of Caribbean Literatures* 3, no. 3: 161–70.

———. 2004. "Under Women's Eyes: Literary Constructs of Afro-Caribbean Masculinity". In *Interrogating Caribbean Masculinities: Theoretical and Empirical Analyses*, edited by Rhoda Reddock, 289–308. Kingston: University of the West Indies Press.

———. 2006. "Fashioning Women for Brave New Worlds: Evolving Literary Representation of Caribbean Women". *Feminist Africa* 7. http://www.feministafrica.org.

———. 2010. "No Money, No Love: Representations of the Social Impact of Poverty in Media, Popular and Literary Discourse". *Caribbean Review of Gender Studies* 4. St Augustine: University of the West Indies.

———. 2011. "The Child as Progenitor: Trauma and the (Un)making of Self". *Tout Moun* 1, no. 1.

———. 2012 "Play Mas Bachannal: Towards a Pedagogy of Jouvert and Identity Politics". In *Approaches to Teaching Anglophone Caribbean Literature*, edited by Supriya Nair, 235–55. New York: Modern Languages Association.

Morgan, Paula, and Roanna Gopaul. 1997. "Spousal Violence: Spiralling Patterns in Trinidad and Tobago". Proceedings of "Family and the Quality of Gender Relations" (workshop), March 5–6: 88–111. Kingston: Institute of Social and Economic Research.

Morgan, Paula, and Valerie Youssef. 2006. *Writing Rage: Unmasking Violence in Caribbean Discourse*. Kingston: University of the West Indies Press.

Morrison, Toni. 1987. *Beloved*. New York: Vintage International.

Naipaul, Seepersad. 1946. *Gurudeva and Other Tales*. Port of Spain: [np].

Naipaul, V.S. 1954. Letter to Henry Swanzy. Naipaul Special Collection. Main Library, University of the West Indies, St Augustine, Trinidad.

———. (1959) 1974. *Miguel Street*. London: Heinemann.

———. (1961) 1969. *A House for Mr Biswas*. Harmondsworth, UK: Penguin.

———. (1962) 1969. *The Middle Passage: Impressions of Five Societies – British, French and Dutch in the West Indies*. Harmondsworth, UK: Penguin.

———. (1967a) 1969. *Mimic Men*. Harmondsworth, UK: Penguin.

———. 1967b. "Tell Me Who to Kill". In *In a Free State*, 59–102. Harmondsworth, UK: Penguin.

———. 1972. *The Overcrowded Barracoon and Other Articles*. Harmondsworth, UK: Penguin.

———. 1987. *The Enigma of Arrival*. Harmondsworth, UK: Penguin.

———. (1988) 2000. *Reading and Writing: A Personal Account*. New York: New York Review of Books.

———. 1999. "Reasoning with the Indians". In *Enterprise of the Indies*, edited by George Lamming, 52–56. Tunapuna: Trinidad and Tobago Institute of the West Indies.

———. 2001. "Two Worlds". Nobel Lecture. http://www.nobelprize.org/nobel_prizes/literature/laureates/2001/naipaul-lecture-e.html.

Nunez, Elizabeth. 2006. *Prospero's Daughter*. New York: Ballantine.

Perry, Bruce D. 2000. "Trauma and Terror in Childhood: The Neuropsychiatric Impact of Childhood Trauma". Child Trauma Academy, August. http://www.childtrauma.org.

Persaud, Lakshmi. 1990. *Butterfly in the Wind*. Leeds: Peepal Tree.

Philip, M. NourbeSe. 2008. *Zong!* Middletown, CT: Wesleyan University Press.
Powell, Patricia. 1994. *A Small Gathering of Bones*. Oxford: Heinemann.
Rahim, Jennifer. 1990. "Beginning". In *Creation Fire: A CAFRA Anthology of Caribbean Women's Poetry*, edited by Ramabai Espinet, 28. Toronto: Sister Vision.
Ramchand, Kenneth. (1970) 2004. *The West Indian Novel and Its Background*. Kingston: Ian Randle.
Ramchand, Kenneth, and Cecil Gray, eds. 1972. *West Indian Poetry*. Port of Spain: Longman.
Rhys, Jean. 1966. *Wide Sargasso Sea*. Harmondsworth, UK: Penguin.
Rohlehr, Gordon. 1988. "Images of Men and Women in the 1930s Calypsos: The Sociology of Food Acquisition in a Context of Survivalism". In *Gender in Caribbean Development*, edited by Patricia Mohammed and Catherine Shepherd, 235–309. Kingston: Paria.
———. 2007. *Transgression, Transition, Transformation: Essays in Caribbean Culture*. San Juan: Lexicon Trinidad.
———. 2012. "Calypso, Education and Community in Trinidad and Tobago: From the 1940s to 2011". In *Culture, Education, and Community Expressions of the Postcolonial Imagination*, edited by Jennifer Lavia and Sechaba Mahlomaholo, 183–210. London: Palgrave Macmillan.
Rothberg, Michael. 2008. "Decolonizing Trauma: A Response". *Studies in the Novel* 40, nos. 1–2: 224–34.
Rothe, Dawn. 2009. *State Criminality: The Crime of All Crimes*. Plymouth, UK: Lexington.
Rupprecht, Anita. 2007. " 'A Very Uncommon Case': Representations of the *Zong* and the British Campaign to Abolish the Slave Trade". *Journal of Legal History* 28, no. 3: 329–46.
———. 2008. " 'A Limited Sort of Property': History, Memory and the Slave Ship *Zong*". *Slavery and Abolition* 29, no. 2: 265–77.
Sabat, Steven R., and Rom Harré. 1994. "The Alzheimer's Disease Sufferer as a Semiotic Subject". *Philosophy, Psychiatry, and Psychology* 1, no. 3: 145–60.
Scarry, Elaine. 1985. The *Body in Pain: The Making and Unmaking of the World*. New York: Oxford University Press.
Selvon, Samuel. 1987. "Three into One Can't Go: East Indian, Trinidadian, West Indian". In *India in the Caribbean*, edited by David Dabydeen and Brinsley Samaroo, 13–25. London: Hansib.
Senior, Olive. 1985. "Colonial Girls School". In *Creation Fire: A CAFRA Anthology of Caribbean Women's Poetry*, edited by Ramabai Espinet, 192. Toronto: Sister Vision.

———. 1986a. "Bright Thursdays". In *Summer Lightning and Other Stories*, 36–53. Kingston: Longman Caribbean.

———. 1986b. "Country of the One-Eyed God". In *Summer Lightning and Other Stories*, 16–25. Kingston: Longman Caribbean.

———. 1989. "The View from the Terrace". In *Arrival of the Snake-Woman and Other Stories*. London: Longman Caribbean.

———. 1991. *Working Miracles: Women's Lives in the English-Speaking* Caribbean. Kingston: Institute of Social and Economic Research, University of the West Indies.

———. 1994. *Gardening in the Tropics*. Toronto: McClelland and Stewart.

Smith, Frederick. 2005. *Caribbean Rum: A Social and Economic History*. Gainesville: University Press of Florida.

Soca Warriors. 2009. Socawarriors.net "Talk Yuh Talk!". Accessed 4 February 2013. http://www.socawarriors.net/forum/index.php?topic=47681.0.

Stuempfle, Stephen. 1995. *The Steelband Movement: The Forging of a National Art in Trinidad and Tobago*. Kingston: University of the West Indies Press.

Thomas, Deborah. 2011. *Exceptional Violence: Embodied Citizenship in Transnational Jamaica*. Durham, NC: Duke University Press.

Trinidad Guardian. (1962) 2012. Commemorative reprint, August.

Trouillot, Michel-Rolph. 1970. *Haiti, State Against Nation: The Origins and Legacy of Duvalierism*. New York: Monthly Review.

Van Manen, Max. 1990. *Researching Lived Experience: Human Science for an Action Sensitive Pedagogy*. New York: State University of New York Press.

Vickroy, Laurie. 2002. *Trauma and Survival in Contemporary Fiction*. Charlottesville: University of Virginia Press.

Visser, Irene. 2011. "Trauma Theory and Postcolonial Literary Studies". *Journal of Postcolonial Writing* 47, no. 3: 270–82.

Walcott, Derek. 1958. *Ti-Jean and His Brothers*.

———. (1970a) 1986. "Laventille". In *Derek Walcott: Collected Poems, 1948–1984*, 85–88. London: Faber and Faber.

———. (1970b) 1998. "What the Twilight Says". In *What the Twilight Says: Essays*, 3–35. London: Faber and Faber.

———. (1974) 1998. "The Muse of History". In *What the Twilight Says: Essays*, 36–64. London: Faber and Faber.

———. 1980. *Remembrance* [1977] and *Pantomime* [1978]. New York: Farrar, Straus and Giroux.

———. (1981) 1992. "The Spoiler's Return". In *Derek Walcott: Collected Poems, 1948–1984*, 432–38. London: Faber and Faber.

———. (1988) 2010. *Steel*. In *Marie LaVeau and Steel*. New York: Farrar, Straus and Giroux.

———. (1993) 1998. "The Antilles: Fragments of an Epic Memory". In *What the Twilight Says: Essays*, 65–86. London: Faber and Faber.

Wallace, Molly. 2011. "Will the Apocalypse Have Been Now?" In *Criticism, Crisis and Contemporary Narrative: Textual Horizons in an Age of Global Risk*, edited by Paul Crosthwaite, 15–30. New York: Routledge.

West, Cornel. 1977. "The Ignoble Paradox of Western Modernity". Foreword to *Spirits of the Passage: The Transatlantic Slave Trade in the Seventeenth Century*, edited by Madeline Burnside and Rosemary Robotham, 8–10. New York: Simon and Schuster.

Williams, Eric. 1991. "Capitalism and Slavery". In *Caribbean Slave Society and Economy*, edited by Hilary Beckles and Verene Shepherd, 120–29. Kingston: Ian Randle.

Winer, Lise. 2008. *Dictionary of Trinidad and Tobago English*. Montreal: McGill-Queen's University Press.

Wolfensohn, James. 2000. Keynote address, Conference on World Poverty and Development: A Challenge for the Private Sector, 3 October. http://go.worldbank.org/UT37CTHQU0.

Wurmser, Leon. 1994. *The Mask of Shame*. New York: Jason Aronson.

Young, Robert J.C. 1995. *Colonial Desire: Hybridity in Theory, Culture and Race*. London: Routledge.

Youssef, Valerie. 2011. "Crimes Against Children: Challenging Their Media Representations". In *In a Fine Castle: Childhood in Caribbean ImagiNations. Tout Moun* 1, no. 1.

INDEX

Notes: If one writer has multiple works discussed, those works are listed only under the author's name.
Page numbers containing "n" refer to notes: 214n7 means note 7, starting on page 214.

abolitionists, 31, 214n7, 215n13
abuse
   alcoholism and, 178–80, 182–83
   of children, 22–23, 39, 41–42, 178–79
   embodiment of, 113–14, 115, 117–18, 124, 143
   of human rights, 106
   as self-perpetuating, 180, 182–83, 184
   by system, 189
   transcendence of, 173
Adisa, Opal Palmer, 8
Afro-Caribbean nationals, 52–53, 61–64
   female, 65, 154
   and identity, 89–90
   male, 61–64, 99
   in Trinidad, 85, 99
Afro-creoles, 54, 55, 61
   dance as embodiment of, 63–64
ageing, 22, 130, 133. *See also* Alzheimer's disease
aggression, 133, 150. *See also* violence
   shame as cause, 78, 79, 133
Alcoholics Anonymous, 175–76, 183

alcoholism, 23, 162–84
   and abuse, 178–80, 182–83
   in calypso, 162, 165–66, 182
   causes, 176, 177–79, 180–81, 182, 184
   as coping strategy, 164, 169
   and death, 165, 168–69, 180
   as disease, 176, 183–84
   festivals and, 165, 166–67, 177–78, 182
   in fiction, 169–75, 182–84, 201
   gender and, 182
   healing process, 180–82
   and home, 167, 171, 173, 174
   impacts, 171, 183–84
   as source of shame, 167, 173, 174, 179
   in Trinidad, 164–66, 168, 177–78
   and violence, 169–75, 201
Allen, Carolyn, 51
Alzheimer's disease, 22, 129–30
   impacts, 132, 141
   as ontological collapse, 131, 133, 134–35
amnesia, 89–91. *See also* forgetting; memory
   as Caribbean history, 6–7, 100

233

anger, 78, 133. See also aggression
Annie John (Kincaid), 220n4
anonymity, 114. See also masking
Anthony, Michael, 170–75
aporia, 15
archives
    place as, 100–101
    sea as, 37, 46
    self as, 12–13
    use of, 36, 44

bad-johns, 95, 96. See also crime
Bakhtin, Mikhail, 163–64
Balaev, Michelle, 15–16
Baron Samedi, 109, 113
Barrow, Christine, 191
Base Colonies in the Western Hemisphere (High), 137–38
Beckles, Hilary, 30, 48, 204, 214n5
"Bed Bug/Redemption" (Mighty Spoiler), 91, 207–8
"Beginning" (Rahim), 146
Belize, 68
belonging, 154. See also community
Benítez-Rojo, Antonio, 49, 50, 53, 64
Bhabha, Homi, 73
    The Location of Culture, 67
    "The World and the Home", 71
birthplace. See nationalism
blackness, 33, 57, 90, 154–55. See also Afro-Caribbean nationals
Black Power movement, 86–87
blame
    acceptance of, 127–28
    denial of, 178, 179, 188
    for historical trauma, 81, 84
    of self, 121, 122
body. See also embodiment
    dissolution of, 115–16, 119, 121, 124, 143

    gendered, 19, 34
    maternal, 142
    and memory, 122, 137, 143, 144
    and narrative, 137
    and pain, 117–18
    policing of, 59, 76
    racialized, 19, 40–41, 49–50, 154–56
    traumatized, 137, 142
The Body in Pain (Scarry), 117, 119, 120
bonded labour. See indentureship
Boulter, Jonathan, 12–13
Braithwaite, Lloyd, 59
Brathwaite, Edward Kamau, 52
    The Development of Creole Society in Jamaica, 50
"Discoverer", 5, 27
Britain. See also empire; Englishness
    immigrants in, 40
    and slave trade, 29, 47
Britain's Black Debt (Beckles), 204
Brodber, Erna, 7–8, 56, 150, 157, 215n11
    Jane and Louisa, 7, 46, 220n3
    Louisiana, 46
    Myal, 32, 46
    The Rainmaker's Mistake, 8, 46, 90
Brontë, Emily, 58
"browning", 154
Buelen, Gert, 13
Burnham, Forbes, 222n4
Burrows, Victoria, 3–4, 46
Burt, Al, 108
Butterfly in the Wind (Persaud), 28

cagoulars, 108–9
calypso. See also individual calypsonians
    alcohol as theme, 162, 165–66, 182
    as collective memory, 138
    as critique, 87, 92, 190–91
    female singers of, 194

gender relations as theme, 190–94
  as healing, 205
Capitalism and Slavery (Williams), 214n4
Caribbean (region). *See also* identity; nation; *specific countries*
  African influences in, 50
  Alzheimer's disease in, 130
  identity in, 2–3, 54, 154
  migrations from, 53, 77, 99
  migrations to, 27–28, 69, 186
  natural disasters in, 2, 23
  as Other, 73
  postcolonial, 18, 70
  status in, 199–200
  trauma as foundation, 17–18, 161, 186
Caribbean Rum (Smith), 164–65
Caribbean Voices (BBC programme), 72
carnival arts, 21, 83, 85
Carter, Martin, 20, 194–97
Caruth, Cathy, 15, 72
Cascade (Lalla), 22, 129, 130, 131, 132–36
  language in, 134–36
  memory in, 136–37, 144–45
caste, 73, 81, 167–68
Cereus Blooms at Night (Mootoo), 9, 170
Chaguaramas (US base in Trinidad), 132, 137–38
Chariandy, David, 22, 141. *See also* Soucouyant
children. *See also* child-shifting; fathers; mothers
  abuse of, 22–23, 39, 41–42, 178–79
  as mediators between worlds, 171, 174
  orphaned by migration, 149, 150
  orphaned by violence, 126–27
  part-born, 38–39, 40–41
  retaliation by, 170–75
  trauma in, 23, 143, 146–47, 152–53
child-shifting, 148, 149–52
Chin, Stacyann, 160
chronotypes, 163–64
chutney (music genre), 165, 167–68
Clarke, Edith, 150
Cliff, Michelle
  "The Land of Look Behind", 148–49, 204
  No Telephone to Heaven, 4
cognitive dissonance, 156, 159–60
Collingwood, Luke, 30, 31
Colonial Desire (Young), 58
colonialism, 18
  aftermath, 46–47, 69, 204
  and nationalism, 68–69
  and patriarchy, 57
  persistence of, 46–47, 204
  and racialized difference, 49–50, 56–57
  and self-hatred, 65
  and trauma, 13–14
  and unhomeliness, 71
  and violence, 5, 122
colourism. *See* racism
community, 94–96. *See also* home; village life
  collective shame in, 134
  and crime, 97, 128
  as identity, 84, 154, 176
  and reinvention, 42–43
Congress of the People (Trinidad), 217n2
Conrad, Joseph, 58
contempt, 79. *See also* aggression
corruption, 6, 69–70, 112–13. *See also* Duvalier regime
Craps, Stef, 13, 14
"Creole: The Problem of Definition" (Allen), 51

"Creoleness" (Harris), 49, 50, 66
creolization, 35, 50–51. *See also* Afro-creoles; Euro-creoles; race
crime, 98, 99
    and children, 126–27, 147
    collectivity and, 97, 128
    collusion with, 126
    in fiction, 108, 218n3
    in Laventille, 87–88, 89, 95, 96
    media treatment of, 95, 147
    state, 105–6, 126, 127
    steelband and, 96–97
crisis, 10–11, 17
Criticism, Crisis and Contemporary Narrative (Crosthwaite), 10–11
critique, 10–11
    calypso as, 87, 190–91
Cultural Trauma (Eyerman), 84

Dabydeen, David, 37, 38–43, 46, 65
D'Aguiar, Fred, 5, 32–36, 37, 46
Daily Express (Trinidad), 87–88, 93–94
dance, 34, 36, 63–64, 205, 216n5
Danticat, Edwidge, 21–22, 109–28. *See also The Dew Breaker*
    Breath, Eyes, Memory, 106, 107, 109, 110–11, 122
Darfur, 13
Das, Veena, 47
Dauge-Roth, Alexandre, 13
death
    alcohol and, 165, 168–69, 180
    fear of, 216n6
death squads. *See* Tontons Macoutes
debasement, 33–35, 195
decolonization, 4, 65, 86, 93
dementia, 130, 134–35. *See also* Alzheimer's disease
Derrida, Jacques, 12
Desperadoes Steel Orchestra ("Despers"), 92, 94–98
"Developmental Perspectives on Psychic Trauma in Childhood" (Eth and Phynos), 152
The Dew Breaker (Danticat), 21–22, 106, 122–23
    "The Book of Miracles", 126
    "The Book of the Dead", 124–25
    "The Bridal Seamstress", 120–21
    Dew Breaker character, 109–10, 123–24
    embodiment in, 113–14, 115, 117–18, 124
    fathering in, 111–13, 115, 123, 124
    identity loss in, 116–18
    interrogation in, 119–20
    masking in, 114, 117
    "Monkey Tails", 112
    realities in, 126–27
    recuperation in, 122–28
    redemption in, 123, 124–25, 127
Diedrich, Bernard, 108
difference, 114, 115, 154–56. *See also* racism
    colonialism and, 49–50, 56–57
Di Prete, Laura, 137
disasters (natural), 2, 23, 197–201
disembodiment, 115–16
displacement, 2–3, 8–9
    and identity, 95, 154–55
    in Naipaul, 79–80, 100
    in Trinidad, 9, 21, 75
dissociation, 12, 58, 90–91, 183. *See also* displacement
    in children, 152, 157
    as coping strategy, 122, 152, 156
dissolution
    of body, 115–16, 119, 121, 124, 143
    of self, 116, 153, 155
diversity, 8, 18

Dockray, Martin, 215n10
"Drunkard of the River" (Anthony), 170–75
  archetypes in, 171, 174–75
drunkenness. *See* alcoholism
Duvalier, François "Papa Doc", 106, 107, 108, 109, 113
Duvalier, Jean-Claude "Baby Doc", 106, 108, 112
Duvalier regime, 21–22, 106, 107–8, 110, 118–19

education, 77, 87–88, 199
Elder, J.D., 192
embodiment. *See also* disembodiment
  of abuse, 113–14, 115, 117–18, 124, 143
  dance as, 63–64
  of memory, 122, 137, 143, 144
  of pain, 117–18
  of power, 113–14, 115
  of racism, 19, 40–41, 49–50, 154–56
  of trauma, 137, 142
empire
  dismantling of, 3, 4–5
  as pornographic project, 41, 65
  products of, 72–73
Englishness, 57, 58
entertainment industry, 97–98
entrapment, 89, 90–91, 179–80
Envisioning Caribbean Futures (Meeks), 101
"The Equalizer" (Singing Sandra), 194, 211–12
Eth, Spencer, 152
Euro-creoles, 59, 66
  vs Afro-creoles, 54, 61
  male, 54, 55–56, 59–60, 65
  narratives of, 51–66
Europe, 6, 34–35, 46

Exceptional Violence (Thomas), 5
Eyerman, Ron, 12, 84

family, 125, 176, 191. *See also specific family roles*
fantasy, 80, 141, 157
fathers, 111–13, 115, 124. *See also* patriarchy
  absent, 123, 160
  abusive, 170, 178–79
  alcoholic, 170, 174
  longing for, 157–58
  lost, 111–12
fear, 158–59, 180
  of death, 216n6
  of miscegenation, 75
  and shame, 78, 79
Feeding the Ghosts (D'Aguiar), 5, 32–36, 46
fiction, 14–15, 19. *See also* narrative
  alcoholism in, 169–75, 182–84, 201
  children in, 147, 148
  and crime, 108, 218n3
  and history, 31–32
  identity in, 3–4, 8–9
  and reality, 44, 108
films, 80–81
flashbacks, 71–73, 100, 120–21, 122
folk culture, 8, 14, 52, 86, 139, 143
Foreign Bodies (Di Prete), 137
forgetting, 22, 42–43, 132, 143. *See also* amnesia; memory
fragmentation, 126
  of voice, 36, 44–45
Freedman, Karyn, 153, 159
Freud, Sigmund, 12–13, 14–15

gang violence, 2, 98, 99–100, 101
gates, 56–57, 73, 74
gaze (of Other), 19, 34, 55–56, 77

gender. *See also* gender relations
   politics of, 9, 65–66
   and roles played, 59, 61, 64–65
gender relations, 4–5, 59–60
   in calypso, 190–94
   in media discourse, 188–89
   in poverty, 196, 199
genocide, 11, 13
Gilroy, Paul, 29, 38
globalization, 2, 51, 97–98, 185–86
Goodison, Lorna, 160
Gopaul, Roanna, 201–2
Gospel Hymns (Sankey), 222n6
government
   criticism of, 93, 94
   of Trinidad and Tobago, 94, 98, 99
Grant, Lennox, 97–98
Greene, Graham, 108
Gregson v. Gilbert (1783), 31, 36, 44
Growling Tiger (Neville Marcano), 190
Gurudeva and Other Tales (S. Naipaul), 219n2
Guyana, 222n4

Haiti, 21–22
   destabilization of, 107–8, 111
   under Duvalier regime, 105, 106, 107–8, 110, 118–19
   natural disasters in, 197–98
Harré, Rom, 132
Harris, Wilson, 49, 50, 66
Hartman, Sadiya, 29, 33, 34, 35
healing, 14, 15, 205–6
   from alcoholism, 180–82
   calypso as, 205
   narrative as, 127–28, 157
   women as, 123
Hearne, John, 5, 46
Heart of Darkness (Conrad), 58
High, Stephen, 137–38

history, 31–32. *See also* memory
   amnesia as, 6–7, 100
   as memory, 136–37
   reconstructing, 11, 134–35
   sea as, 46
   as traumatic, 12–13, 89–90
Hodge, Merle
   Crick Crack, Monkey, 160
   For the Life of Laetitia, 151, 160
Holocaust (Second World War), 11, 13
home, 60, 70, 76, 155, 157–58. *See also* community; unhomeliness
   alcoholism and, 167, 171, 173, 174
   as entrapment, 179–80
hougans, 109
hunger. *See* poverty
hyperarousal, 100, 152, 159
hypernesia, 100

"I Am Becoming My Mother" (Goodison), 160
identity, 12, 17, 98, 176. *See also* identity, cultural
   in Caribbean, 2–3, 54, 154
   displacement and, 95, 154–55
   in fiction, 3–4, 8–9
   loss of, 89–90
   social, 56–57, 59
   victimhood as, 16, 114–15, 116–17
identity, cultural, 70, 84, 144. *See also* trauma, cultural
   ancestral roots, 6, 86, 89–90, 164
   loss of, 89–90
   and nation, 54, 69, 82
   search for, 86–87
The Impact of Migration on Children in the Caribbean (UNICEF), 149
imperialism, 1–2, 47, 48, 77, 138. *See also* empire
inbetweenness, 72–73, 174

incest, 9, 170, 194, 211–12
indentureship, 8–9, 28, 164–65, 203–4
independence, 67–68, 141. *See also* nation
individuation, 39–40
Indo-Caribbean nationals, 40. *See also* specific writers
  and alcohol, 164–66, 168, 177–78
  and caste, 73, 81, 167–68
  and identity, 8–9, 21
  music of, 165, 167–68
  as writers, 8–9
inequality, 43, 140, 165
  in gender relations, 4–5, 65
  social, 18, 22, 41, 65, 190
  structural, 1–2, 185–86
injustice, 41, 44, 47, 138, 143. *See also* Duvalier regime
Ismond, Patricia, 91
isolation, 60, 62–63

Jamaica, 52, 68, 136
  gang violence in, 99–100, 101
Jensen, George, 175–76, 221n4
Jesse James (film), 80
journeys, 27–28, 29–30, 38. *See also* Middle Passage

ka, 124–25
Kanhai, Rosanne, 170
Kelsall, James, 215n10
Kincaid, Jamaica, 160, 220n4
Kingston (Jamaica), 101
Knowles, Beyonce, 97–98
kumblas, 158, 220n3

LaCapra, Dominic, 32
Ladoo, Harold Sonny
  No Pain Like This Body, 9, 170
  Yesterdays, 9

Lalla, Barbara, 197. *See also Cascade Arch of Fire*, 4
Lamming, George, 4–5, 6
  Natives of My Person, 4, 46, 65
  Water with Berries, 4–5
language. *See* voice
Laventille (Trinidad), 6, 85–86, 98
  crime in, 87–88, 89, 95, 96
  as Middle Passage legacy, 83, 85, 88–89
  in popular imaginary, 84, 85, 88, 100–101
  sociocultural location, 83, 100
  Walcott on, 83–84, 85, 87
Levy, Andrea, 152
"A Limited Sort of Property" (Rupprecht), 47–48
Lord Invader (Rupert Grant), 138, 208–9
loss, 12–13, 38–39, 127. *See also* amnesia
love
  commodification of, 192–93
  and memory loss, 136, 144–45
  and reinvention, 42–43, 125–26
  as transcendence, 173
  and violence, 41–42
Lovelace, Earl, 7

Macbeth (Shakespeare), 46
Mansfield, William Murray, 1st Earl of, 31
Marshall, Paule
  "Barbados", 52, 53, 54–55, 57–60, 62–66
  Brown Girl, Brownstones, 53, 216n5
  Praisesong for the Widow, 216n2, 216n5
martyrdom, 114, 115
masculinity, 5, 55, 58, 150. *See also* men
masking, 114, 117, 133–34

The Mask of Shame (Wurmser), 77–78
media, 205–6
   and crisis, 10, 17
   domestic violence in, 187–90
   and Laventille, 83–84, 95
   and social issues, 84, 147, 194
   and trauma, 12, 189
Meeks, Brian, 101
melancholia, 12–13, 15
Melancholy and the Archive (Boulter), 12–13
memory, 19. *See also* forgetting; re-memory
   ancestral, 158
   collective, 12, 14, 15, 84, 136–37, 138
   embodied, 122, 137, 143, 144
   intrusive, 47, 71–73, 79, 140
   loss of, 136, 144–45
   of trauma, 12, 14, 15, 153
men. *See also* gender; masculinity; violence
   Afro-Caribbean, 61–64, 99
   Euro-creole, 54, 55–56, 59–60
   expectations of, 191–92, 201
   privileged, 151
   young, 7, 171
Mendes, Alfred, 221n5
metalepsis, 196
metaphor, 42–43, 141–42, 147
Middle Passage, 21, 88–90. *See also* ships; *Zong* massacre
   as encounter between worlds, 37, 39
   Laventille as legacy, 83, 85, 88–89
   silence around, 5, 28, 29
The Middle Passage (Naipaul), 68–69, 72–73
Mighty Sparrow (Slinger Francisco)
   "Drunk and Disorderly", 162, 165–66, 182
   "Jean and Dinah", 138

   "No Money, No Love", 192–93, 209–10
Mighty Spoiler (Theophilus Philip), 91, 207–8
migration, 149, 195–96, 197
   to Caribbean, 27–28, 69, 186
   enforced, 69
   to metropolis, 77, 99
   to North America, 53, 132
   to Trinidad, 83, 85
miscegenation, 66, 156. *See also* creolization
   fear of, 75
   and upward mobility, 58–59, 151, 154
Mohammed, Patricia, 190–92
"Money Is King" (Growling Tiger), 190
Moody, Dwight L., 222n6
Mootoo, Shani, 9, 170
Morgan, Paula, 187, 201–2
   experiences of alcoholism, 163
   experiences of Alzheimer's disease, 130–31
   experiences of child-shifting, 151
   "Fashioning Women for Brave New Worlds", 220n5
   Writing Rage (Morgan and Youssef), 187
Morrison, Toni, 214n3
mothers, 40, 77. *See also* Cascade; children; *Soucouyant*
   as enablers, 175, 178, 180
   as symbolic matriarchs, 54, 55, 132, 142, 160, 173, 196
mourning, 12–13, 14, 48
movies, 80
multiculturalism, 82, 177
music, 23, 95–96, 205. *See also* calypso
   chutney, 165, 167–68
   steelband, 94, 96–97, 98–99, 100
   women in, 97–98, 167–68, 194

My Mother Who Fathered Me (Clarke), 150

Naipaul, Seepersad, 81, 219n2
Naipaul, V.S., 21, 68–70, 72–73, 78–82, 191
   acerbic vision, 73, 81
   ambivalence in, 73, 75, 79–80
   and caste, 73, 81
   A House for Mr Biswas, 70, 73–75, 81
   In a Free State, 217n4
   Miguel Street, 219n2
   Mimic Men, 70
   "The Overcrowded Barracoon", 81
   "Reading and Writing", 80
   "Tell Me How to Kill", 76–77, 81
   unhomeliness of, 8, 71–73
naming, 35, 36, 55, 166
narcissism, 76, 77–78
narrative. *See also* fiction
   as communal, 48, 84
   decoding, 134–36, 137
   as healing, 127–28, 157
   location in, 53–54, 60
   meaning-making in, 176
   as mourning, 48
   otherness in, 64–66
   and reality, 44, 108
   as resistance, 44
   of self, 205–6
   symbolization in, 141–42, 205
   of transcendence, 184
   of trauma, 11–12, 17
   of the unspeakable, 44, 47
nation, 4–5, 51, 68–70, 86. *See also* independence
   in Caribbean, 18, 67–68, 70
   cultural identity and, 54, 69, 82, 100
   as home, 70

natural disasters, 2, 23, 197–201
Nunez, Elizabeth Harrel, 5, 46

oppression, 1–2, 15, 43, 59–60, 158, 189. *See also* injustice
Other. *See also* otherness
   containment of, 56–57
   desire for, 58, 65–66
   self and, 73
   silencing of, 63
   as unknowable, 62
otherness
   creolization as, 50
   female, 54–55, 59–60, 61, 65–66
   isolation and, 60, 62–63
   in narrative, 64–66
   reversal of, 205
The Other Side of Paradise (Chin), 160

"Pablo's Fandango" (Mendes), 221n5
pain, 117–18, 120. *See also* torture; trauma
panmen. *See* steelband
Papa Doc and the Tontons Macoutes (Diedrich and Burt), 108
patriarchy, 57, 64–65, 111–12, 201. *See also* fathers
peasantry, 107, 198–99, 200. *See also* village life
People's Education Movement (Trinidad), 87
People's National Movement (Trinidad), 87, 217n2
Perry, Bruce D., 152
Persaud, Lakshmi, 28
phenomenological approach, 163–64
Philip, NourbeSe, 5–6, 36–37, 44–46
Phynos, Robert S., 152
plantation society, 3, 5, 164, 204. *See also* empire

plantation society (continued)
    creolization as response to, 50, 51, 53
    persistence of, 49–50
political critique, 93, 94
Port of Spain (Trinidad), 6, 85, 87. See also Laventille
postcolonialism, 46, 71
poverty. See also upward mobility
    coping strategies, 201
    defining, 185–86
    impacts, 23, 138, 189, 191
    literary expressions of, 194–201
    and shame, 191–92, 201
    as trauma, 194–95, 197
    urban, 7, 21, 196
    and violence, 189–90, 192, 201
Powell, Patricia, 160
power. See also powerlessness
    embodied, 113–14, 115
    of language, 116, 135
    and sexuality, 5, 141
powerlessness
    and alcoholism, 180
    and domestic violence, 173, 201
    responses to, 113–14
Prospero's Daughter (Nunez), 5, 46
prostitution, 138, 140
PTSD (post-traumatic stress disorder), 11, 122, 141, 152–53

race, 40, 51, 70, 161. See also creolization; racism
    in social order, 56–57, 151–52, 154, 204
racism, 77, 186
    colonialism and, 49–50, 56–57
    embodied, 19, 40–41, 49–50, 154–56
    internalized, 40, 41, 57
    legacy of, 5, 20–21

Rahim, Jennifer, 146
Ramchand, Kenneth, 3
Ramleela ritual, 87
rape, 111, 122, 170
"Ravi" (AA member), 176–83
reality
    fragmentation of, 126
    narrative and, 44, 108
Rebecca (film), 80
rebirth, 61, 63
redemption, 43, 123, 124–25, 127
religious beliefs, 15, 164, 181–82, 201
religious festivals, 165, 166–67, 177–78
re-memory, 118–19, 123, 142–43
Researching Lived Experience (Van Manen), 163, 176
resistance, 170
    cultural, 44, 96–97, 100
Rhys, Jean, 3–4, 58, 215n12
Roberts, G., 150
Rohlehr, Gordon, 3, 99
    "Calypso, Education and Community", 87–88
    "Images of Men and Women in the 1930s Calypsos", 191–92, 194
Rope (film), 80
Rothberg, Michael, 14
Rothe, Dawn, 105–6
rum, 162, 164–65. See also alcoholism
"Rum and Coca-Cola" (Lord Invader), 138, 208–9
"Rum Sweet Rum" (Kanhai), 170
"Rum Till I Die" (Samaroo), 165, 167, 168–69, 183
Rupprecht, Anita, 30, 47–48
Ruskin, John, 37, 38, 42
Rwanda, 13

Sabat, Steven, 132
Samaroo, Adesh, 165, 166, 183

Sankey, Ira David, 222n6
Scarry, Elaine, 117, 119, 120
Scenes of Subjection (Hartman), 29, 33, 34, 35
sea. *See also* Middle Passage
   journeys on, 27–28, 29–30, 38
   as metaphor, 37, 46, 91
Sebastian, Jamel, 188
self, 77
   displacement and, 95, 154–55
   dissolution of, 116, 153, 155
   hatred of, 40, 41, 57, 65
   liberation of, 85–87
   making of, 160, 179, 205–6
   memory and, 136
   narratives of, 205–6
   and Other, 73
self-deception, 47–48, 179
self-esteem, 153, 178–84, 186
Selvon, Samuel, 50–51
Senior, Olive
   "Bright Thursdays", 151–52, 153–54, 155–61
   on child-shifting, 149–50, 151
   "Colonial Girls School", 216n4
   "Country of the One-Eyed God", 150
   "Hurricane Story, 1903", 197, 198–99
   "Hurricane Story, 1944", 197, 198, 199–201
   "Meditation on Yellow", 27
   "The View from the Terrace", 52–53, 54, 55–57, 58–62, 63, 64–66
   Working Miracles, 150
separation, 39–40. *See also* child-shifting
servants, 59, 62–64
sexuality
   commodification of, 192–93, 196
   otherness and, 59–60
   and power, 5, 141
shame, 40, 76–79, 118
   and aggression, 78, 79, 133
   and alcoholism, 167, 173, 174, 179
   collective, 134
   defilement and, 139, 140
   fear and, 78, 79
   memory of, 139–40
   over Africanness, 90, 154–55
   poverty and, 191–92, 201
   as traumatizing, 77–78, 123–24, 143, 157, 173–74
   and unhomeliness, 78, 95
   visibility and, 133–34
ships (slave), 29–30, 43
   as inbetweenness, 72–73
   as multilingual universe, 45–46
   as social structure, 33–34
silence, 46, 156. *See also* voice
   breaking of, 5, 45, 63–64
   imposition of, 62–63
Sinclair, S.A., 150
Singing Francine (Edwards), 194
Singing Sandra (DesVignes-Millington), 194, 211–12
slavery, 29. *See also* slaves; slave trade
   legacy of, 5–8
   as originary trauma, 84, 203–4
   and violence, 99–100, 122
slaves
   alcohol and, 164
   as chattels, 31, 33, 214n5
   child-rearing practices, 148–49
   descendants of, 89, 90–91
   as human, 33
   as inhuman, 29, 34–35
   voices of, 36
Slave Ship (Turner painting), 37–38
slave trade, 5, 28–29, 30, 33–35. *See also* Middle Passage; ships; slavery

slave trade (*continued*)
    Britain and, 29, 47
    as crime against humanity, 48, 204
    as psychosexual encounter, 39, 41–42
A Small Gathering of Bones (Powell), 160
Small Island (Levy), 152
Smith, Frederick, 164–65
Soucouyant (Chariandy), 22, 129–32, 134–35, 138–44
    defilement and cleansing in, 139, 140, 144
    language in, 135, 137, 140
    memory in, 136–37
    redemption in, 144, 145
    soucouyant myth in, 139, 141–42
State Criminality (Rothe), 105–6
steelband, 94, 96–97, 98–99, 100
The Steelband Movement (Stuempfle), 86, 94–95
storytelling
    in Alcoholics Anonymous, 175–76, 183
    as coping strategy, 179, 183, 205
Storytelling in Alcoholics Anonymous (Jensen), 175–76, 221n4
stress. *See* trauma
Studies in the Novel (2008), 13
Stuempfle, Stephen, 86, 94–95
subjugation, 6, 43. *See also* oppression
sublime (aesthetics of), 38, 42
supernatural
    Duvalier use of, 109, 113
    trauma as (haunting), 120–21, 156–57
The Sure Salvation (Hearne), 5, 46
symbols, 141–42, 205

tabanca, 168
terminality (culture of), 99
terrorism, 107–8, 109, 111. *See also* torture; violence
theatre
    debasement as, 33–35
    indigenous, 86–87
    terrorism as, 111
Thomas, Deborah, 5, 48, 99–100
"Three Words Towards Creolization" (Benítez-Rojo), 49, 50, 53
Tontons Macoutes, 22, 106–7, 108–10
torture, 36, 42, 114–17. *See also* torturers
torturers, 116–17, 119–20, 123, 127
transcendence, 43–44, 184
    love as, 173
    of metaphor, 141–42
    of place, 94–96
    of trauma, 144–45, 185
trauma, 10. *See also* healing; loss; PTSD; *specific traumas*
    belatedness of, 46–47, 71–73, 122, 153
    as Caribbean foundation, 17–18, 161, 186
    catalysts of, 39–40
    in children, 23, 143, 146–47, 152–53
    colonialism and, 13–15
    and contagion, 15–16
    coping strategies, 121, 122, 143–44, 159, 201
    cultural, 12, 84
    as cyclical, 19, 100, 122–23, 174–75
    definitions of, 14–15
    embodied, 137, 142
    as haunting presence, 120–21, 156–57
    hyperarousal response to, 100, 152, 159

individual *vs* social, 11–12, 14, 16
intergenerational impact, 128, 142, 161
legacies, 153, 203
media discourse on, 12, 189
memory of, 12, 14, 15, 153
narratives of, 11–12, 17, 81, 141–42
persistence of, 19, 100, 203, 204–5
postcolonial, 14–15
public discourse on, 17
re-experience of, 71–73, 100, 120–21, 122
self-blame for, 121, 122
and shame, 77–78, 123–24, 143, 157, 173–74
theories of, 11, 13–15, 31–32
transcendence of, 144–45, 185
transmission of, 15–16, 41, 84, 143
as unspeakable, 5, 11–12, 14–15, 16, 22, 36, 143, 160–61
and worldview, 153, 160
Trauma and Survival in Contemporary Fiction (Vickroy), 11–12
"Trauma and Terror in Childhood" (Perry), 152
Trinidad and Tobago, 68–69, 97–99, 137. *See also* calypso; Indo-Caribbean nationals; Laventille
  alcohol consumption in, 165–66, 172, 177–78
  carnival arts of, 21, 83, 85
  development in, 94, 98, 99
  education in, 87–88
  gang violence in, 98, 99
  government of, 94, 98, 99
  migration to, 83, 85
  pre-independence, 9, 21, 75
  steelband in, 94, 96–97
  US occupation (1940s), 22, 132, 137–38

Trinidad Express, 93–94, 97–98
Trinidad Guardian, 67–68, 187–90
Trouillot, Michel-Rolph, 107
Turner (Dabydeen), 37, 38–43, 46
Turner, J.M.W., 37–38
"Two into Three Won't Go" (Selvon), 50–51

Unclaimed Experience (Caruth), 72
underdevelopment, 90, 105, 106
unhomeliness, 60, 71–73, 81, 143. *See also* home
  shame and, 78, 95
UNICEF, 149
United National Congress (Trinidad), 217n2
United Nations Conference against Racism (2001), 204
United States
  Caribbean nationals in, 57
  occupation of Haiti, 107
  occupation of Trinidad, 22, 132, 137–38
  racist history, 47–48
"The University of Hunger" (Carter), 20, 194–97
upward mobility, 154, 160, 185, 199–200. *See also* poverty
  education and, 23, 199
  miscegenation and, 58–59, 151, 155–56
  race and, 154, 155–56
  women and, 58–59, 154

Van Manen, Max, 163, 176
Vickroy, Laurie, 11–12
victimhood, 15, 84, 127, 147
  as identity, 16, 114–15, 116–17
village life, 75, 76–77, 127, 172–73. *See also* community; peasantry

violence, 1–2. *See also* gang violence; violence, domestic
  alcohol and, 169–75, 182, 201
  as bestial, 29, 33, 116, 123, 149, 174, 182
  and children, 126–27, 148
  colonialism and, 5, 122
  as everyday presence, 10, 22–23, 148
  gender-based, 110, 122, 200–201
  as legacy of slavery, 99–100
  love and, 41–42
  state, 106, 110–11, 127
  steelband and, 96–97
violence, domestic, 8–9, 22–23
  alcohol and, 169–70, 173
  justification attempts, 188–89
  media reports on, 187–90
  poverty and, 189–90, 192, 201
  roots of, 173, 192–93, 201
Visser, Irene, 14–15
voice, 35, 115–16, 120. *See also* silence
  and forgetting, 42–43
  fragmented, 36, 44–45
  power of, 116, 135
  silencing of, 46, 115, 120
  unsilencing of, 5, 63–64
voodoo, 109, 111, 116
vulnerability. *See also* children
  ageing and, 136
  female, 110, 122, 132, 170, 196, 201
  human, 134, 144, 195
  of island societies, 2, 67, 132
  male, 35, 58, 65–66, 127
  masking of, 114
  as source of shame, 78
  of torturers, 112–13, 117

Walcott, Derek
  "The Antilles", 87
  "Laventille", 1, 6, 21, 86, 88–89, 90–91, 92
  on Laventille, 83–84, 85, 87
  "The Muse of History", 6–7, 89
  Pantomime, 7
  "The Spoiler's Return", 91–93, 98
  Steel, 83, 219n2
  Ti-Jean and His Brothers, 86, 90
  "What the Twilight Says", 6, 7, 86
Wallace, Molly, 213n2
Waterloo Bridge (film), 80
Wellington, Alisha, 188
West, Cornel, 29, 48
West Indian Federation, 68
West Indies. *See* Caribbean; nation
whiteness, 57, 62
Whiteness and Trauma (Burrows), 3–4, 46–47
Wide Sargasso Sea (Rhys), 3–4, 215n12
Williams, Eric, 87–88, 138, 214n4
wives, 58–59, 60. *See also* women
  submissive, 173, 175, 201
  as symbolic, 200–201
Wolfensohn, James, 185–86
women, 65. *See also* mothers; rape; wives
  Afro-Caribbean, 65, 154
  and child-bearing, 61–62
  coping strategies, 200–201
  family role, 150, 191, 192–93, 200–201
  in Haiti, 109, 110
  as healing power, 123
  in music, 97–98, 167–68, 194
  as objects of desire, 62–63, 151
  as Other, 54–55, 59–60, 61, 65–66
  as prostitutes, 138, 140
  silencing of, 42
  soucouyant as symbol, 141–42

as targets (of violence), 110, 122, 170, 173, 201–2
torture of, 36, 42, 119
and upward mobility, 58–59, 154
white, 3–4
working, 193
writers
   as healers, 205
   Indo-Caribbean, 8–9
   and self-fashioning, 205–6
   and traumatic encounter, 46, 48

Writing Rage (Morgan and Youssef), 187
Wurmser, Leon, 77–78
Wuthering Heights (Brontë), 58

Yawney, Carole, 165
Young, Robert, 58
Youssef, Valerie, 187

Zong! (Philip), 5–6, 36–37, 44–46
Zong massacre, 20, 30–31, 47–48
   judicial proceedings, 31, 36, 44

www.ingramcontent.com/pod-product-compliance
Lightning Source LLC
Chambersburg PA
CBHW031806220426
43662CB00007B/547